WORKING ABROAD

THE COMPLETE GUIDE TO OVERSEAS EMPLOYMENT

TWENTY-THIRD EDITION

GODFREY GOLZEN & JONATHAN REUVID

KOGAN
PAGE

First published in 1977

Twenty-third edition 2002

Kogan Page Limited
120 Pentonville Road
London N1 9JN

© Godfrey Golzen and contributors 1977, 1979, 1980, 1981, 1982, 1983, 1984, 1985, 1986, 1987, 1988, 1989, 1990, 1991
© Kogan Page Ltd and contributors 1992, 1993, 1994, 1995, 1996, 1997, 1999, 2000, 2002

Every effort has been made to ensure information in this book is up to date at the time of printing. Where no revisions to country profiles were received from individual embassies the text from the twenty-second edition has been used.

British Library Cataloguing in Publication Data

A CIP record for this book is available from the British Library.

ISBN 0 7494 3786 3

Typeset by Saxon Graphics Ltd, Derby
Printed and bound in Great Britain by Thanet Press Ltd, Margate

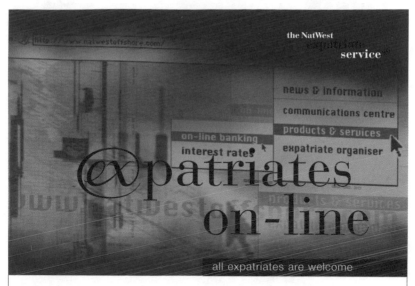

the NatWest
service

news & information

communications centre

products & services

on-line banking

interest rates

expatriate organiser

@xpatriates
on-line

all expatriates are welcome

We realise that moving outside of your home country may be tinged with apprehension - so you'll see that our website offers much more than financial information.

It's been designed with your busy new lifestyle in mind and ensures appropriate and up-to-date information is displayed in one place.

Our extensive range of products and information enables you to choose the elements which will make our service fit your personal requirements.

You don't have to be a NatWest customer to feel part of our Internet community.

to
plore

web site:	**www.natwestoffshore.com**
phone:	44 1534 282164
fax:	44 1534 282665
e-mail:	expats@natwestoffshore.com

Contents

Acknowledgements

Over the years many individuals and organisations have helped us with information and advice on various aspects of working and living abroad, and in updating information for successive editions. We wish to extend our thanks to Margaret Stewart for her contributions to several previous editions; Tony Smith of the International Safety Council, Chicago; Susan Jackson for writing the chapter on the education of expatriates' children; the Centre for International Briefing, Farnham Castle, Surrey; the Department for International Development for information on the situation in developing countries; the European Council of International Schools; Innes Anderson of Anderson Sinclair & Co for detailed advice on the financial planning chapter; Colin Bexon of Hay Management Consultants for information on job opportunities; R J B Anderton of Anderton & Son for his help on the chapter on letting your home; Louis Conrad of the Conrad School of Languages for help on the section on learning a language; John Thompson and colleagues of PricewaterhouseCoopers; Barry Page from Arthur Andersen; the members of foreign embassies and high commissions in London and the press offices of various government departments (particularly DSS, DfEE, HM Customs) who have helped in the revision of the text; and readers who have written in with criticisms, information and suggestions.

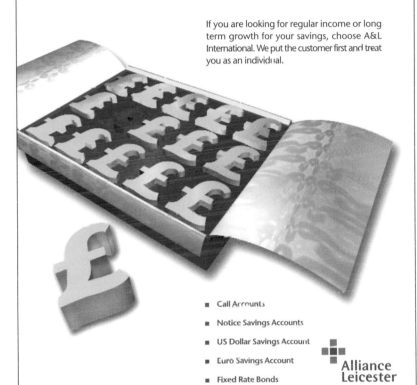

Moving Overseas is not the same as moving locally, It is most important to employ a specialist moving company that dedicates itself to international moving. Across the street is not across the world.

Limit your choice to members of recognised International Associations such as FIDI or OMNI, at the very least a member of the Overseas Group of BAR who will be able to give you financial bonding security.

The next step is to arrange for a pre-move survey of the items you would like to take with you overseas. The surveyor will be able to help advise what is best to take or not and to discuss your move in details. The survey will establish

- The content of the consignment
- Any parking restrictions at the origin and destination point
- Your timetable, moving in and out dates
- If storage is required short or long term (at origin or destination)
- Any special needs or concerns you may have
- The cost of your intended move

Following the surveyor's visit you should be allocated a single contact person to move manage your shipment from door to door, providing continuous direct line support throughout the process.

You should receive assistance in completion of customs documentation. Help with insurance for the furniture and if required assistance with other relocation issues such as home and school search, cultural training etc. are all available.

Choose carefully and you will be rewarded with a move that is relatively stress free and exceeds you expectations. Peace of mind is always worth paying that little bit extra for.

Yes!

The perfect paper for living and working abroad!

Daltons Weekly has hundreds of **properties abroad** for sale in every issue.

This is complemented by a great selection of **overseas businesses** for sale.

Available at all good newsagents every Thursday.

Before your departure, arrive at self storage.

When you're going abroad, we're here to make things easier.

As Europe's no1 self storage specialist, we can provide secure, clean and dry storage rooms for everything you're leaving behind, whether you have a few bags to store or all your furniture and household appliances. And as the only keyholder you can rest easy, knowing your belongings will be undisturbed while you're away.

We also offer all the accessories you might need, from packing cases to bubble wrap and tape, and even insurance if you want additional peace of mind.

A choice of long or short term contracts and easy payment options, which includes direct debit, also saves you trouble.

Prices start from just £5 a week. So, give us a call and then just leave it with us.

FOR MORE INFORMATION,
PHONE US FREE ON:
0800 122 522

About BDO Stoy Hayward

We are the UK member firm of BDO, a multinational accounting organisation, which since 1963 has grown to be the sixth largest in the world with:

2,000 Partners

20,000 Staff

Over 550 offices operating in 100 countries

World-wide fee income of US$2.3bn

BDO International is well placed to serve both individuals with global taxation issues and multinational growing businesses in the UK and overseas. We provide a comprehensive range of audit, assurance, corporate finance and taxation services.

BDO Global Expatriate Tax Services

For expatriates, tax, social security and pension issues tend to be more complex than for most. For example, how can double taxation be avoided or how do you cope with different tax and social security issues in various countries?

You may be letting your house or have continuing UK sources of income. In some cases, emigration can bring tax advantages and this may need to be looked at.

At BDO Stoy Hayward, our global network of expatriate tax experts offers an in-depth understanding of the issues facing employees working or planning to work overseas and maintains a personal service that is suited to your specific circumstances.

Reducing the burden of international and social security compliance

Complying with unfamiliar and constantly changing tax legislation in foreign countries is a daunting task for the employee looking to work or currently working abroad. BDO Stoy Hayward can remove this burden by ensuring that all host obligations are met, as well as providing ongoing tax advice in the UK. Our services include:

- Pre-departure planning meetings and briefings with executives to deal with home country issues and any pre-assignment tax planning
- Arrival meetings in the host country to familiarise executives with the tax implications of their assignments
- Dealing with all home and host country tax returns and filing obligations to keep responsibilities up to date and avoid interest and penalties
- Hypothetical tax calculations and Inland Revenue documentation
- Payroll issues
- Liaison with and tax documentation for tax authorities worldwide

- Advice on the implications of being a non-UK resident landlord
- Social security advice
- Pension planning advice
- Stock option advice
- Double taxation treaty advice
- High level International tax planning

For foreign nationals repatriating or moving on to their next assignment, timely advice before the end of the UK secondment can also prevent needless tax liabilities arising.

Reducing the cost of international assignments

Effective planning for expatriate executives relies on extensive, accessible knowledge of the home and host country tax law. Using our global network we can ensure that assignment costs are kept to a minimum. BDO Stoy Hayward can offer:

- reviews of company and expatriate policies and remuneration packages. It is important for compensation packages to be carefully structured in order to ensure tax efficiency for both the employer and assignee.
- tax equalisation and protection mechanisms to deal with varying tax exposure for employees worldwide.

Planning points

They are many planning opportunities for employees working abroad, below are just a few to consider:

- **Secondment length** affects both the employer and employee tax and social security obligations;
- It is important to consider the **start date of an assignment,** by moving it forward or backwards, tax savings can be maximised.
- **The structure of the compensation package** can in certain countries minimise tax and social security costs, for instance by substituting benefits for a proportion of salary.
- Always consider **reporting obligations.** Even when there are no tax obligations there are sometimes reporting obligations. If these are ignored the penalties can be high.
- In some host countries, **employer pension contributions** are taxable and employee contributions are not deductible, therefore planning is essential.

Contact us

For further information on the services BDO Stoy Hayward can offer to expatriates and their employers please call Chris Maddock or Andrea Reed on 020 7893 3423 or email expat@bdo.co.uk

THE NEW SCHOOL ROME

Education for life

Via della Camilluccia, 669 00135 ROMA
E-mail: info@newschoolrome.com

Tel. 0039063294269   Fax 0039063297546
Internet: www.newschoolrome.com

Company profile

Towers Perrin is one of the world's largest firms of human resources and actuarial consultants. UK clients include 80 of the current Financial Times Top 100 companies, over 70 of which receive pension and employee benefit advice. In addition to pensions and benefit consultancy, Towers Perrin provides a range of broader human resources services including advice on remuneration, organisational change, employee communication and human resource management. It is therefore able to advise organisations on all aspects of people and performance. Towers Perrin's international network is one of the largest and most respected of its kind: it gives its consulting staff a multinational perspective, enabling them to comment and advise on worldwide policies and issues.

For more details about our services, please access our website at **www.towersperrin.com**

Towers Perrin

Argentina	Italy	Singapore
Australia	Japan	South Africa
Belgium	Malaysia	South Korea
Bermuda	Mexico	Spain
Brazil	Netherlands	Sweden
Canada	New Zealand	Switzerland
France	People's Republic	United Kingdom
Germany	of China	USA

Introduction

JOB PROSPECTS FOR UK EXPATRIATES

The reputation of British expatriates is still highly regarded abroad and their salary rates are very competitive against labour recruited from the USA and the other Western European states. In reality, US and European contractors frequently turn to the United Kingdom to recruit workers for their overseas projects at salary rates below those demanded by their own nationals. This type of contract is normally lucrative in salary terms for the UK national and has the added advantage that the contractor frequently provides good living and contract conditions.

The ability to earn significant salaries overseas, together with the chance to avoid UK taxes, sounds like Utopia. However, in fact, the expatriate worker is faced with a new set of problems. Many of these will be outside work and will involve his or her family and social life. Working abroad requires a substantial adjustment in attitudes towards work and life in general. The ability to adapt to the new environment is absolutely essential, together with a willingness to make the best of things as they are in the new surroundings. Attempting to change the new surroundings to a British way of life is bound to be frustrated and to result in the resentment of the host country.

Lucrative overseas employment can solve many problems and may seem like the answer to a prayer. But it also creates problems, which may result in broken marriages, ruined careers and disturbed children. In accepting a job overseas you are taking a substantial risk and you should calculate how big the risk is in your

MERIDIAN FUNDS BVI

A REFRESHING APPROACH TO OFFSHORE FIXED RATE INVESTMENT

MERIDIAN Funds were launched in 1998 under the auspices, and regulation, of the highly investor protective British Virgin Islands 1996 Mutual Funds Act and 1997 BVI Money Laundering protection legislation. The 1996 Act being the most investor protective and regulatory controlled legislation which has been enacted by any offshore jurisdiction providing for the oversight and licensing, by the Registrar of Mutual Funds, of all aspects of a Funds affairs.

The centrepiece Fund of the Group is the boutique styled Meridian Income Bond which provides a refreshing, and badly needed, alternative to bank deposits. Being independent of any other banking or institutionally controlled influence this investment is able to provide investors with fixed rate returns which reflects a truer return on an investment, and an interest rate philosophy which is not hampered by external onshore parent companies or any government interest rate interference. Deposit rates are also enhanced by the strict control of overheads and charges and the company policy of implementation of a high level of technological systems all of which have been developed in-house. In short the investors, and not the company, are treated as the beneficiaries of the investment philosophy. There are a number of advantages in investing in this vehicle not the least of which are the very attractive rates on offer: currently rates for 12 months terms are 7.8% p.a. for £ sterling, 7.6% p.a. for $ US and 6.0% for Euros. Good rates of return are available for 3 month investments and, in incremental terms, up to 10 years for those who require a fixed rate for that period of time. All rates are fixed for the agreed period of the investment regardless of any changes in rates during the investment period, which are only applicable to new investors, and all investments guarantee the return of the original investment. Despite being named as an Income Bond there is no requirement to take income. In the event an investor wishes to do so he will receive quarterly a sum equal to 25% of the gross annual interest rate. Thus someone who invests £10,000 at 8% p.a. will receive £200 per quarter for the agreed duration of the investment. For those who do not require income the investment will be rolled over on an annual basis, at the agreed rate, for the duration of the term of investment.

In order to compliment the Income Bond Meridian Funds have three Equity Funds viz. North American Fund, European Fund and Asian Fund, all of which are designed to give support to investors in the fixed rate vehicle. Investors are able to shelter in the comfort of the fixed rate fund for periods from 3 months and upwards and are then able to transfer instantly, by sending a fax, to an equity fund of their choice in order to enjoy a period of equity growth. The reverse can be applied just as quickly when running for shelter during times of equity crisis. An active investor can then manage his portfolio within the same group of funds.

Investment is open to all with minimums of US$ 2,000, £ 1,200, and Euros 2,000.

Information is available on the excellent company website at www.meridianfundsbvi.com and brochures are available from Meridian Funds, Sea Meadow House, P.O.Box 116, Road Town, Tortola, British Virgin Islands. Tel. + 1 284 4943399 (Extn 340). Fax. + 1 284 4943041. E-mail: admin@meridianfundsbvi.com

particular case. Very often you will find that there is a direct corre-
lation between risk and salary. For example, working for a major
company such as British Aerospace in Saudi Arabia carries much
less risk than working for a Saudi company. The rate of pay offered
will probably be very different, with the Saudi company offering
much higher pay, but the security and facilities which British
Aerospace provide would not be available. However, even working
for British Aerospace will not stop or cure all the problems caused
by working overseas. It will also not give workers immunity if they
break the laws of the host country.

People work overseas for many different reasons and are moti-
vated to do so by many different things. It is difficult to believe
anyone who says that money is not one of the major incentives.
The duration of overseas employment is also varied. Some people
just work a one- or two-year contract to help pay off the mortgage,
or to produce the capital to start a business. However, such short-
term contracts attract many applications and usually tend to be
taken up by 'permanent expatriates' – those people who have
spent much of their working lives abroad.

Increasingly, though, employers are looking to replace expatriation with short-term assignments or even commuting to locations, where practically possible. New technology has encouraged
such changes and the introduction of 'virtual assignments' has
meant that professionals can manage projects from their own
country, with regular visits to their international office. While this
might avoid the problems traditional models of expatriation face –
such as the upheaval of family and home – an entirely new set of
problems arise, such as the burden of frequent travel, which will
also be investigated further on in this book.

Career development is another common reason for working
abroad and is particularly important for those working in multinational and international companies, government bodies, banks and
organisations with large export markets.

An expatriate returning to the UK faces as many adjustments to
life and work as he or she does in going out to an overseas job.
Picking up the threads of a career in the UK can be extremely
difficult and overseas experience is not always regarded
favourably. Employers with no previous experience in overseas
work themselves may think that you are returning from a very

alien and low technology environment, and doubt your ability to cope with new technology and life in the UK.

Recruiting organisations need to find workers who can perform a specified job in an overseas environment. It is easy to find candidates who can do the job in a British environment but only a small proportion can survive and succeed overseas. Their second task is to ensure that any applicant they select is aware of all the problems and difficulties he or she is likely to encounter in the country he or she is going to work in. They do not want the candidate to be surprised by conditions when he or she arrives, resulting in a premature termination of contract. This is bad for the individual and may affect his or her future employment prospects. It is bad for the company since it is very disruptive and involves them in substantial replacement costs. It is bad for the recruitment agent since it undermines the confidence of the client and can also turn him or her totally against the idea of using British workers.

Given that you have decided, after careful consideration of your family and your career, to find work overseas, you will need to identify the best way of achieving this, and to decide in which overseas countries you wish to work. Working in the Middle East is very different from working in Africa, which is also poles apart from working in the USA, Europe or the Far East. Carrying out research on your host country before departure will help, and the resource section at the back of this book will help get you started on this. However, more often than not it is not until you arrive in your new home that the differences in work and home environment, and whether or not you will be able to fit in comfortably, will become apparent.

The overall number of jobs for UK expatriates has declined quite markedly in recent years and the jobs most affected are for unskilled, semi-skilled, skilled, clerical and administrative workers. Many of these types of job are now filled by workers from the Far East and the Indian sub-continent where wage rates are much lower. The same market forces have resulted in some of the more senior jobs which have traditionally been filled by Americans being switched to less costly British labour.

Frequently, salaries are only 10–20 per cent above current UK rates, but of course the ability to avoid tax and deductions from salary and the receipt of free accommodation and other benefits still make contracts financially attractive.

FAMILY CONSIDERATIONS

Perhaps the most fundamental question an expatriate must resolve is whether he or she is going to take up a post on an unaccompanied status or whether he or she is looking for accompanied postings. Many people who apply for overseas jobs have not thought out the problems and have not reached a family agreement on the type of posting required. One of the major irritations affecting international recruiters is that some candidates apply for single-status jobs and then at the final interview state they are only prepared to accept an accompanied status situation. This results in a complete waste of time and money for both parties and is guaranteed to reduce your chances of getting employment through that agent.

Before you even decide to apply for an overseas job you must discuss and agree with your family the status of posting that you are prepared to take, the countries you would want to work in, and the minimum remuneration and benefits package you will accept. Only when you have decided these points are you in a position to start making job applications. Furthermore, many dual-income couples will need to investigate job opportunities for an accompanying partner in the new location, as many are no longer prepared to give up their own career for the sake of a foreign sojourn. The issues affecting the 'trailing spouse' are fully discussed in Chapter 6.

USING TECHNOLOGY

Advances in communications technology have certainly made the expatriate's life easier. Keeping in contact with colleagues, friends and family can be done with ease. If you haven't already done so, become acquainted with the Internet. This has become an invaluable aid for the international community and provides quick and cheap global communication. It also provides excellent information on any subject you care to think of, including country-specific information, job opportunities, government advice and so on. The 23rd edition of *Working Abroad* acknowledges the impact of the Internet on the expatriate community and where possible has included Web site addresses for relevant information. Where there are no Web sites available we have included the postal address and telephone number instead. However, Web site addresses change frequently, as does the content, and we are unable to take responsibility for these factors. Once you are on the right track using the links provided by many Web sites it should prove a worthwhile and fruitful journey, arming you with the information required to settle into your foreign assignment.

THE EMPLOYER'S PERSPECTIVE

A new departure from previous editions of the book is the inclusion as Chapter 2 of a section focused on the development of internationally mobile employee (IME) strategy, employment policies and the administration of IMEs. The chapter primarily addresses companies with international business operations, which are engaged in the assignment of employees to overseas appointments for varying periods.

If you are not in the position of working for a company that may offer you overseas employment and do not expect to do so, you may prefer to omit this chapter from your reading. However, if you are considering company employment in an overseas operation the chapter may provide some understanding of the corporate mindset.

CONCLUSION

The rewards of working abroad can be high and usually offer the chance to make significant savings. The amount of your savings depends largely on the location chosen and your attitude to life abroad.

Perhaps the expatriate who finds life the most difficult is the married person with teenage children, since in many countries, secondary education is either unavailable or extremely expensive. The alternative of a UK boarding school is also expensive, and tends to break up the family unit.

We strongly recommend that if you are seriously contemplating a job overseas you should research the job market very carefully. You should try to decide whether you have the ability to survive and succeed overseas and whether, where appropriate, your family can also adapt to the new lifestyle. Once you have made this decision honestly you must identify the countries that offer the rewards and conditions you require.

NEW CONTRIBUTORS

There are two new professional contributors to this 23rd edition of *Working Abroad*. BDO Stoy Hayward, the international accountancy firm, has authored the chapter and checklists in Part Two detailing the effect on personal taxation of working abroad (Chapter 3). BDO Stoy Hayward practises in many of the countries featured in Part Five and has contributed personal taxation briefings for expatriates moving to those territories.

In Part One, Chapter 2, Managing Internationally Mobile Employees, is the product of content provided by Towers Perrin, the leading international human resources management consultancy, and discussion with two of its practitioners.

Part One:

Job Opportunities and the Employer's Perspective

1 Independent Job Opportunities

It is difficult, if not impossible, to form any precise idea of the number of UK citizens currently working overseas. Despite the flood of human resource statistics which flows from Whitehall, there is no central register of expatriates. The broad trend can, however, be adduced by examining people's intentions, looking at the range of jobs on offer, and the numbers of applications for particular posts. The peak was probably reached in 1976. Thereafter, rising unemployment in many countries, political uncertainties in the Middle East and parts of Africa and perhaps more optimism about prospects at home combined to make people more cautious. Moreover, reductions in UK tax rates have tended to reduce financial incentives to work and live overseas.

However, expatriate employment, though continuing to be an attractive prospect to UK jobseekers, is no longer the Klondike it used to be. At present only the most intrepid and seasoned expatriates would consider taking up postings in most Middle East countries. Economic and political problems have affected the expatriate job markets in Africa and Latin America, and the outlook for most tiger economies of the Far East and Pacific is uncertain once again following China's accession to the World Trade Organisation. Compensating factors are a continuing demand in specific areas of employment, notably in the financial and retail service sectors, and the growth in short-term contracts.

This shading off has been accompanied by a trend towards greater stability in salaries, as well as some degree of uniformity in the remuneration packages being offered by different employers for comparable jobs, as competition for expatriate labour diminishes. In many parts of the world remuneration in sterling terms has only risen by the level of UK inflation.

Opportunities have diminished more markedly at technician and supervisory levels, because of competition from qualified personnel in developing countries who are prepared to accept much lower salaries, and also because of the gradual emergence of skilled workers among local nationals as the fruits of training schemes come on-stream. On the other hand, at more senior grades the relatively low level of British executive salaries by international standards continues to make UK managers an attractive proposition – especially those who are prepared to be reasonably flexible about working and living conditions. The typical American expatriate employee will often expect to take with him or her the standard of living associated with an executive lifestyle in the US. Consequently, more senior jobs are going to British or European personnel.

FINDING A JOB ABROAD

So how do you set about trying to find a job abroad? Both new and old forms of media provide ample opportunities for jobseekers looking from their home country. And for the brave, there is always the choice of turning up on spec to search out job opportunities in the chosen destination. However, the pros and cons of this last alternative should be fully understood and are discussed further on.

Newspapers

Not only the nationals and the Sunday newspapers but also the trade press carry overseas job advertisements. Graduates can look in annual career directories for details of overseas employers. It stands to reason that any employer wishing to recruit UK personnel will advertise in the UK press, but there is another good reason why the 'overseas vacancies' pages are worth scanning: they give a very good indication of the going rates of salary and benefits in particular parts of the world. Indeed, even if you have been made an offer without having replied to an advertisement, it is worth looking closely at these pages over a few issues to make sure that the remuneration package being put to you is in line with market rates.

However, if you are actually looking for a job, do not just confine your reading to the ads. It is worth reading any news and features that relate to the countries you are interested in. Not only will news of general or specific developments – a new type of industry opening up, for instance – give you background information that might be very useful in an interview, but it might also in itself be a source of job leads. Indeed, if you can read the papers in the language of the country you would like to work in, so much the better. They will go into potential job-lead information in more depth, and of course they contain job advertisements. How useful these are likely to be to the British jobseeker depends somewhat on the country in which the paper is published. In the Far East, for instance, employers would almost exclusively be looking for locals when advertising in a local paper. But in the EU, a response from a suitably qualified EU national might well produce a positive result. Indeed, in some European countries there is a trend towards taking on British people for overseas jobs. Quite a number of European countries are involved in projects in the Middle East and in other resource-rich countries where English is the dominant language. In those cases they are beginning to think in terms of putting some UK nationals on location as well as their own people.

Apart from the major newspapers, some countries have also developed their equivalent of career publications. Published every two weeks, *Overseas Jobs Express*, 20 New Road, Brighton, Sussex BN1 1UF (tel: 01273 699777, fax: 01273 699778, e-mail: editor@over seasjobsexpress.co.uk, Web site: www.overseasjobsexpress.co.uk) carries international recruitment advertising and provides information and news about working abroad. This excellent paper costs £75 a year, or £29.95 for three months. *Overseas Jobs Express* also publishes several books, including *Finding a Job in Canada* and *Finding a Job in Australia*, both £9.95, as well as a number of titles for young people wanting to live and work abroad.

There are also a number of news-sheets which are advertised from time to time, but some of them, it must be said, are fly-by-night operations and you would be ill-advised to part with your money without seeing a sample copy or to subscribe for more than six months at a time.

The Internet

One of the most effective ways of looking for a job abroad is to search the wide range of Web sites offering information for job-seekers. There are a number of ways in which the Internet can help and these resources are listed in Irene Krechowiecka's book *Net That Job!* (Kogan Page, £8.99). Useful categories include:

☐ Careers libraries in schools, colleges and universities.
☐ Professional associations and journals.
☐ People doing the job you are interested in. You can 'talk' to people via the Internet using a service such as Internet Relay Chat.
☐ Job advertisements, job descriptions and person specifications.
☐ Employers and employment agencies.
☐ Promotional organisations.

Many large employers have job advertisements and descriptions for every area of work and provide application forms online. Interesting sites are listed in the directory at the back of this book, but two good examples of employer Web sites can be found at Shell International on www.shell.com and Hewlett-Packard on www.europe.hp.com/Jobposting. Another invaluable resource is The Monster Board, which has information and sites in Canada, Australia, Belgium and The Netherlands on www.monster.com. Most large employers have sites and they are well worth a visit to assess what kinds of international opportunities are available. The advantages of carrying out a job search on the Internet are as follows:

☐ The main sources of information on vacancies are unchanged. However, they are made more accessible to all by means of the WWW.
☐ Searching for vacancies on the Web should be quicker and more effective than by other means. Dedicated search tools make finding appropriate jobs in newspapers and with agencies quick and straightforward.

- ☐ There are simple ways of arranging to be notified of suitable vacancies by e-mail.
- ☐ Some employers encourage and facilitate speculative applications via their Web sites.
- ☐ CV databases enable you to make your skills and abilities known to a large audience of potential employers.
- ☐ Web-based vacancy searches should enhance, not replace, other means of job hunting.

Source: *Net That Job,* **Irene Krechowiecka**

FINDING A JOB ON SPEC

Possible sources of job information are, of course, legion and they change constantly. Apart from keeping a close watch on the papers, as good a move as any is to get in touch with trade associations connected to the country in which you are interested or local chambers of commerce there. They will not be able to give you any job leads as such, unless you are very lucky, but they can usually give you lists of firms or other organisations that have a particularly close connection with the UK. Preliminary leads of this nature are essential if you are going to a country to look for a job on spec, though except in the EU you should never state this as your intention when entering a country. In most places now you need to have a job offer from a local employer in order to get a work permit, so you should always state that you are entering as a visitor, whatever your subsequent intention might be. It must be said, however, that some countries do not permit turning a visitor's visa into a work permit – that is something you will have to check on, discreetly, before you go.

In general, however, going abroad on spec to find a job is not a good idea. Even in the EU, where it is permitted, some jobseekers have had unhappy experiences unless they are in a 'hot' area such as electronics. By far the best plan is to get interviews lined up before you go or at least get some expressions of interest from potential employers – they will probably not commit themselves to more than that from a distance, even if there is a job possibility. To do more might put them under an embarrassing moral obligation when you turn up on their doorstep, having spent a lot of time and money to get there.

British jobseekers now have greater access to vacancies in Europe with the introduction of the EURES (European Employment Services) computer network, which provides jobseekers with free information and guidance on current opportunities throughout the EU. The database includes up-to-date information on living and working conditions in other member states. In Britain, anyone interested in working abroad can access the EURES database, and obtain advice from a Euroadviser, via their local Jobcentre. *The Overseas Placing Unit* (OPU) of the Employment Service produces a useful information booklet *Working Abroad*, as well as a series of guides entitled *Working in...*, concerning specific countries. These deal with entry requirements, information sources, benefits, liabilities, taxation, state of the market and cultural notes. The OPU also holds information on work overseas in specific professions. Write with your details to Overseas Placing Unit, Level 1, Rockingham House, 123 West Street, Sheffield S1 4ER (tel: 0114 259 6051).

Further useful information on the EU and its members can be accessed via Public Information Relays (PIR), European Documentation Centres (EDC) and Euro Info Centres (EIC) set up in libraries or at regional government offices or Business Links. Contact your local library for details of your nearest source of EU information.

Writing on-spec letters to potential employers is a subject that is well covered elsewhere. In essence what you have to do is address yourself to something that you have identified as being the employer's need or possible need – this is where researching the background and looking for job leads comes into play. For instance, if you have read in *Der Spiegel* or in *Frankfurter Allgemeine Zeitung* of a German firm being awarded a large contract in the Middle East, it is likely that they will respond in some way, provided your letter demonstrates that you have relevant experience. Even if they intend advertising the job, the fact that you have taken an intelligent interest in their activities will count in your favour. It is rarely worthwhile advertising in the situations wanted column, though writing to headhunters is a good move, especially if you are qualified to work in one of the fields in current demand: electronic engineering, financial services and retailing. Letters should be kept short and your CV should not exceed two pages – highlighting and quantifying achievements, rather than just listing posts you have held. With technical jobs you may have to show that your knowledge of the field is up to date with current developments, especially in areas where things are changing rapidly.

When a job is actually advertised, the interview will probably be in London, or your fare will be paid if you are called upon to travel abroad. Here again, the rules for replying to an advertisement are no different from those relating to UK employers: read the text carefully and frame your reply and organise your CV in such a way as to show that you meet the essential requirements of the job. As one Canadian employer put it recently, paraphrasing, no doubt, John F Kennedy's much quoted presidential address, 'The question to ask is not what I can gain from moving to your company, but what your company (or organisation or school) can gain from me.'

If you need to arrange your own travel, companies such as The Visaservice, 2 Northdown Street, London N1 9BG; tel: 020 7833 2709; 24-hour information line: 0891 343638 (50p at any time); fax: 020 7833 1857, Web site: www.visaservice.co.uk specialises in processing applications for business, working-holiday and tourism visas and passports on your behalf, which is particularly useful for those living outside London, where most embassies and consulates are located. Most professions have specialist agencies to help find work both nationally and internationally, and these could be a first port of call. Non-professional jobs such as au-pairing or voluntary work are also well served and details are given further on in this chapter.

SPECIALIST AREAS

Engineers and technicians

These terms cover many grades of expatriate worker, from truck drivers and road builders to site supervisors and project directors. Many overseas companies, especially airlines and construction companies, recruit directly in the UK by advertising in UK newspapers. Examine all such offers carefully. Many companies will arrange for technicians going abroad to meet compatriots on leave, who can answer their questions.

However, this is one area where opportunities are now very limited indeed. Workers from countries such as Korea, the Philippines and Pakistan now predominate at this end of the labour market.

At the top end of the scale, the Malla Technical Recruitment Consultancy at 173–175 Drummond Street, London NW1 3JD (tel: 020 7388 2284, fax: 020 7387 8312, e-mail: recruit@malla.com, Web site: www.malla.com) has a register of international engineering experts on all subjects who are leased out on contract worldwide.

The professionally qualified

The professions and qualifications most in demand overseas are medicine, agriculture and food, process engineering, finance, civil engineering and construction. In general, positions in these areas can best be found through the companies themselves or through management consultants and headhunters (executive search consultants). Many consultants specialise in particular professions such as accountancy.

Some are on a small, specialist scale. An example of an international, multi-purpose agency is International Training and Recruitment Link Ltd (ITRL, 56 High Street, Harston, Cambridge CB2 5PZ; tel: 01223 872747, fax: 01223 872212). ITRL recruit only for the Middle East, the Far East and North Africa. They are a major international training and recruitment agency specialising in executive, managerial, technical and scientific fields. They are particularly involved with construction, maintenance and operations, engineering, oil and petrochemicals, health care, hospitals, and general financial and commercial management.

People with professional qualifications will obviously consult their appropriate professional association or trade union. In the medical profession, jobs are usually found through advertisements in the medical press. BMA members are advised to contact the International Department at the British Medical Association (BMA House, Tavistock Square, London WC1H 9JP; tel: 020 7383 6491, fax: 020 7383 6644, www.bma.org.uk) for information and advice on working abroad. Most intending emigrants would prefer to work in North America and Australasia, but opportunities are limited. Within the EU there is recognition of medical qualifications. Remuneration is highest in Germany and Denmark, followed by France, Belgium and Luxembourg, with the UK towards the bottom of the scale. But there is unlikely to be much of a 'brain drain' to Europe since there is already a surplus of doctors in training and the profession is becoming particularly overcrowded in Italy and Scandinavia.

The developing countries, by contrast, are in urgent need of doctors and nurses. The average doctor/patient ratio in these countries is about 1:10,000 compared with 1:750 in the UK; in some areas it is as high as 1:80,000, rural areas being almost completely neglected. The International Health Exchange (8–10 Dryden Street, London WC2E 9NA; tel: 020 7620 3333, fax: 020 7379 1239, e-mail: info@ihe.org.uk, www.ihe.org.uk) helps provide appropriately trained health personnel for programmes in countries in Africa, Asia, the Pacific, Eastern Europe, Latin America and other areas seeking assistance. It maintains a register of health workers for those actively seeking work in developing countries and areas requiring humanitarian aid.

International demand for UK nurses has been reduced by worldwide recession and radical health service reforms in many countries, but opportunities still exist, particularly in the USA and the Middle East, for those with sound, post-registration experience and qualifications. The International Office of the Royal College of Nursing, 20 Cavendish Square, London W1M 0AB; tel: 020 7409 3333, www.rcn.org.uk provides overseas employment advice to its members, and overseas vacancies appear in weekly nursing journals such as *Nursing Standard*, on sale at newsagents.

Another useful publication is the CEPEC *Recruitment Guide*, which lists agencies and search consultants in the UK, including full details of their overseas work areas. CEPEC is itself a human resource consultancy and specialises in employee counselling, outplacement and career management. Further details from CEPEC, Lilly House, 13 Hanover Square, London W1R 9HD; tel: 020 7629 2266, fax: 020 7629 7066, e-mail: enquiries.focus@notesgw.compuserve.com, www.cepec.co.uk

In the UK the Department for Trade and Industry (DTI) provides information on the mutual recognition of professional qualifications at degree level and above and has overall responsibility for the operation of the UK Certificate of Experience Scheme, which is run by the British Chambers of Commerce on behalf of the DTI. The Department for Education and Employment (DfEE) provides advice on qualifications below degree level.

Further information can be obtained from DTI at Bay 212, Kingsgate House, 66–74 Victoria Street, London SW1E 6SW; tel: 020 7215 4648, fax: 020 7215 4489, and from DfEE at Room E4b, Moorfoot, Sheffield S1 4PQ; tel: 0114 259 4151, fax: 0114 259 4151, e-mail carol.rowlands@dfee.gov.uk, who can advise on international recognition of qualifications. Copies of the DTI/DfEE publication *Europe Open for Professions* are available from either organisation.

Information on the Certificate of Experience Scheme is available from the Certification Unit, British Chambers of Commerce, Westwood House, Westwood Business Park, Coventry CV4 8HS; tel: 024 7669 5688.

Finally, one can get a direct comparison between any UK qualifications and those recognised in any EU country via the National Academic Recognition Information Centre. However, you can only do this from abroad to the local jobcentre equivalent by asking to contact the local NARIC representative.

Business schools

For high-flyers, a possible route into the overseas job market is a course at one of the European business schools – either a short executive programme or a full-scale MBA. The latter course is in huge demand and is offered by a very large and ever-increasing number of schools worldwide, whether on a full-, part-time or distant basis. The Internet is also being adopted as a learning medium. However, one should weigh up its worth with care, given the effort, time and expense involved. A book and directory of business schools approved by the Association of MBAs is the annual *AMBA Guide to Business Schools* (FT/Pitman).

Another possibility lies with the Open University Business School, which offers a range of six-month courses on a distance-learning basis:

OUBS Customer Relations Centre, PO Box 625, Milton Keynes MK1 1TY; tel: 01908 654321 (24 hrs). The longest established European business school is INSEAD. Founded over 40 years ago, in 1959, today the school is widely recognised as one of the most influential business schools in the world. Its global scope and multicultural diversity make it the model for international management education. Located in Fontainebleau, France, INSEAD runs a 10-month MBA programme, a PhD programme and shorter executive development courses with a focus on general management in an international environment. Holders of the MBA can find jobs through the INSEAD Career Management Service. The emphasis is on international business management. Each year several hundred companies find that INSEAD is an excellent source for recruiting talented, multilingual and geographically mobile managers with high potential. Over one-third of graduates go on to start their own business sometime in their career. Students come from more than 50 countries with no single nationality dominating.

The majority of MBA students come as non-sponsored individuals. Various scholarships and loans are available. INSEAD is clearly a good investment for your future if you have the right background. Courses are taught in English but a fair knowledge of French is required. A third language is required in order to graduate and courses in German and Spanish are available. For further information contact INSEAD, MBA Admissions, Boulevard de Constance, F-77305 Fountainebleau Cedex; tel: +33 1 60 72 40 05, fax: +33 1 60 74 33 00.

Department for International Development

The Department for International Development (DfID) manages Britain's programme of aid to developing countries. The range of skills required under the programme is vast and constantly changing. Workers are drawn from a large number of backgrounds and professions such as agriculture, education and engineering.

The minimum requirement for most vacancies is usually a professional qualification and at least two to three years' relevant experience, including some in a developing country. A limited number of postgraduate study awards are also offered. Successful applicants are usually given assignments of up to two to three years as either a cooperation officer, employed by the DfID and 'on loan' to the overseas client government, or as a supplemented officer, under contract to the relevant government on local salary, with a supplement provided by the DfID to equal UK pay level.

Where the DfID needs immediate expert advice, consultants are used on appointments lasting from a few days to several months. Such assignments are open to both employed and self-employed specialists. The DfID also provides assistance to the United Nations and its specialist agencies (eg International Labour Office) in recruitment to field programmes, as well as the Junior Professional Officers Scheme.

For further information please write, enclosing a CV, to the Service and Resource Development Group, Room AH304, Department for International Development, Abercrombie House, Eaglesham Road, East Kilbride, Glasgow G75 8EA (tel: 01355 844000, fax: 01355 844099).

The British Council

The British Council (10 Spring Gardens, London SW1A 2BN; tel: 020 7930 8466, www.britishcouncil.org) promotes Britain abroad. It provides access to British ideas, talents and experience through education and training, books and periodicals, the English language, the arts, science and technology.

It is represented in 109 countries, 209 libraries and information centres and over 118 English language schools and has offices in 228 towns and cities. The Council provides an unrivalled network of contacts with government departments, universities, embassies, professional bodies and business and industry in Britain and overseas.

The British Council is an independent and non-political organisation. In developing countries it has considerable responsibilities for the DfID in the field of educational aid, and in recent years it has become involved in the design and implementation of education projects funded by international lending agencies such as the World Bank.

The Council also acts as an agent for governments and other employers overseas in recruiting for contract teaching and educational advisory posts in ministries, universities, training colleges and secondary and primary schools. The Council usually guarantees the terms of such posts and sometimes subsidises them. In these appointments it works closely with the DfID. Teachers are also recruited on contract for the Council's network of English language schools.

Vacancies include teacher trainers, curriculum designers and British studies specialists for posts in projects or for direct placement with overseas institutions. Candidates must be professionally qualified and have appropriate experience.

Appointments are usually for one or two years initially and often renewable by agreement. Vacancies are advertised in *The Times Educational Supplement, The Guardian* and other journals as appropriate.

Teaching English as a foreign language

EFL teachers are in demand in both the private and public education sectors abroad. Public sector recruiting is usually done by the government concerned through the British Council; private recruitment varies from the highly reputable organisation (such as International House) to the distinctly dubious. Most EFL teachers have a degree and/or teaching qualification. An RSA/ Cambridge TEFLA qualification will also be required. A four-week RSA/Cambridge Certificate in TEFLA (Teaching English as a Foreign Language to Adults) is available at International House in London and Hastings, and at a number of other centres. The course may also be taken on a part-time basis. Experienced EFL teachers may gain a further qualification, the RSA/Cambridge Diploma in TEFLA (essential for more responsible posts). The University of Cambridge Local Examinations Syndicate (tel. 01223 553311) can provide comprehensive lists of the centres running courses leading to these awards, worldwide.

Bear the following points in mind when applying for an EFL post abroad:

☐ Will your travel expenses be paid? Some schools refund them on arrival or at the end of the contract.

☐ Is accommodation provided? If so, is it free or is the rent deducted from your salary? Is your salary sufficient to meet the deduction? If you find your own accommodation, are you helped to find it, especially if your knowledge of the local language is modest? Does the school lend you money to help pay the accommodation agency's fee and deposit? If the accommodation is provided, does it include hard or soft furnishing, and what should you bring with you?

☐ Contracts and work permits. Will you have a contract, how long for, and will the school obtain the permits to legalise your position in the country?

☐ Salary. Are you paid by the hour, week or month? If you are paid by the hour, is there a guaranteed minimum amount of teaching available for you? Do ensure that you can survive financially in the face of cancelled classes, bank strikes and numerous public holidays. Are there cost-of-living adjustments in countries with alarming inflation rates? Salaries are generally geared to local rates, but do make sure they are adequate. In sterling terms, one may earn a very low salary (in Rabat, for instance) yet enjoy a higher standard of living than a teacher earning double in Italy, or three times as much in Singapore.

☐ How many hours are you expected to teach? Be wary of employers who expect you to teach more than about 25 hours a week (remember you need additional time to prepare lessons). What paid leisure time do you expect? This is variable, but two weeks at both Easter and Christmas is fairly common.

☐ What type of student will you be teaching? Children or adults, those learning general English or English for special purposes (ESP)?

☐ What levels will you be teaching and what course books will be used? Will there be a director of studies to help you over any initial difficulties and provide some form of in-service training?

A knowledge of the local language is an asset; in some situations, it is absolutely essential. Without it, one's social contacts are restricted to the English-speaking community which, in some areas, is virtually non-existent.

_____

24

Locating the vacancies

1. International House recruits teachers only for its own affiliated schools, of which there are 100 in 26 countries. Vacancies elsewhere can be seen on the IH noticeboard in the Staffing Unit, 106 Piccadilly, London W1V 9FL (tel: 020 7491 2598, fax: 020 7491 2679, e-mail: 100645;1547@compuserve.com, www.international-house-london.ac).

2. Advertisements appear in publications such as *The Times Educational Supplement* (Fridays) and *The Guardian* (Tuesdays).

3. The British Council Central Management of Direct Teaching recruits EFL teachers for the British Council's Language Centres around the world. It can be contacted at 10 Spring Gardens, London SW1A 2BN (tel: 020 7930 8466, www.britishcouncil.org). British Council vacancies are also advertised in the press. The British Council Overseas Appointments Services recruits for posts funded directly by overseas employers. It can be contacted at Medlock Street, Manchester M15 4AA, tel: 0161 957 7384; fax: 0161 957 7397.

4. The Centre for British Teachers, CfBT Education Services, 1 The Chambers, East Street, Reading RG1 4JD (tel: 0118 952 3900, fax: 0118 952 3924, e-mail: intrecruit@cfbt-hq.org.uk, www.cfbt.com) recruits teachers for English language teaching projects in Brunei, Oman and Turkey and educational specialists for consultancies on donor-funded projects in Eastern Europe, Africa, Asia and India.

5. The Central Bureau (c/o British Council, 10 Spring Gardens, London SW1A 2BN, tel: 020 7389 4929; fax: 020 7389 4426) compiles guides on a range of paid and voluntary work opportunities worldwide.

Voluntary work

Those who are technically skilled or professionally qualified and who would like to share their skills with developing countries could apply to VSO (Voluntary Service Overseas). VSO has over 1,750 skilled people working in 58 countries: in Africa, Asia, the Caribbean, Eastern Europe and the Pacific. Placements are in education, health, natural resources, technical trades, engineering, business, communications and social development. Volunteers are aged from 20 to 70, usually 23–60, with no dependent children. Accommodation and a modest living allowance are provided by the local employer. Flights, insurance and other allowances are provided by VSO. Posts are generally for two years, but many volunteers stay longer.

Working as a VSO volunteer is very much a two-way process; volunteers often feel that they learn more from the society and culture they are involved with than they can possibly contribute. For further information contact The Enquiries Unit, VSO, 317 Putney Bridge Road, London SW15 2PN, tel: 020 7780 7500, fax: 020 7780 7576, Web site: www.oneworld.org/vso/.

Checklist: Independent job opportunities

1. Research professional and national media for overseas jobs.
2. Investigate opportunities on the Internet and place your CV with databanks on the WWW.
3. Check out the possibilities of turning a visitor's visa into a work permit before you look for a job on spec.
4. Contact your trade or professional associations for overseas vacancies and guidance on employment conditions and what to expect.
5. Consider taking a qualification, such as an MBA, in a foreign business school as a way to open doors overseas.
6. Examine the pay and conditions of language schools.
7. Have realistic expectations of short-term work such as au pairing or working on a kibbutz, and ensure that all details are given in writing before departure.

2 | *Managing Internationally Mobile Employees*

This chapter is primarily for organisations seeking guidance on the development of their human resource (HR) strategies and on reward packages for employees sent abroad, whether:

☐ on short- or longer-term assignments either as comnuuters or locally resident to support local business needs, for example to provide project skills or management expertise; or
☐ as permanent relocations to fulfil a particular local role; or
☐ as part of a globally mobile executive cadre who frequently move from country to country.

An understanding of the employer's perspective is also important to company managers and specialist skilled staff who are asked to work abroad in any of these capacities or for whom international experience is a prerequisite for career advancement into senior management positions. Individual readers who are not working now, or do not intend to work, in a corporate environment, may prefer to omit this chapter and go forward to Part Two.

PREPARING THE BUSINESS CASE

Who needs a mobile workforce?

The need to fill overseas appointments with managers or skilled staff selected from an employer's home base or another of its overseas operations, rather than with local nationals, can arise at any time. This applies equally to large multinational organisations and to smaller companies, whose activities have extended from the domestic market into as little as one overseas manufacturing location or a handful of export markets. The degree of globalisation may vary within the following continuum:

☐ from companies engaged in the export of goods and/or services only;
☐ to international companies (including those with loosely associated, autonomous operations in just a few locations);
☐ to multinationals with operations in a number of different countries in more than one region, having common business processes and systems (especially financial controls and IT);
☐ to global corporations covering most, if not all, developed and transition economies, with universal branding, integrated marketing and manufacturing strategies and centrally controlled financial, corporate planning and HR functions.

The background to this continuum is an unstoppable trend of globalisation that has been characterised as 'The continued and growing economic interdependence of countries, the increasing volume and variety of cross-border transaction' (International Monetary Fund, 1997 – *World Economic Outlook*).

Why have an IME policy?

The large organisations in the multinational and global categories will certainly have in place HR policies for the management of internationally mobile employees (IMEs).

Smaller organisations, whose IME requirements are occasional or sporadic, may be tempted to manage expatriate assignments on an *ad hoc* basis without articulating an IME strategy or reward policies. Besides being poor management practice, lack of clearly defined policy is dangerous and can lead to unwelcome outcomes.

For example, in the case of an international company that has decided to develop a new manufacturing operation involving a transfer of technology from the home plant, the only course of action may be to send a senior factory manager for a period of two to three years to handle the start-up and to develop a local management capability. An external appointment is not really feasible, because of the technology transfer, and there may be no more than one, or perhaps two candidates. In these circumstances the company's opportunistic decision to invest may be matched by the preferred or only candidate's equally opportunistic demands for the most favourable reward package that the employee can achieve. In the absence of an established reward policy, the company might find it impossible to resist the employee's more exorbitant demands and, worse still, the appointment risks setting a precedent that the company would not wish to repeat.

A familiar client scenario for Towers Perrin, the international human resource management consultancy, is that in which a new client describes an overseas appointment that it plans to make and asks 'How much do we need to pay?' Invariably, Towers Perrin's advice is for the client to take a step back and develop a business case for the assignment before considering the package. Necessary conditions for preparing the business case are that the client has already developed its business strategy and can analyse its motivation for making the appointment.

INTERNATIONALLY MOBILE EMPLOYEE (IME) STRATEGY

Who are the stakeholders?

A first step in the strategy development process is recognition by the corporate employer that there are four interested parties or players to each international staff transfer:

- [ ] the home country operation from which the employee is transferred;
- [ ] the host country operation to which the employee is transferred;
- [ ] the overall corporation and its group interest;
- [ ] the employee who is sent on assignment.

The interests of each player differ widely as Chart 2.1 demonstrates.

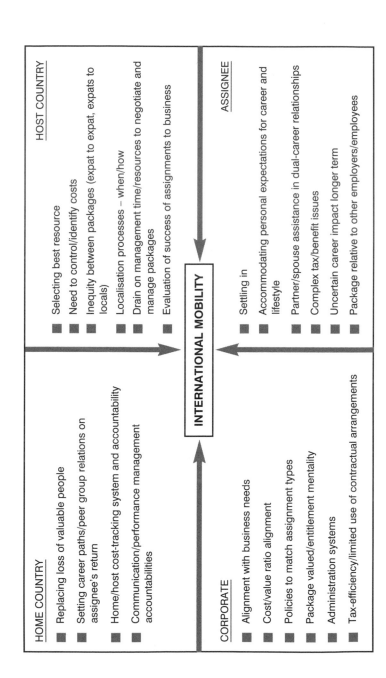

HOST COUNTRY

■ Selecting best resource
■ Need to control/identify costs
■ Inequity between packages (expat to expat, expats to locals)
■ Localisation processes – when/how
■ Drain on management time/resources to negotiate and manage packages
■ Evaluation of success of assignments to business

HOME COUNTRY

■ Replacing loss of valuable people
■ Setting career paths/peer group relations on assignee's return
■ Home/host cost-tracking system and accountability
■ Communication/performance management accountabilities

INTERNATIONAL MOBILITY

ASSIGNEE

■ Settling in
■ Accommodating personal expectations for career and lifestyle
■ Partner/spouse assistance in dual-career relationships
■ Complex tax/benefit issues
■ Uncertain career impact longer term
■ Package relative to other employers/employees

CORPORATE

■ Alignment with business needs
■ Cost/value ratio alignment
■ Policies to match assignment types
■ Package valued/entitlement mentality
■ Administration systems
■ Tax-efficiency/limited use of contractual arrangements

Chart 2.1 International mobility – the players and their issues

What are their issues?

The key issues concerning management of the home country and host country operations are self-explanatory; for both of these players the transfer of skilled and experienced employees is inevitably a disruptive event that will affect the smooth running of their local businesses. Similarly, for the assignee and his or her family the key concerns are clearly definable, although the order of importance attached to each issue will vary. The various issues are discussed separately in the sections that follow.

The corporate issues are necessarily more complex, involving the need to balance the interests of the home and host operations with overriding group interest, which include building and maintaining a cadre of effective, experienced and well-motivated IMEs. Particular attention is given to reward strategy, selection criteria and career management later in this chapter.

What are the business drivers?

The next step in strategic planning is to analyse the external reasons for deploying IMEs in terms of global business strategy, which drives organisational capabilities and requirements and, in turn, generates the need for mobility. In smaller, export-orientated companies the dominant international business motivation is likely to remain opportunism; for international companies the dominant focus will probably be business control and technology transfer in selected markets. For truly multinational companies, the international business focus becomes management of the group's portfolio of businesses while the global corporation, by definition, is focused on managing a worldwide business.

The organisation structures of these four types of company in the globalisation continuum follow their international business focus. Export-orientated companies are usually organised by function or division, but the next level of international companies relies on centralised core competencies with local coordination.

In multinational corporations the organisational balance shifts towards decentralised, nationally self-sufficient subsidiaries. Finally, the global corporation seeks to develop an integrated 'borderless' structure that fosters interdependence within a strong corporate culture.

What are the likely IME profiles?

These organisation requirements in turn determine the sourcing of key talent and the characteristics of international personnel expatriates. Export-orientated companies can only draw their IMEs from the headquarters country, which is their sole source of key talent. International companies may have a choice between their headquarters country and key operating countries to source mid-career executives and business specialists but the number of 'from-to' alternatives is likely to be limited.

Within multinationals, the alternative combinations drawn from developed operations countries or headquarters will grow and include younger executives who are given international exposure and experience within career development programmes.

In global corporations, IMEs are drawn from worldwide centres of excellence and include senior as well as mid-career executives with business specialist and developmental staff deployed in growing numbers in new markets.

Within these parameters, each company individually needs to define:

☐ the business need;
☐ the extent to which local managers can be used;
☐ at what levels and which functions international managers will perform.

What are the resourcing aims?

Following these definitions, the company will be able to set its HR policies for the development and deployment of IMEs. For example, one UK-based global corporation has ruled that top management positions in any country must be filled by local nationals with international experience.

Further examples, in contrast, are the diverse IME strategies of two automotive global corporations for their joint ventures in China. Volkswagen, the Chinese market leader in passenger car manufacture, has established a management structure in its Shanghai plants where Chinese and German managers work in parallel positions at each management level from general manager to departmental managers. All management responsibilities and decisions are taken on a partnership basis.

Fiat-Iveco took a quite different approach when developing their van manufacturing joint venture at an established Chinese factory in Nanjing. Over a two-year period, a total of some 200 Chinese employees were taken to Italy for six-month periods to be trained and work in an Iveco factory manufacturing similar vehicles. After the programme there are just two Italian managers left in Nanjing, one marketing expert and one manufacturing manager, both operating in largely mentoring roles. One by-product of the programme, surprising to visitors, is that the entire Chinese management team speaks fluent Italian.

Even in smaller international or export-orientated companies there are some functions that are almost always performed by expatriates from the headquarters country. Start-ups in a new territory or training to deliver skills in local markets inevitably involve expatriate management. In post-acquisition situations it is normal to import an expatriate general manager and financial controller, unless there is a long-established and successful local operation within the group from which the positions can be filled.

How are the IME categories defined?

Development of IME strategy also involves determining the different categories of IME and the types of people to be assigned. Expatriate assignments may be categorised by length of appointment – six months or less, perhaps, in the case of training local staff for skills or technology transfers; two to five years (which may even result in localisation at the end of the assignment) in the case of senior line management appointments. Appointees for these assignments are usually drawn from mid-career managers at sub-divisional board level and, in the case of technology transfer appointments, may include case-hardened older managers who may be at retirement age post-assignment.

There has been a growing trend towards so-called 'commuter' appointments where the IME travels from his or her base every week. Very often the commuting approach is adopted at the instigation of the appointee whose family are unwilling to move, and may not represent the employer's first choice for assignments of longer than six months. Although the considerable cost of moving a partner and family may be avoided, commuting generates many strains on the employee, both socially and on work performance, and may have an adverse effect on peer relationships with local managers who resent the apparent privilege and reduced involvement.

In multinationals and global corporations there is a further category of junior developmental IMEs who are being given early international experience both to load the pipeline of available talent and to cement organisational and cultural integration within the company. Junior developmental assignees are normally in their mid-20s to 30s, often without family commitments, possibly having single status.

Finally, in the global corporation there will be a cadre of career internationalists employed at headquarters level and drawn from any country within the span of the group's activities who are committed to moving from one international assignment to the next. They are the cultural glue of the organisation and the world is truly their oyster.

REWARD STRATEGY

In the light of the company's articulated IME strategy, management should now turn to determining reward strategy and compensation policies. In the case of the smaller company considering a single assignment to meet an *ad hoc* business opportunity, the IME strategy will assist in making the business case and fixing the reward package in terms of the confirmed need for an expatriate appointment and a reasoned cost/benefit analysis.

How to develop appropriate reward programmes?

A successful reward strategy encompasses much more than the compensation package, although that may be the key practical element in ensuring that the appointee, partner and family set off on the assignment with confidence and in a positive frame of mind. Towers Perrin typically work with organisations to develop a checklist of globally mobile programme components, each of which they discuss with their clients in order to determine the degree of significance. This will enable the company to prioritise the key elements of the reward programme, as:

1. critical to success;
2. important to be fair and equitable;
3. limited importance but cannot ignore.

An example of this Towers Perrin's matrix is reproduced overleaf as Chart 2.2 – *Relative importance of globally mobile programme components*. Towers Perrin work with the organisation to determine to what extent these different components should be given different priorities for the various categories of assignees that the company may potentially have, as shown in the chart.

If you are in the business of designing your company's reward strategy or a prospective candidate for an expatriate appointment, you may like to complete the matrix for relevant positions.

What are the key reward issues?

Paramount among the employer's reward strategy principles is the objective of moving the assignee's motivation from a package value/entitlement mindset towards a personal focus on career development through the acceptance of overseas assignments and/or an international career. This may be more difficult in the case of smaller companies where the range of opportunities for IMEs is limited, or inappropriate in the case of older managers for whom a single overseas assignment precedes retirement.

Indeed, retirement is a key issue in reward strategy and pension benefits are recognised as a major element in the compensation package. There is a natural fear on the part of many IMEs who are members of a pension plan in the home territory that their entitlements will be affected adversely by secondment to an overseas operation.

PROGRAM COMPONENTS	SENIOR EXECUTIVES	HIGH POTENTIALS	CAREER INTER-NATIONALISTS	KEY REGIONAL/LOCAL EXECUTIVES	SKILL GAP TRANSFERS	REGIONAL TRANSFERS	DEVELOPMENTAL TRANSFERS
Career planning							
Base salary							
Short-term incentives							
Long-term incentives							
Retirement							
Health care							
Expatriate support services							
Special needs (tax, housing, education, spousal career)							
Flexibility							
Assimilation							
Next assignment support							
Communications							
Integration with corporate programmes							

KEY: 1. Critical to success   2. Important to be fair and equitable   3. Limited importance but cannot ignore

Chart 2.2 Relative importance of globally mobile programme components

How to address retirement benefits

Here, as in many other areas of reward strategy, a flexible approach by the employer is required commensurate with the nature and duration of the assignment.

In the case of short-term or traditional two- to three-year assignments the best approach is to maintain the employee in the home pension plan. If the pension scheme rules do not permit membership during absence, the company might need to substitute an unfunded promise for the assignment period or enrol the IME in membership of the host operation pension plan (if there is one). As a last resort, the loss of future entitlement can be compensated for by extra basic pay. In the case of internationalist staff the most favoured alternatives are to enrol the IME in the home or host country or headquarters plan with unfunded top up where a global standard has been promised or to enrol in the group international pension plan (if there is one). In fact, there is an increasing trend towards implementing international plans, sometimes established in an offshore location. Advantages of such plans include:

☐ continuity of retirement provision, regardless of where the IME works;

☐ security of benefits (depending on design and financing method);

☐ greater equity among IMEs of different nationalities and locations of employment;

☐ planned design, which can incorporate much more flexibility than local plans to address diverse employee needs;

☐ readier adaptability to any other wealth accumulation programmes for executives;

☐ potentially simpler administration than a multiplicity of local plans.

For IMEs who are transferred permanently, the preferred options are to enrol in the host plan for the whole period of service or retain membership of the home plan for all or part of past service and enrol in the host plan for future service.

What are the trends?

In addition to employer recognition of pension and other benefits as key parts of total reward, Towers Perrin identify five further trends:

☐ increasing emphasis on tailoring IME reward to business needs by matching segmentation of policies to the recognition of diversity;
☐ a movement towards performance-driven packages;
☐ some use of global/regional packages;
☐ simplification of allowance structures;
☐ stronger emphasis on employee communication and family support.

In the context of this book, the last two trends in the above list demand additional comment. Surveys of IMEs have shown that a flexible approach to the award and administration of allowances is a very important factor for expatriate employees.

Where the employer has no particular concerns other than cost, judgements can be left to the employer. For example, in the matter of family travel allowances, where the company provides for a home visit once a year, it might allow the option of disbursing an equivalent sum if the family decided to spend that time travelling in the region of the host country or elsewhere. Similarly, flexibility may be given to the removal allowances for moving home, setting up in new accommodation and returning home at the end of the assignment. For example, rather than disbursement against invoices up to a prescribed limit, the employer might consider a lump sum approach with, say, two-thirds paid up front and the balance on return.

Moreover, host housing provision typically forms an important (and costly) part of the overall package. Companies are now becoming more cautious of the need to control these costs and are offering cash allowances of a level to provide appropriate (but not luxurious) accommodation, which the IME then uses, or supplements, to meet the family's particular housing needs.

Successful reward is not just about cash

Communication by the company with the assignee and his/her family both before and during the assignment is now recognised as an important factor in helping IMEs to prepare for the transfer and to settle in. Family support extends to helping the family investigate and decide on the most appropriate schooling for children and is focused strongly on helping partners to resolve dual-career issues. For partners who decide to step out from their home country careers for the period of the assignment, financial assistance is often given to obtain a job in the host country or to maintain professional education standards during absence from work. However, few if any companies would directly compensate the partner for loss of income during their absence.

Returning to the second item on the list of further trends identified by Towers Perrin, a corollary to the tailoring of IME reward to business needs is the absolute necessity that any diversity within the categories should be seen to be equitable and that there should be a justifiable logic for differentiation between categories.

In conclusion on the topic of reward strategy, Chart 2.3 overleaf is a reproduction of Towers Perrin's total reward model for multinational and global corporations. Under a successful reward strategy, the tangible transactional elements of pay and benefits strengthen and are themselves supported by the intangible relational outcomes of individual learning and development and the communal work environment.

SELECTION

We have already referred to the problems that international companies face when there is a dearth of candidates for an expatriate appointment. For multinationals and global corporations the solution lies in creating a talent pool from which IMEs can be selected as assignments arise. With this objective in mind, the company should assess incoming staff on their potential for international assignments when hiring.

Towers Perrin list the most common required competencies for international managers as:

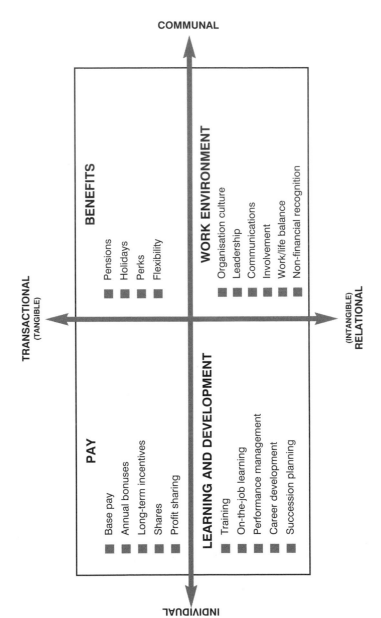

COMMUNAL

BENEFITS
- Pensions
- Holidays
- Perks
- Flexibility

WORK ENVIRONMENT
- Organisation culture
- Leadership
- Communications
- Involvement
- Work/life balance
- Non-financial recognition

TRANSACTIONAL
(TANGIBLE)

RELATIONAL
(INTANGIBLE)

PAY
- Base pay
- Annual bonuses
- Long-term incentives
- Shares
- Profit sharing

LEARNING AND DEVELOPMENT
- Training
- On-the-job learning
- Performance management
- Career development
- Succession planning

INDIVIDUAL

Chart 2.3 A total reward model

- [ ] cultural sensitivity;
- [ ] interpersonal skills;
- [ ] listening;
- [ ] flexibility/adaptability;
- [ ] ability to learn;
- [ ] personal ambiguity tolerance;
- [ ] emotional stability;
- [ ] technical competencies.

Relationship and self-enhancement skills are placed ahead of technical skills and abilities.

What are the important selection criteria?

Of course, selection is a two-way process. Given the emphasis that employers now place on accommodating partner needs, companies understand that acceptance of an expatriate appointment is a collective family decision and have become mindful of the factors in expatriate partner suitability. Interestingly, Towers Perrin have found that employers and employees agree on the relative importance, in descending order, of the following characteristics, although in a recent survey a rather higher percentage of employers than employees mentioned each factor, except for language skills:

- [ ] family flexibility;
- [ ] personal resilience;
- [ ] personality;
- [ ] cultural sensitivity;
- [ ] interpersonal skills;
- [ ] international experience;
- [ ] employability;
- [ ] language skills.

Within the company the selection process for each appointment ideally involves the HR and finance functions and line management within the division to which the appointee will be assigned. However, the whole process of IME selection is a minefield as the following collection of facts and figures demonstrates:

☐ the cost of intended assignments is normally 2 to 3.5 times the home package;

☐ 40 per cent of international assignees (IAs) return early;*

☐ 97 per cent of IAs agree success is directly related to the happiness of their partner;

☐ 20 per cent of companies involve partners at the selection stage;**

☐ 25 per cent of businesses are looking at changing their selection procedures;**

☐ 50 per cent of IAs would like changes to be made to selection procedures.

Sources: * Kealey **CBI/Umist 1995

Towers Perrin believe that the overall global demand for IMEs may be shrinking as companies realise that they can do better with local employee development programmes, and that the Internet revolution has made it easier to manage multinationals remotely, particularly in terms of financial controls, monitoring, technical input and consultancy advice. The increasing reluctance of companies to guarantee repatriation of IMEs to their home operations at the end of longer-term assignments may be symptomatic of this trend. There is also some evidence that the global trend towards outsourcing key functions has also impacted the incidence of expatriate placements.

CAREER MANAGEMENT

Managing careers and expectations is a crucial aspect of growing and maintaining a pool of talented IMEs. Unsuccessful placements and disaffected managers who believe that the organisation has reneged on its promises quickly taint the well of talent from which IMEs are drawn and developed. The objective of moving personal motivation from the compensation package to career fulfilment will only be achieved if there are sufficient case histories that demonstrate that the company cares about, plans and develops the careers of individuals.

Critical to manage career expectations

Succession planning is an important aspect of career management and in the field of international appointments it is normal to include in the expatriate assignee's job description participation in the task of identifying, selecting and training a replacement to ensure continuity.

Given that there are no prior commitments to job security in today's business world, it is normal for a contract of expatriate employment to specify the term of the appointment, to set out a procedure for discussing repatriation in the final six to 12 months of the appointment and to provide for an extended period of notice – say six months – in the event that a further appointment is not on offer.

Performance management is an integral part of HR best practice and career management, even if the reward package does not include an element of performance-related compensation. Annual appraisals including a review of personal performance against responsibilities and tasks and the joint setting of objectives for the next year are the norm among multinationals and global corporations, as well as some smaller companies. They are conducted either by group/home office management in the case of senior appointments or by regional or local management superiors.

For IMEs performance reviews may be an important point of contact with home country management colleagues but regular liaison throughout the year between home and host country with colleagues and peers is essential to the appointee's well-being and effectiveness.

IMPLEMENTATION/ONGOING ADMINISTRATION

Towers Perrin recommend that the process of managing international assignees should be fully integrated by the HR function responsible for administration. The process involves the following consecutive phases:

☐ profiling the assignment;
☐ screening, assessment and selection;
☐ pre-departure preparation;
☐ supporting and managing performance;
☐ pre-return (or next assignment) preparation;
☐ managing re-entry or next assignment;
☐ evaluation.

The transition phases are particularly stressful for the assignee and his/her family; companies experienced in expatriate placement are careful to provide as much information and administrative support as possible in handling the logistics of the move abroad and the family's return. In larger corporations the development of peer group family circles among other expatriates in the host country have been particularly helpful in acclimatising new arrivals to the unfamiliar environment and culture.

Good communication is critical to success

Transition, either return to the home country or localisation within the host country, may also involve some reduction in the compensation package. This is an issue that needs careful handling and communication. In some cases, companies may phase out the additional allowances or benefits over a period rather than withdraw them immediately.

Enhanced communication is an ongoing theme in the effective implementation of IME strategy, including handbooks and newsletters for family consumption and a company Web site giving full information on company policy in all HR areas. All too often company perceptions of IME satisfaction or dissatisfaction with aspects of IME reward strategy differ keenly from reality, as do employee perceptions of what the corporate strategy may really be. Such misconceptions are invariably rooted in communications failure.

Payroll and tax are other sensitive areas in IME administration. Very often companies prefer to keep the details of IME reward packages confidential from local host company operations and will continue to pay expatriates from the centre, making appropriate tax deductions. Some global and multinational corporations have chosen to form service companies that employ all IMEs and lease out their services to the operations to which they are assigned. In this way the individual remuneration details are hidden within an overall leasing charge. It is sometimes suggested that registration of such service companies in tax havens will reduce the taxation burden. However, this device is unlikely to benefit IME employees, who are generally taxed according to their place of domicile rather than employment.

The home base or headquarters should remain responsive to the daily needs of expatriate employees and their families. Cutting the umbilical cord between the employee and the home office generates insecurity and there ought to be at least one member of HR staff with responsibility for the welfare of IME expatriates who is able to provide a helpline service.

In summary, Towers Perrin remind the administrators of IME strategy of the main objectives for each stage in the expatriate cycle:

☐ *Pre-departure.* Create and sustain a sufficient and high-calibre demand pool for assignments.
☐ *On assignment.* Facilitate business delivery consistent with strategy and justify expatriate spend.
☐ *Package.* Provide competitive and comprehensive compensation and benefit programme to retain key staff.
☐ *Next assignment.* Integrate valuable assignment knowledge within the organisation to ensure continuity of the cycle.

Checklist: The employer's perspective

1. Avoid making expatriate appointments without preparing a business case first.
2. Identify where your company stands in the globalisation continuum.
3. Develop an IME strategy for your company.
4. Define your company's business need for IMEs, the extent to which local managers can be used and the levels and functions where IMEs will perform.

5. Define reward strategy and develop compensation policies according to your company's IME strategy to be equitable within and justifiable between job categories.
6. Move your IMEs motivation from a package value/entitlement mindset to focusing on career development.
7. Recognise that retirement is a key issue in reward strategy, particularly for older IMEs.
8. Simplify and allow flexibility of allowance structures.
9. Emphasise employee communication and family support.
10. Recognise the needs of dual-career partners.
11. Place relationship and self-enhancement skills ahead of technical skills in IME selection criteria.
12. Manage IME career development and plan for succession.

Checklist: Employment conditions

If you have been offered employment abroad, bear in mind that you will incur a whole range of expenses which would not arise if you were employed here. It is vital to consider these expenses and to check whether your remuneration package covers them, either directly or in the form of fringe benefits.

If you are going to work for a reputable international company, it will probably have a standard reward package that includes the fringe benefits that it is prepared to offer. But if your employer is new to, or inexperienced in, the game of sending people to work abroad (especially if he or she is a native of the country to which you are going and therefore possibly not aware of expatriates' standards in such matters as housing) here are some of the factors you should look at in assessing how good the offer really is.

To help you arrive at realistic, up-to-date answers to the following questions, it is worth trying to talk to someone who has recently worked in the country to which you are thinking of going, as well as reading the relevant sections in this book.

If you are discussing the terms of an executive appointment abroad you may find Chart 5.1 at the end of Part Five useful. Prepared by Towers Perrin it compares the executive perquisites that are commonly granted to executives of larger public companies in 25 locations around the world. More details from Towers Perrin's 'Worldwide Total Remuneration 2001–2002' may be found at www.towersperrin.com.

1. **Family**
   (a) Is your employer going to help your partner find a job or to identify other opportunities such as further education or voluntary work?
   (b) If your employer is not able to help your partner find work, do they have a policy of reimbursing for loss of income?
   (c) Is your partner involved in the briefing sessions provided by your employer before departure?
   (d) Does your employer provide a support network for your partner?
   (e) Will your employer provide details of schools?
   (f) Do you have contacts provided by your employer to talk to before you move?
   (g) Is your employer going to meet the cost of travel out from the UK for your family as well as yourself?

2. **Accommodation**
   (a) Is your employer going to provide accommodation? If so:
   - [ ] of what standard?
   - [ ] how soon will it be available after you arrive?
   - [ ] is it furnished or unfurnished? If furnished, what will be provided in the way of furniture?
   (b) If accommodation is not free, but there is a subsidy, is this assessed:
   - [ ] as an absolute sum? In this case, is it realistic in the light of current prices? If not, is there any provision to adjust it?
   - [ ] as a proportion of what you will actually have to pay?
   (c) Who is going to pay for utilities (gas, water, electricity, telephone)?
   (d) If there is no subsidy and accommodation is not free, are you sure your salary, however grand it sounds, is adequate? Do not accept the job unless you are sure about this.

(e) Will the employer subsidise or pay for you and your family's hotel bills for a reasonable period until you find somewhere to live? Is the figure realistic in the light of local hotel prices?

3. **Removal assistance**

   (a) Will you be paid a disturbance allowance? Is it adequate to cover the cost of shipping (and, possibly, duty at the other end) for as many household and personal effects as you need? Will your eventual return to the UK as well as your departure be taken care of?

   (b) What arrangements will be made:

   ☐ to cover legal and other fees if you have to sell your UK home?

   ☐ to cover the difference, if you have to let your UK home while you are away, between the rental income and such outgoings as insurance, mortgage interest and agent's management? Will you be compensated for any legal expenses you incur, eg to get rid of an unsatisfactory tenant?

   ☐ to cover the cost of storing household effects?

4. **Personal effects and domestic help**

   (a) Will you be paid a clothing allowance, bearing in mind that you will need a whole new wardrobe if you are going to a hot country? Will it cover just your clothes, or those of your family as well?

   (b) Will your employer pay for or subsidise household items (eg air conditioning) that you will need in a hot climate and that are not included in an accommodation package?

   (c) Will your employer provide/subsidise the cost of domestic servants? If not, is your salary adequate to pay for them yourself, if they are necessary and customary in the country and at the level at which you are being employed?

   (d) Is a car going to be provided with the job – with or without driver?

   (e) Will the employer pay for or subsidise club membership and/or entrance fees?

   (f) Will you be paid an allowance for entertaining?

5. **Leave entitlement**
   (a) If your children attend UK boarding schools, what arrangements are there for them to join you in the holidays? Will the employer pay for their air fares and if so will this be for every holiday or only some of them? If the latter, can you arrange for them to be looked after at Christmas or Easter?
   (b) What arrangements are there for your own leaves? Does the employer provide return air fares to the UK or another country of your choice? Will these cover your family? And for how many holidays?

6. **Personal finance**
   (a) Will the employer pay for/subsidise all or any additional insurance premiums you may incur? In some countries (eg Saudi Arabia) it is advisable to insure your servants. The cost of motor vehicle insurance may be inordinately high because of poor roads and low driving standards.
   (b) If social security payments are higher than in the UK (eg in some EU countries), will your employer make up the difference?
   (c) Will the employer contribute to your medical expenses if free medical attention is not available or is inadequate?

7. **Salary**
   (a) If your salary is expressed in sterling, would you be protected against loss of local buying power in case of devaluation? Equally, if your salary is in local currency, would it be adjusted for a rise in sterling against that currency?
   (b) Is your salary in any way index-linked to the cost of living? How often are the effects of inflation taken into account in assessing and adjusting your current level of remuneration?
   (c) If there are any restrictions on remittances, is your employer prepared to pay a proportion of your salary into a UK bank or that of some other country with a freely negotiable currency?

8. **Language**
   (a) Will your employer contribute towards language teaching for you and/or your partner?

9. **Legal status**
   (a) Is the legal status of your appointment clear? If you are held to be your employer's sole or principal representative, you may be personally liable in some countries for any obligations incurred, eg the payment of corporate taxes or social security contributions.
   (b) Have all the terms of the job and the provisions of the remuneration package been confirmed in writing concerning the contract and conditions of employment subject to English law and, if not, do you or your advisers clearly understand how they should be interpreted should a dispute arise?
10. **Working for a foreign company**
   (a) If the job is with a foreign company, particularly a locally based one rather than a multinational, there are a number of points that need special attention:
      ☐ are the duties of the job clearly spelt out in writing in a contract of employment?
      ☐ are the normal working hours laid down? How long will your journey to work be?
      ☐ are all matters affecting pay, including when it is due and whether you will be paid for overtime, clear and in writing?
      ☐ if there is a bonus, are the conditions under which it is due unambiguous?
      ☐ are there satisfactory arrangements for sick pay?
      ☐ would there be any restriction on your changing jobs if you got a better offer from another employer or decided to leave? (This one obviously has to be handled with particular tact!)
      ☐ do leave conditions clearly specify whether the leave is home or local? For the former, has the employer unambiguously declared the intention of paying your return air fare and that of your partner/family.
      ☐ will legitimate expenses be paid in addition to salary?
   (b) Have you taken any steps to check the bona fides of the prospective employer, eg through a Chamber of

Commerce (the local/British Chambers of Commerce to be found in many main centres are often more obliging and better informed than commercial sections of British embassies), bank, trade association, or Dun & Bradstreet's Business Information Services?

11. **Personal protection**
   (a) Is there a legal obligation on the employer in a high-risk country to continue to pay your salary if you are taken hostage?
   (b) Will the employer offer you a special training course to cope with the risks involved in living in a very high-risk country?

(Much of the content of this chapter was provided by Valerie Vardy and Mike Langley of Towers Perrin whose collaboration the authors gratefully acknowledge.)

Part Two:

Managing Personal Finance

3 Impact on Personal Taxation of Working Abroad

DOMICILE AND RESIDENCE

When leaving the UK on secondment you must consider the impact on your residence and domicile status, as this will dictate how you are treated for taxation. In the April 2002 budget, it was announced that there would be a review of the rules on residence and domicile, so you should check if any of these changes affect your situation prior to departure.

The concepts

Domicile is a complex issue, but is broadly the country of your permanent home. It is an indication of where you intend to reside indefinitely, and the country to which you ultimately intend to return. Your domicile of origin is inherited from your father at birth, and will continue to follow that of your father while you are a minor (this is known as domicile of dependence). Establishing a new domicile of choice is extremely difficult, and in the case of someone with a domicile in the UK is only achieved when emigrating permanently to another country, with no intention of returning to the UK.

Your residence status reflects your immediate intentions and whereabouts, and is therefore likely to be affected by an overseas assignment. Tax law in the UK distinguishes between 'residence' and 'ordinary residence'. Whereas residence is a question of physical presence and intention, ordinary residence equates broadly to habitual residence and considers the individual's behaviour over the short and medium term.

United Kingdom nationals leaving the UK for an assignment abroad will remain UK residents for tax purposes unless the overseas employment contract and the absence abroad span at least one complete UK tax year (6 April to 5 April). Even where this is the case, if, during the assignment, the individual's visits to the UK exceed 183 days in total in any one tax year or an average of 91 or more days per year across four tax years, UK-residence status is retained.

When working abroad you should always consider the host country's definition of residence and domicile. You should be aware that most countries that do not have a legal system inherited from that of the UK do not have the concept of 'domicile' as understood in the UK. Note that they may use the word 'domicile' or its equivalent in their language to mean no more than a place of abode.

Having UK domicile and or residence status does not preclude you from becoming a resident or domiciliary of the host country under its domestic tax law. In these circumstances, care should be taken to avoid double taxation where possible.

UNITED KINGDOM TAXATION

The UK taxation of the expatriate who does not break UK residence

If you remain resident and domiciled in the UK, your liability to UK income tax on your worldwide employment and investment income will continue. Capital gains and inheritance taxes will also be chargeable irrespective of the location of the relevant assets. It is explained below how the correct use of foreign tax credits, double tax treaties and effective planning can prevent double taxation and mitigate your exposure to UK tax.

One advantage of remaining a UK resident is that you remain

eligible for tax-efficient investments like ISAs. However, losing UK residence need not result in losing your right to make tax-deductible pension contributions (see below).

The non-UK resident expatriate

A non-UK resident is taxable in the UK on employment income relating to duties performed in the UK only. If these UK duties are, however, merely incidental to the individual's overseas employment, the respective income will not be liable to UK income tax. Nevertheless, you may still be liable to UK income tax on employment income received while a non-resident, in the case of bonuses, termination payments and stock-option exercises (if you were UK resident when the option was granted). As these items are earned over a period of time, the Inland Revenue may tax a proportionate amount of the income, which relates to the period of UK residence.

If you are a non-UK resident, income from your foreign investments is outside the scope of UK income tax. Even if you are UK resident, it will not be chargeable to UK tax, provided that you are not UK domiciled and that you do not bring any of the income into the UK. Income from UK investments such as rental income from UK property will continue to be liable to UK income tax.

Capital gains tax is not avoided by simply being non-UK resident at the time the gain arises. Under a relatively recent rule, individuals who have been resident or ordinarily resident in the UK during any part of four out of the previous seven tax years and leave the UK become liable to capital gains tax on their return on any gains made during their absence. Absences of five years or more, however, negate this rule, and it applies (broadly) only to assets already held by the individual when he or she leaves the UK. Individuals who left the UK prior to 17 March 1998 also avoid this charge. Note that the terms of a double tax treaty between the UK and the new country of residence may override the charge. Specific advice should be sought if disposals that could come within the rule are likely.

You should note that, subject to certain conditions, capital gains tax is not usually chargeable on the sale of your UK property if it was your only or main residence. Advice should be sought to ensure the maximum advantage is taken of this generous relief. You should always be aware that a potential tax charge may arise in your new country of residence if you sell property after your departure from the UK.

For UK domiciliaries, an inheritance tax charge may arise on any transfer of assets, irrespective of their location and of the residence status of the donor at the time of death. Individuals who are not UK domiciled should note the 'deemed domicile' provisions if they have been UK-resident for 17 out of the last 20 years. Specific advice should always be obtained before making any gifts.

If you remain employed by your UK firm while overseas, you may continue to make contributions and receive employer contributions to your occupational pension scheme. This continues for an indefinite period provided that you eventually intend to return to the UK. If your contract of employment is with the overseas entity, you may continue to participate in the scheme only if you intend to, and do, return to the UK within 10 years. The overseas consequences of maintaining a UK pension scheme should always be considered.

It is now also possible to continue making contributions to a personal or stakeholder scheme if you are non-UK resident provided that certain conditions are met. When non-UK resident, you will no longer be eligible to take out new tax-efficient investment schemes, such as ISAs, although you may continue to contribute to existing schemes. Tax relief on life assurance premiums, should you still be eligible for this, is also revoked for your period of residence outside the UK.

YOUR EMPLOYMENT PACKAGE

Employers have many options when considering how to structure an assignee's remuneration package. The decision is based on many factors, with tax being just one. Set out below are the three main categories of expatriate package, and the type of expatriate to whom they are usually offered.

Tax equalisation

The principle is that the expatriate will continue to pay the same amount of tax as he or she would have done had he or she continued working in his or her home country (on the home-country package). Under this scheme, the employer continues to deduct an amount equal to the usual home-country tax (hypothetical tax). The employer is then responsible for paying the individual's tax liability, wherever it arises. As this tax payment is a cash item paid on behalf of the employee, it is, in itself, a taxable payment and must be grossed up. The employer meets any additional liability (for example, an employer settling tax on behalf of an employee liable to 40 per cent actually has to pay tax at $100/40 = 67$ per cent). As this is an expensive method of remunerating an assignee, this type of package is usually restricted to executives, assignees who require incentivising, or peripatetic expatriates, who do not wish to deal with many different tax authorities. Companies with large expatriate populations will also tend to use this method as it encourages mobility.

Tax protection

This method is less expensive for the employer, although it is harder to administer. The idea, again, is that the expatriate will not pay any more tax than he or she would have done had he or she remained working in his or her home country. No hypothetical tax is withheld, the individual actually pays the host country tax up to the lower of the actual tax liability in the host country and his or her home-country tax liability. If the host country tax liability is higher, the employer will meet the difference.

This method would usually be offered to the same category of expatriate as above or by companies sending expatriates to countries with lower tax rates. It can discourage mobility as assignees will be keener to move to lower-tax countries from higher-tax countries.

Laissez faire

This method does not involve the employer at all (apart from any local responsibilities like employer social security contributions). The individual is simply responsible for his or her own tax liability in the host country. This may be beneficial if the host country tax rate is lower than the home country's.

This method is often applied where it is the expatriate who

is keen to take the assignment, where companies have had little experience of remunerating international assignees, or where companies are continually sending expatriates to lower-tax countries.

PLANNING POINTS

Timing

As explained above, non-UK residence is only achieved if the overseas employment contract covers a complete UK tax year. If the assignment was planned to begin on say, 20 April, you may consider bringing the starting date forward by a few weeks to, say, 5 April.

There are tax reliefs for overseas assignments of less than two years, the details of which are set out below. The Inland Revenue may reject any claims to relief if it is evident that the assignee had knowledge that the assignment length would be greater than two years. Indicators such as work permits and assignment letters may be used as evidence.

An overseas assignment that lasts for less than 183 days in a tax year will not usually give rise to an income tax liability in the host country, subject to the terms of the double taxation treaty (if there is one). Remember that in most countries, unlike the UK, the tax year is the calendar year, so there may be scope for some planning on this point.

If you are about to be granted share options, you should consider carefully whether it is beneficial for you to be granted them before or after your departure. The options are likely to be taxable somewhere and your marginal tax rates in each country should be considered.

Non-contractual termination payments may be exempt from UK tax altogether, if the employment involved many years of foreign service. You should seek advice if you expect to receive such a payment, as the tax savings can be considerable.

Avoiding double taxation

The UK has ratified treaties with 103 countries to avoid double taxation of individuals and companies on the same income in two different countries. This situation usually arises during short-term secondments. Although the treaties vary, and should be examined in depth before assuming qualification, the general rules to be eligible for tax-free status in the host country are:

- [ ] you should not be present for more than 183 days (in a fiscal year or 365-day period, depending on the treaty);
- [ ] you should remain employed by your home country office;
- [ ] the costs of your assignment must be borne wholly by the home country.

In some circumstances, double taxation is unavoidable. In these cases, the Inland Revenue will usually allow a credit for foreign taxes paid, up to the amount of UK tax suffered.

Expatriate tax reliefs and allowances

Even for expatriates who do not break UK residence, there are a number of tax reliefs available that should not be overlooked. These include the following.

For assignments that are not expected to exceed two years, the Inland Revenue will usually compensate you for incurring additional living costs that arise due to the temporary nature of your absence. A UK tax deduction is allowed for the cost of the overseas accommodation, travel and subsistence amounts. Equally, if these amounts are reimbursed by the employer, the Inland Revenue will not seek to tax them.

The following reimbursed expenses are not taxable in the UK:

- [ ] qualifying relocation costs up to £8,000, when leaving the UK, and returning from the assignment;
- [ ] outbound and return airfare costs for you, and your family;
- [ ] limited home-leave flights.

A tax-free allowance of £10 per night is available to cover incidental expenses when working abroad.

All individuals who are Commonwealth or EEA nationals are entitled to a personal allowance deductible from their income taxable in the UK. This treatment is also extended to nationals of certain other countries with which the UK has a double tax treaty. This allowance is £4,535 for the 2001–2 UK tax year and will be £4,615 in 2002–3.

Investments (for tax purposes only)

If you are going to become a non-UK resident, you may consider moving your UK investments offshore prior to your departure, to avoid any UK tax on income arising from those investments while you are overseas. Before you return to the UK, you should close down all interest-bearing overseas bank accounts if you do not wish to pay tax on the interest in the UK. If you wait until you have regained UK residence to do this, the interest accruing since UK residence resumed will be taxable in the UK.

CONCLUSION

The key item to remember about expatriate taxation is *plan in advance.* You may be able to save yourself a substantial amount of tax by merely adjusting the terms of your assignment package, but this must be weighed up against the personal and commercial needs of your secondment.

Checklist: Leaving the UK

1. *Plan ahead.* Consult a tax professional to ensure that your remuneration package and investment portfolio have been structured tax efficiently.
2. *Inform the Inland Revenue.* File a departure form P85. Take care with the wording of this document, as it will form the basis of the Inland Revenue's evaluation of your residence status.
3. *Inform your bank.* If you do not expect your UK bank interest to exceed your tax-free personal allowance it is possible for non-UK residents to receive bank interest gross while

overseas. This will save you from having to file a tax return to obtain any refund of withholding tax due. If you believe your UK-source income will exceed your tax-free personal allowance, you may wish to set up an offshore bank account so that your bank interest is not liable to UK tax.

4. *Prepare your payroll department.* In many cases, you will need to stay on the UK payroll in order to continue making UK pension and UK National Insurance (social security) contributions. If you are going to become non-UK resident, apply for an NT (no tax) code to prevent withholding of payroll withholding tax (PAYE) from your salary. If you are going to remain UK-resident and expect to suffer foreign tax on your earnings, you should apply for the relevant credit to be factored into your PAYE code number, to avoid excessive withholding of tax during the year.

5. *Inform your pension provider.* Check whether you remain eligible to make tax-deductible contributions to your company, personal or stakeholder scheme.

6. *File a UK tax return.* There are many reliefs and allowances available to expatriate assignees (the main items are covered- above), most of which must be on your UK tax return. A further repayment of UK tax is usually due, as personal allowances are given in full each year.

7. *Register in your host country.* If you do this on arrival, you avoid the risk of large tax bills at the end of its tax year.

Checklist: Returning to the UK

1. *Plan ahead.* Seek advice if you have made capital gains, received large payments such as termination payments, or have a complex investment portfolio.

2. *Close offshore accounts.* This prevents the UK from taxing the accrued interest.

3. *De-register with the host country.* Ensure you have informed the appropriate authorities of your departure, to prevent any attempt to dispute your actual date of departure.

4. *Register with the Inland Revenue.* File an arrival form P86. This form will dictate your tax treatment from your date of return onwards and will validate your tax treatment during your

4 *Financial Planning and Asset Management*

For most people, working abroad means a rise in income. For those in countries with a low rate of income tax, or, as is the case in some countries in the Middle East, without income tax, it may be the first chance they have had to accumulate a substantial amount of money, and this may indeed be the whole object of the exercise. Expatriates are therefore an obvious target for firms and individuals offering financial advice on such matters as tax, mortgages, insurance schemes, school fee funding, income building plans and stock and 'alternative' investments. Most of them are honest, but some are better than others, either in choosing investments wisely or in finding schemes that are most appropriate to the needs and circumstances of their client, or both. At any rate the expatriate with money to spend is nowadays faced with a wide variety of choices, ranging from enterprising local traders, proffering allegedly valuable antiques, and fly-by-night operators, selling real estate in inaccessible tropical swamps, to serious financial advisers and consultants. The Internet might also help independently minded investors in remote locations, and provides another option.

ALTERNATIVES FOR INVESTING SURPLUS INCOME

There are really only three types of objectives in investment: growth, income, and growth with income. The choice of one main objective usually involves some sacrifice in regard to the other. A high degree of capital appreciation generally implies a lower level of income and vice versa. Growth with income is an ideal, but generally it means some growth with some income, not a maximisation of both. Ultimately, the objective is the preservation of capital in bad times and the increase of wealth in good ones, but your adviser cannot perform miracles. If he is lucky enough to catch the market in an upward phase he may be able to show quick results, but normally investment is a process that pays off over a longer period and through the course of varying market cycles.

INVESTMENT THROUGH UK OR OFFSHORE MANAGED FUNDS

There are many investment opportunities in the offshore fund markets, from specialised funds in individual countries to international ones spread across many industries. There are equally many ways of investing: regular investments, lump-sum purchase of units, periodic and irregular investments. It is also possible to invest in commodity markets and there are specialists trading in gold, silver, diamonds, sapphires and metals generally. Another innovation is the currency fund, which regulates holdings of foreign exchange and aims to predict fluctuations in exchange rates.

Your consultant should be able not only to inform you of the various schemes available, but also to advise on the degree of risk, the quality of management available and the combination of investments most likely to achieve your aims.

For those who prefer the safety of banks or building society deposits, there is now a concession to non-residents – interest is paid without tax being deducted at source. However, you will have to inform your bank about your non-resident status. A building society may also require you to open a separate, non-resident account.

You may still be assessed for income tax on any interest earned in the year of your return to the UK. For this reason, there are a number of advantages in taking up the facilities that UK banks offer non-residents to open an account in one of the established tax havens, notably the Channel Islands and the Isle of Man.

In all cases, though, there are important tax considerations before you return to the UK. You should discuss these with your adviser at least six months before then, so that the necessary plans can be drawn up.

SCHOOL FEES PLANNING

There are many schemes available for school fees planning. These schemes aim to provide you with a tax-free income at a specified date for a predetermined length of time. They need not necessarily be used for educational purposes, and some readers may feel that if the employer is paying school fees, as is often the case, there is no need to take out such a policy. However, parents should bear in mind that it is highly advisable not to interrupt children's education, and taking out such a policy would obviously be a good way of ensuring that your child could go on with his or her education at the same school, even if your employment with that employer ended.

PENSIONS AND LIFE ASSURANCE POLICIES

One of the most important aspects of financial planning for expatriates relates to pensions. Most people will have been members of a UK scheme and will have been either 'contracted in' or 'contracted out' of the government pension provisions. If your employer has contracted out – that is, made their own arrangements for you within the guidelines laid down by the government – you will normally retain the full benefits of the scheme, even if you are not resident in the UK. If your employer has contracted in, you will lose your right to the benefits once

your contribution ceases. Private, contracted out schemes usually include a lump-sum death benefit as well as provision for benefits for disability.

This assumes that you are going to work abroad for a UK employer. If this is not the case, you will have to make your own arrangements with the help of your adviser, unless your employer abroad has a scheme of their own. Most multinationals do have such schemes, but they may have set up a pension fund in the country of residence and that country may have rules of its own and be subject to local legislation. Therefore, even if your employer is providing a scheme, you should ask for your adviser's comments on it.

People working overseas can now take a Jersey pension linked to a UK tax-exempt pension fund. The contract is linked to the With Profit Fund of a select number of life offices. Termination benefits can be taken wholly in cash and free of any tax deduction in Jersey. Benefits can be taken at any age, and there is no limit imposed on contribution. The scheme is essentially for the benefit of those expatriates not planning to return and take up residence in the UK.

The right way to buy life assurance is through an independent professional adviser, outlining to him or her what you feel your needs are. In fact, even if you already have a policy, either on your own account or through your employer, there are a number of points you should check:

1. You should advise the company issuing the policy of a change of residence status.
2. You should check that your policy has no restrictions about overseas living.
3. You must ensure that you have set up a suitable system for paying premiums in your absence (eg via a banker's order).

Assuming, however, that you do not already have adequate life assurance, your adviser is likely to come up with one of four basic life assurance schemes:

1. Term assurance: this pays a fixed sum if you die within a specified time (eg before the age of 55).
2. Whole life: this pays a fixed sum irrespective of when you die.

3. Endowment: this gives you a sum of money at a fixed date, and is not only related to death. It is often used as a way of insuring mortgage payments; the mortgage is paid off when the policy matures.
4. Family income benefit: this gives an income after death and would usually be used to provide for your spouse and children. As a rule this would be taken out to give cover until all your children reach maturity.

All these policies may be taken out for a fixed sum and can be with or without profits. There may also be other variants, the most common of which is the facility to turn term assurance into an endowment policy. Your main concern, however, may be the degree of cover you require and this depends on the level of commitments that would be incurred by your family in the event of your death. A rule of thumb in most cases is that the capital sum provided should be five times the individual's annual income, combined with cover of between a half and three-quarters of annual salary until the children in the family reach maturity. You need not necessarily take out an insurance policy in sterling. There are foreign currency policies and, even though they are more expensive than sterling ones, for long-term expatriates in certain tax situations these may have aspects to recommend them. Again you will need professional advice in assessing your particular circumstances and choosing a scheme.

OFFSHORE BROKER BOND

The offshore broker bond whose asset is a fund is also an interesting option. This is administered in a tax haven by a subsidiary of one of the major UK life offices, who appoints an independent financial adviser to manage the underlying assets. The adviser in this case will be wearing two hats, both as fund manager and broker, so he needs to have good reasons for recommending his own fund.

The advantages of the broker bond are in the tax treatment and its efficient route to the stock and bond markets. All the investment decisions are made for you. Broker fund managers have the time and resources, not always available to the individual investor, to select investments to make the best use of your capital.

OFFSHORE INSURANCE POLICIES

The legislation relating to these has become increasingly complicated. Tax-mitigating benefits available through offshore insurance policies to those working abroad, but intending to return to the UK, have gradually been eroded by the Chancellor in his Finance Acts.

Life policies can be encashed free of tax and financial advisers suggest taking out a large number of single policies (rather than one large one) and encashing them separately and in small numbers. This effectively creates a tax-free income.

There are also some other tax-mitigating schemes related to offshore insurance policies. These are technically very complex. They are also subject to change as the Inland Revenue and financial experts play their cat and mouse game with tax loopholes. You should therefore check the latest position with an independent UK adviser before undertaking any offshore insurance commitment.

RETURNING TO THE UK

All aspects of pension and investment planning need to be reviewed if you are returning to the UK, or you may leave yourself open to tax problems that could easily have been avoided with good advice. You should therefore notify your financial consultant at least 12 months before the tax year of your return so that he or she can make arrangements to mitigate tax liabilities.

SHORT-TERM CONTRACTS

Someone going abroad on a short-term contract of two years or less is in a somewhat different investment position from those who have committed themselves to longer spells or intend to remain working abroad. Certainly you should be very careful about taking on investment or pension plan schemes that require regular payments over periods longer than your contract. For instance, there was the case of a doctor in the Gulf on a two-year contract who was persuaded to invest £1,500 a month in a unit-linked life assurance scheme with a 10-year duration. Clearly, on what he could reasonably expect to earn back in the UK, he had no hope of keeping up payments on that scale – yet to extricate himself from that commitment, once this became clear to him, cost six months' premiums: £9,000!

In the opinion of some investment consultants, non-resident expatriates on short-term contracts might be best advised to put their savings deposit into a Channel Islands bank account. As not ordinarily resident non-residents they would not have to pay income tax on the interest up to the tax year of their return. Speculative investments tend to be risky on a short-term profit basis. When looking for longer-term profits, expatriates on two-year contracts or less are liable to be caught within the UK capital gains tax network unless they are able to realise their profits in the tax year before they return. If they endeavour to do so having regained UK resident status, they would be liable for CGT, even though the investment had initially been made when they were non-resident and not ordinarily resident.

LETTING AND INSURING YOUR HOME WHILE ABROAD

Most home owners going to live abroad for a limited period will be looking for a tenant to live in their house or flat while they are away. There is, of course, an obvious alternative, which is to sell, but then there is the question of storage of your effects – the average storage charge for the contents of a typical three-bedroomed house will be £50–£60 per week – and, more to the point, the fact that when you do return to this country you will have no place of your own to go to. Even if you do not intend to return to the house you lived in when you come back, it may be advisable to retain ownership because your house represents a fairly inflation-indexed asset.

The case for letting, as opposed to leaving your home empty, hardly needs to be put today when crime and vandalism are constantly in the headlines. The government, recognising the difficulties for owners leaving their homes and wishing to encourage the private landlord, introduced the 1996 Housing Act which came into force on 27 February 1997. This Act created two new types of tenancies – Assured and Assured Shorthold – and simplified the many provisions of the various Rent and Housing Acts from 1965 to 1988, thus making letting safer and easier. The Assured Tenancy offers much comfort for security of tenure to a tenant while the Assured Shorthold guarantees possession to a landlord at the end of a tenancy. It is not possible here to define the various differences between these two forms of tenancy, but there are specific aspects of which the owner-occupier needs to be aware. However, lettings to large companies where the occupier is a genuine employee being housed by the company temporarily are excluded from the Act. It should be noted that a letting to a member of the Diplomatic Corps who has immunity is inadvisable, as the individual would be outside the jurisdiction of British courts. It is essential, therefore, for the owner to obtain proper advice before deciding which form of tenancy to choose. All new tenancies are automatically Assured Shorthold tenancies unless parties agree otherwise.

Assured shorthold tenancies

1. These can be for any length of time if both parties agree. However, the landlord will not be able to seek a court order for possession before the end of six months unless there has been a breach of the tenancy agreement.
2. The tenant may apply to the Rent Assessment Committee during the period of the tenancy to fix the rental at a 'market' figure during the first six months. However, on the expiry of the original term, the owner is entitled to require the tenant to pay a higher rental and the tenant is not entitled to go back to the Rent Assessment Committee. It is therefore preferable to have relatively short lease periods.
3. Two months' notice has to be served that the landlord requires possession before or on the day the fixed term comes to an end and, if the tenant refuses to leave, the courts must grant possession, after the expiry of the notice.

The benefits of an assured tenancy are as follows:

- [ ] there is very little rent control;
- [ ] there is no restriction on the initial rent;
- [ ] premiums can be taken (although this is unlikely to be a marketable facility);
- [ ] rents can be increased during the tenancy, provided there is a term in the agreement;
- [ ] even where not so provided the landlord may serve notice under the Act to increase the rent.

In the last instance, the tenant may go to the Rent Assessment Committee who must fix the rent at a 'market' figure, not at the previous imposition of what was, perhaps unfortunately, called a 'fair' rent.

Possession of the property can still be obtained by virtue of former owner-occupation and the service of the appropriate notice on the tenant before the commencement of the tenancy. Additional provisions for a mandatory possession order have been included in the new Act, such as two months' arrears of rent, and there are a number of discretionary grounds on which possession can be granted, even if the owner does not wish to return to the house. However, there is one specific disadvantage with the Act if the owner is unfortunate enough to have a tenant who refuses to leave when the owner wishes to reoccupy. This is the provision under the Act where the owner is obliged to serve two months' notice advising the tenant that he or she requires possession and on what ground(s) prior to any proceedings being commenced. This undoubtedly will extend the period needed before a possession order is granted by the court and owners would be well advised to take out one of the various insurance policies now available to cover hotel costs, legal fees, etc, and as a minimum to make sure that either alternative accommodation is temporarily available in the event of a return home earlier than expected or the tenancy is terminated well before the projected date of return.

Assured tenancies

1. An assured tenancy may be for a fixed term or periodic, ie month to month.

2. The tenant must be an individual, not a limited company.
3. The tenant must occupy the house or flat as his or her only or principal home.
4. There are various terms that should be provided in the agreement and in particular a provision for the rent to be increased by notice in writing.

As must now be obvious to the reader, the rules do nothing to encourage the owners to attempt to let the property or manage their home themselves while away, and the need for an experienced property management firm becomes even more important than in the past. A solicitor might be an alternative but, although possibly more versed in the legal technicalities than a managing agent, he or she will not be in a position to market the house to the best advantage (if at all) and solicitors' practices do not usually have staff experienced in property management, able to carry out inspections, deal with repairs, arrange inventories and to handle the many and various problems that often arise.

Having obtained advice to ensure that you have the correct form of tenancy, you now need to find an experienced and reliable estate agent (ideally, he or she should be a member of the Royal Institution of Chartered Surveyors, the Incorporated Society of Valuers and Auctioneers, the Association of Residential Letting Agents or the National Association of Estate Agents) specialising in property management who will be well versed in both the legal and financial aspects of the property market.

Property management

Property management is a rather specialised branch of estate agency and you should check carefully that the agent you go to can give you the service you need, that he or she is not just an accommodation broker, and that he or she is equipped to handle the letting, collection of rental and management of your property, as well as the more common kinds of agency work. Your solicitor should be able to advise you here, but to some extent you will have to rely on your own judgement of how ready and satisfactory the agent's answers are to the sort of questions you are going to want to ask. There are several specialised firms well equipped to deal with your affairs.

In the first place the agent you instruct should have a clear idea of the kind of tenant you can expect for your property, and preferably be able to show you that he or she does have people on his or her books who are looking for rented accommodation of this kind. Obviously the rental and the tenant you can expect will vary with what you have to offer. A normal family house in a good area should attract someone like the executive of a multinational company who is in a similar, but reverse, position to your own: that is, someone working here on a contract basis for a limited period of time who may well provide a stable tenancy for the whole or a substantial part of your absence. A smaller house or flat would be more likely to attract a younger person who only wants the property for a limited period or who, at any rate, might be reluctant to accept a long-term commitment because of the possibility of a change in professional circumstances or marital status. Equally, if you are only going to be away for a shortish period like 6 to 12 months, you are going to be rather lucky to find a tenant whose needs exactly overlap with your absence. You would probably have to accept a slightly shorter period than your exact stay abroad.

For your part you should bear in mind that tenants, unlike house purchasers, are usually only interested in a property with almost immediate possession, but you should give the agent, wherever possible, at least two or three months' warning of your departure in order that interest may be built up by advertising, mailing out details, etc, over a period of time.

Rent

How much rent you can expect will also vary with what you have to offer and where it is, but the point to bear in mind is that rents are not usually subject to bargaining like a house price. Bargaining, if there is to be any, is more likely to occur over the terms of the lease which are set out below. Do not, therefore, ask for an unrealistically high figure in the expectation that the tenant will regard this as a starting point for negotiation.

Your agent, if he or she knows the job, will be able to advise you on the rental you should ask, though if you have not had previous dealings with him or her it might be advisable to have your solicitor check out the figures or to ask the agent to give you some instances of rentals being charged for similar accommodation. On the other hand, an offer that is a bit less than you had hoped for, but from a good tenant, might be worth taking in preference to a better one from somebody who, for various reasons, looks more doubtful.

Terms of agreement

A property management agent should have, or be able to produce fairly quickly, a draft agreement to cover the specific situation of the overseas landlord. You should show this to your solicitor and how well it is drafted will again be a pointer to how effective the agent concerned is likely to be. The document should cover at least the following points:

1. The intervals of payment – monthly or quarterly – and the length of lease.
2. A prohibition from assigning the lease without your express permission; likewise from keeping animals on the premises or using them for other than residential purposes.
3. An undertaking by the tenant to make good any damage, other than fair wear and tear, to fixtures, fittings and furniture, and to maintain the garden.
4. An undertaking by the tenant to pay for telephone and other services from the commencement of the lease, including Council Tax.
5. An undertaking to allow the landlord, or the agent, regular access to the property for inspection and repair; and two months before the expiry of the lease to allow him or her to take other prospective tenants or purchasers round the property.
6. A clause stating that the lease is terminated if any of the other clauses are broken although the wording has to be carefully drafted to avoid invalidating the agreement.
7. What you, as landlord, are responsible for in the way of repairs: usually the maintenance of the structure and furnishings of the property together with anything left in the property (eg the central heating boiler). You can exclude some items, such as the television, from your responsibility, but

generally the tenant is only liable for specific damage to items left in the house and not for their general maintenance. The government has tightened up safety laws in respect of gas appliances. In November 1994 the Gas Safety (Installation & Use) Regulations 1994 were introduced, forcing landlords to take greater responsibility for the safety of their tenants by regularly servicing and repairing any gas appliances through a British Gas or Corgi registered company. Heavy penalties will be enforced for failing to comply.

8. Any special restrictions you want to impose: if, for example, your house is full of valuable antiques you may wish to specify 'no small children'.

9. The conditions under which the tenancy can be terminated prior to its full period having run and without any breach having taken place.

10. If this is to be an Assured tenancy, notice must be served under Schedule 2, Grounds 1 and 2 of the Housing Act 1988 which notifies the tenant that you are an owner-occupier within the meaning of the Housing Act. This gives the landlord and those members of his or her family who occupied the house before it was let the right to reoccupy it when the lease expires or is terminated, and protects the mortgage.

11. Notice under Sections 47 and 48 of the Landlord and Tenant Act 1987. The former should be on all rent demands; the latter, notifying the tenant of an address in England and Wales at which notices can be served on the landlord, need only be served once on a tenant at the beginning of a tenancy.

Although the agreement is probably the central document in the transactions involved in letting your house, it does not bring to an end all the things you have to think about. For instance, there is the important matter of the contents insurance. Letting your home to a third party is probably not covered in your policy and you will have to notify your insurers (and the people who hold your mortgage) that this is what you are doing. In many instances, insurance companies will not insure the contents if the property is to be let and you will need to check carefully that you have cover and can switch to another company if it becomes necessary. This is covered in greater detail on page 84, under Insurance. At the same time you would be wise to check that the contents insurance covers the full value of what you have left in the house. This check could be combined with making a proper inventory of the contents, which is in any case essential before tenants move into a furnished property. Making an exact inventory is quite a time-consuming business and you should bear in mind that it will also have to be checked at the end of the lease, when you may not be there. There are several firms that provide a specialist inventory service at both ends of the lease, covering dilapidations as well as items actually missing, for quite a modest charge which, incidentally, is deductible from the tax due from the letting. Any good property management agent should be able to put you on to one of them.

It is also essential that landlords are aware of important fire regulations that have recently come into force concerning the supply of furniture and furnishings when letting out accommodation. The Furniture (Fire) (Safety) Regulations 1988, introduced for all landlords on 1 January 1997, make it an offence to supply furniture which does not comply with the regulations concerning fire resistance. Essentially, it covers all upholstery and upholstered furnishings, including loose fittings and permanent or loose covers. These must comply with the following three tests, each of which measures the flame-retardant properties of the furnishings: Cigarette Test; Match Test; Ignitability Test. Heavy penalties will be enforced for failing to comply.

Your managing agent should be able to provide details of exactly what furniture should be replaced and when.

Finding the tenant and getting a signature on the agreement marks the beginning rather than the end of the property management firm's responsibilities. Broadly, these fall under two headings: the collection of rental and the management of the property. The rent is collected from the tenant, usually on a standing order basis, under the terms – monthly or quarterly – as set out in the agreement; and, in the event of persistent non-payment, the agent will instruct solicitors on your behalf to issue a county court summons, or if you have taken out rental or legal insurance, the agent will contact the insurance company.

What can you expect from the agent?

Management is a more complex subject but an experienced property management agent should be able to supply you with a list of the services that he or she can undertake. It is, therefore, also a checklist of the kind of eventualities that may crop up in your absence which, broadly speaking, relate to the collection of rent, the payment of charges such as service charges and insurance, arrangements for repairs to the fabric of the building and its contents, garden maintenance or when forwarding mail.

Thus, apart from the basic business of collecting the rent, the agent can also pay, on your behalf, any charges on the property (eg ground rent, water rates and insurance) that your contract with the tenant does not specify should be paid by him or her. There may also be annual maintenance agreements to pay in respect of items like central heating plant and the washing machine.

Then there is the question of what to do about repairs. As we have indicated earlier, whatever you manage to get the tenant to agree to take care of under the terms of the lease, there are certain responsibilities for maintenance and repair that you have to accept by virtue of your status as a landlord. If repairs are necessary, you will simply have to trust the agent to obtain fair prices for you.

On the other hand, except in the case of essential repairs which affect the tenant's legal rights of enjoyment of the property, you can ask your agent to provide estimates for having the work carried out, so that your approval must be obtained before the job is put in hand. Bear in mind, though, that in certain parts of the world the postal system may not be all that reliable. You may, therefore, find it a good idea to put a clause in the management contract giving the agent freedom to proceed with the best estimate if he or she does not hear from you within a specified period. For the same reason it is also wise to ask the agent to send you a formal acknowledgement of receipt of any special or new instructions you have given. An example of this might be an instruction to inspect the property at regular intervals.

To summarise, the responsibilities of a property management agent are as follows:

☐ collection of rent;
☐ payment of service charges and insurance;
☐ arranging repairs to the building and contents;
☐ garden maintenance;
☐ forwarding mail;
☐ payment of charges on property;
☐ payment of maintenance agreements;
☐ obtaining prices/estimates for repairs.

Depending on how many concessions you have to make to the tenant to get him or her to sign the lease, there may be other articles for which repair and maintenance remain your responsibility. These may include washing machine, TV and the deep freeze. Such responsibilities should be set out in the management contract and you should give the agent the details of any guarantees or maintenance contracts relating to them and photocopies of the actual documents for reference. If no such arrangements apply, you should list the manufacturers' names and the model number and age of each item so that the agent can get the manufacturer to send the repair people along equipped with the right spares.

It is very important that a third party, other than you and the tenant, should be in possession of all this information, particularly when there is likely to be more than one tenancy during your absence; and it is a competent management agent, rather than friends, relatives or even a solicitor, who will be best equipped in this case to find new tenants, to check their references, to draw up new agreements and supervise the handover of the tenancy.

Costs and tax

The costs of all these services vary according to the nature of the package you need. The professional societies already mentioned recommend charges, which would be applicable in most circumstances. For example, letting and collection is usually 10 per cent of annual rental. In the case of management services, expect to find additional charges made (usually 5 to 7 per cent of the annual rent). These are reasonable fees for the quite considerable headaches involved. We have shown enough of them here to indicate that not only is it virtually impossible to administer a tenancy yourself from a distance, but also that these are not matters to be left to an amateur – friend or relative – however well intentioned. In real terms the agent's charges may be reduced because they are deductible against the tax levied in the UK against rental income.

Expatriates letting their houses also derive a further benefit in respect of capital gains tax. Generally, if you let your principal residence, when you come to sell it you can claim exemption from CGT only for those years in which you lived in it yourself. However, if you let it because you are absent abroad this does not apply, provided you come back to live in the house before you sell it.

Finally, in this context, it is worth pointing out that some building societies are now prepared to consider giving mortgages to expatriates for the purchase of a property in the UK *and* to allow them to lease that property for the period of their stay overseas. Up to 90 per cent of the purchase price is available at normal building society rates of interest.

This is an attractive proposition for expatriates, particularly for young executives and professional people who have not yet bought a home in the UK but are earning a substantial income in, say, the Middle East, and for older expatriates perhaps thinking of a retirement home in the UK.

Some agencies supply details of the building societies offering this facility, or you could approach a society directly and explain your position. Should you buy a house as an expatriate and then let it until you return, the earlier recommendation that you leave the management of the property to an experienced and competent agent still applies.

You should check that if a UK property is bought purely as an investment, you would have to time its sale carefully to avoid liability to CGT.

Taxation is too complex a subject and varies considerably in its effects on the individual, preventing any practical advice being offered other than to state the importance of employing the services of an accountant in your absence, but it must be stressed that rent received in the UK is considered unearned income, and is subject to UK tax laws. A new scheme now operates whereby letting agents, or where there are no letting agents, tenants of a non-resident landlord, must deduct tax at the basic rate from the rental income, and pay tax quarterly to the Inland Revenue. These landlords who wish to receive their income with no tax deducted can apply to FICO for approval. Forms are available from: FICO (non-residents), St John's House, Merton Road, Bootle, Merseyside L69 9BB; tel: 0151 472 6208/6209.

Insurance

One important point that is often overlooked by people who let their house or flat is the necessity of notifying the insurers that a change of occupancy has taken place. Insurance policies only cover occupancy by the insured, not the tenants, though it can be extended to do so on payment of what is usually only a small premium. As many insurance companies will not cover properties that are or will be let, notifying the company concerned becomes essential.

What worries insurance companies much more is if the house is left unoccupied for any length of time. If you look at your policy you will see that it lapses if you leave your house empty for more than 30 days or so – a point that is sometimes forgotten by people who go away on extended holidays. If you are going abroad and leave the house empty – maybe because you have not yet succeeded in finding a tenant – the insurers will usually insist that you turn off the main services and that the premises are inspected regularly by a qualified person. That means someone like a letting agent, not a relative or friend. Even if you have let the house without an agent, it may still be advisable to get one to look after the place. A situation could easily occur where the tenant moves out, leaving the place empty and without satisfactory steps having been taken from an insurance point of view. Furthermore, if the worst happens and the house is broken into or damaged, it is imperative that the insurers are notified right away. The effects of damage can be made worse unless they are rapidly attended to, and insurers do not hold themselves responsible for anything that happens between the time the insured eventuality occurs and the time they are notified of it. For instance, if your house is broken into and, a few days later, vandals get in through a broken point of entry and cause further damage, you would not be covered for that second incident unless the insurers had been notified of the first break-in.

Valuable contents are best put into storage and insured there: Pickfords, for instance, charge a premium of 12½ per cent of the storage charge, inclusive of insurance premium tax. For contents worth more than £25,000, a reduction may be possible. For very high-value items, safe deposit boxes are becoming popular, but from an everyday point of view, the important thing is to make sure you are insured for full values. If you insure contents for £15,000 and the insurer's assessors value them at £20,000 you will only get three-quarters of your claim. To keep insured values in line with rising costs, an index-linked policy would be the best buy for anyone contemplating a long stay abroad. A policy specially written for expatriates is available from Europea-IMG Ltd: the Weavers Homeowners Policy. They also offer expatriate motor insurance on private cars being used overseas. All insurance premiums are now subject to insurance premium tax (IPT).

Insuring at full value, incidentally, is equally important when it comes to insuring contents and personal belongings in your residence abroad. Many items will cost much more locally if you have to replace them than they did at the time they were originally bought. There are a few such policies available in the UK, or it may be possible to insure in the country concerned.

Finally, but most important, you should insure against legal and hotel costs when letting your house. Although in principle the legal instruments for quick repossession exist, events have shown that a bloody-minded tenant with a committed lawyer can spin things out to his or her advantage for almost an indefinite period. Premiums, which can be offset against rental income, are in the region of £85 a year.

Also recently introduced, rental protection policies have become available, some providing limited cover at a relatively low premium, others covering the higher rental amounts, which are naturally more expensive. In addition, these policies will normally cover legal and other costs. However, due to wide cover, the insurance companies usually insist on their own credit check and the employment of a managing agent, as well as the usual references.

The same companies will add, as an extra, buildings and/or contents cover when the property is let, often at rates which are competitive to the premiums charged when the property was owner-occupied.

Only selected agents with a professional background offer policies which protect rent, so the choice of a managing agent becomes even more important than before if you want to protect your rental income.

Checklist: Financial planning and the expatriate

1. Check out your financial adviser's credentials.
2. Consider the pros and cons of offshore funds.
3. Check your life assurance policy to make sure that there are no restrictions about overseas living.
4. Consider tax-efficient ways to save for school fees.
5. If your company has a pension scheme in the country of residence, make sure you become acquainted with its rules and local legislation through your financial adviser.
6. Notify your financial adviser at least 12 months before the tax year of your return so that he or she can mitigate tax liabilities.

Checklist: Letting your home

1. Consider the pros and cons of an Assured Shorthold Tenancy versus an Assured Tenancy. Be aware that a period of notice must be given to a tenant to vacate a property.
2. Ask your property management agent to show you what kinds of people he or she has on the books.
3. Try and give the agent two or three months warning prior to the rental date.
4. Seek advice from your solicitor concerning the agent's draft contract.

5. Inform your insurance company of your intention to let your home and check that your contents insurance covers the full value of what you have left in the house.
6. Make a full inventory of the contents.
7. Ensure that your furniture complies with fire regulations.
8. Provide your agent with details of any guarantees or maintenance contracts.
9. Put valuable possessions into storage.
10. Consider insuring against legal and hotel costs.

5 National Insurance, Benefits and Pensions

The desire to earn more money – and to pay less of it in tax and other deductions – looms large for many as a motive for going to work abroad. People who take this step are often temperamentally inclined to be strongly individualistic and self-reliant and as such many feel that they would rather fend for themselves when circumstances get difficult than rely on what they regard as 'state handouts'. Whatever the virtues of this attitude of mind may be, those who have it are more to be commended for their sense of independence than their common sense. The fact is that during your working life in the UK you will have made compulsory National Insurance contributions and you are therefore eligible for benefits in the same way as if you had paid premiums into a private insurance scheme; drawing a state benefit you are entitled to is no more taking a handout than making an insurance claim.

National Insurance has another feature in common with private insurance: you lose your entitlement to benefit if you fail to keep up your contributions, though the circumstances under which this would happen are different from, and more gradual than in, the private sector. Furthermore, you cannot immediately reactivate your eligibility for benefits in full if, your payments having lapsed for a period of time, you return to this country and once again become liable to make contributions. For instance, in order to qualify in full for a UK retirement pension you must have paid the minimum contribution for each year for at least 90 per cent of your working life. In the case of other benefits too, in order to qualify to get them, there must be a record of your having made a certain level of contributions in the two tax years governing that in which benefits are being claimed.

DSS AGENCIES

National Insurance provisions are handled by Executive Agencies of the Department of Social Security. The Contributions Agency deals with all contributions and insurability matters, while the Benefits Agency deals with all matters relating to social security benefits.

NI contribution matters for persons working abroad are handled by the Contributions Agency's International Services, Longbenton, Newcastle upon Tyne NE98 1YX; tel: 0845 915 4811. The International service can provide you with information on your National Insurance liability, voluntary contributions, retirement pension forecasts, healthcare and other benefits. Visit the Web site at www.inlandrevenue.gov.uk/nic/interserv/osc.html. Matters relating to benefits are handled by the Benefit Agency's Pensions and Overseas Benefits Directorate at Newcastle upon Tyne NE98 1BA.

Leaflet NI 38, or for European Economic Area countries leaflet SA29, available from either Agency at Newcastle, or from a local social security office, sets out the basic conditions relating to National Insurance and benefits abroad.

LIABILITY FOR CONTRIBUTIONS WHILE ABROAD

If your employer in the UK sends you to work in another European Economic Area country or in a country with whom the UK has a reciprocal agreement (these are listed in leaflet NI 38) for a period not expected to exceed that which is specified in the EC regulations *or* the reciprocal agreement (RA) involved, you will normally continue to be subject to the UK social security scheme for that period and you will be required to pay Class 1 contributions as though you were in the UK. (The specified period can vary between one year where the EC regulations apply and up to five years depending upon the reciprocal agreement involved.) If your employment unexpectedly lasts longer than 'the specified period', then for certain countries you may remain insured under the UK scheme with the agreement of the authorities in the country in which you are working. Your employer will obtain a certificate for you from the Contributions Agency, International Services, at Newcastle upon Tyne confirming your continued liability under the UK scheme, which you should present to the foreign authorities if required to confirm your non-liability under their scheme. This form, E101, is issued with form E128 which provides health care cover abroad for you and your family for the period of employment in another country.

If you are sent by your UK employer to an EU member state or to a country with which there is a reciprocal agreement in circumstances other than the above, eg for an initial period expected to exceed 12 months or for a period of indefinite duration, then normally you will cease to be liable to pay UK contributions from the date you are posted and will instead become liable to pay into the scheme of the country you are working in. Leaflet SA29 tells you about the European Community (EC) Regulations on social security and their effect on EU nationals. If you would like a copy of leaflet SA29 or would like more information, you can telephone or write to International Services. Alternatively you can get a copy of leaflet SA29 from your local social security office.

If you are sent by your employer to a country other than those in the EU or with which there is a reciprocal agreement you will be liable to pay Class 1 contributions for the first 52 weeks of your posting provided your employer has a place of business in the UK, you were resident in the UK immediately before you took up employment abroad, you remain 'ordinarily resident' in the UK while you are abroad and you are under UK retirement age (currently 60 for women and 65 for men). If you are self-employed you must obtain forms E101/E102/E128.

MAKING VOLUNTARY CONTRIBUTIONS

For non-EU and non-RA countries, when your period of liability for Class 1 contributions ends, you may wish to pay voluntary Class 3 contributions to the UK scheme in order to protect your UK retirement/widow's pension entitlement. We will deal with the mechanics of this later, but at this stage it should be pointed out that if you are going abroad for a British-based firm you will be liable to make the same contributions as if you were employed in this country up to a maximum earnings level of £535 per week (2000/2001 tax year). Your proportion of this contribution will be deducted from your salary, as if you were still working in the UK. Payment of these contributions for the first 52 weeks of your employment abroad will make you eligible to receive incapacity or unemployment benefit and, in the case of a woman, maternity allowance, under the usual conditions applicable to those benefits, on your return to the UK – even though this may be some years later – because Class 1 contributions will be deemed to have been paid in the tax year(s) relevant to your claim. This is subject to the proviso that you remained 'ordinarily resident' in the UK during your absence. If you did not intend to sever your connection with the UK when you went abroad, continuing ordinary residence will usually be accepted. To establish ordinary residence you may need to show that you maintained a home or accommodation in the UK or stored your furniture in the UK during your absence. To maintain entitlement to UK retirement pension or widow's benefits, however, it will usually be necessary to pay Class 3 contributions after the Class 1 period has expired although this may not be necessary for the balance of the year – April to April – in which Class 1 liability ceased. The Contributions Agency, International Services, Room, BP1303, Longbenton, Newcastle upon Tyne NE98 1ZZ can advise you about this. Remember always to quote your National Insurance number and the country involved when you write.

Class 1 contributions are not payable at all in respect of employment abroad if your employer has no place of business in the UK. However, if you work for an overseas government or an international agency such as the UN, you will be able to pay your share of the Class 1 contribution for the first 52 weeks of your employment abroad and so qualify on return to the UK for the benefits named in the previous paragraph.

You may, of course, have been a self-employed person paying the Class 2 rate of £2 a week for the 2000/2001 tax year. These contributions also cover a more limited range of benefits – Jobseeker's Allowance (previously unemployment benefit) and injury or death caused by an industrial accident or prescribed disease are excluded – but like Class 3 contributions, they can also be paid voluntarily if you go to work in an EU country or countries with which the UK has an RA agreement, provided you are gainfully occupied there. However, you *need not* pay Class 2 contributions just because you were self-employed before you went abroad. You can go to the voluntary Class 3 rate (which is £6.55 for the 2000/2001 tax year), but if you want to qualify for incapacity benefit when you return to the UK, provided you were employed abroad you can switch back to Class 2 payments for the two tax years governing the benefit year in which you are due to return.

These rates and conditions apply, of course, as much to women as to men. The right of married women to pay reduced rate contributions has been phased out. If you get married while working abroad you should write to International Services for leaflet CA 13 which explains in more detail your National Insurance position as a married woman. A married woman may consider paying contributions in her own right (eg for retirement pension purposes). See leaflet NI 38.

Leaflet NI 38 contains a form at the back (CF 83) which should be filled in when you want to start making voluntary payments. You can pay by annual lump sum, by arranging for someone in the UK to make regular payments for you, or through direct debit if you have a bank or building society in the UK or Channel Islands.

Class 2 and Class 3 contributions can be paid before the end of the sixth tax year following the one in which they were due. However, although you have six years in which to pay there is a limited period in which to pay at the relevant year's contribution rates. International Services can advise you about this. Whatever method you choose it is important that your contributions are paid on time. For further information see leaflet CA07 – *Unpaid and late paid contributions*. Also see CF411 *How to protect your State Retirement Pension*.

GETTING NI BENEFITS ABROAD

Thus far we have only mentioned the range of benefits available to you once you return to the UK. But is there any way you can become eligible for benefits while still abroad? Generally, the answer is that you can only receive retirement pensions and widow's benefits, but there are important exceptions in the case of EU countries and some others – a full list is given in leaflet NI 38 – with which the UK has reciprocal agreements. How those agreements affect you varies somewhat from country to country, but in essence they mean that the contributions you have paid in the UK count, for benefit purposes, as if you had paid them in the reciprocal agreement country, and vice versa. This is usually advantageous if you do become eligible for benefit while abroad because in relation to the cost of living – or even in absolute terms – UK benefits are lower than many foreign ones. You will, in general, have to pay contributions to the scheme of the country you are working in, so by the same token if you are going to a country with which the UK has a reciprocal agreement, you will have to decide if you want to pay voluntary contributions to the UK in order to maintain UK pension entitlement when you return here. The Contributions Agency can advise you on this. If you have not yet come under the scheme of a foreign country and are paying Class 1, 2 or 3 contributions to the UK while working abroad then, if you think you are eligible for benefit, you should write to the Benefits Agency, Pensions and Overseas Benefits Directorate immediately the contingency governing your claim arises. One important point to bear in mind in this case, though, is that if benefit can be paid, you will only get paid at the UK rate, not that of similar welfare schemes of the country in which you are living. In many cases the latter may be much more generous than UK rates; furthermore, UK rates may bear very little relationship to the cost of living abroad.

In this connection it is also worth pointing out that the UK is by no means the top of the world league table when it comes to the percentage of the pay packet taken up by contributions to social services. In many of the EU countries, in particular, it is significantly higher. This is an important detail to discuss with a prospective employer, because the 'social wage' and what you have to put in to get it obviously have a bearing on the real value of the remuneration package you are being offered.

THE NHS AND HEALTH CARE BENEFITS

In one important instance UK benefits are actually more generous than those of many other countries. We refer here to the UK National Health Service. But medical expenses incurred abroad are definitely not refunded by the NHS, which is only available to people living in this country; so, contrary to popular belief, you will no longer be able to get free NHS treatment in this country once you become permanently resident abroad. Many overseas countries do have reciprocal health agreements with the UK – once again a list is given on the Inland Revenue site – but the services they provide are not exactly comparable with those of the British NHS. Forms E111, E128 and E106 are available from the DSS or post offices especially in the case of E111, which are essential documents in being able to access this reciprocal care. See also leaflet T5 – *Health Advice for Travellers Anywhere in the World*. The range of treatment provided free of charge varies considerably and it is advisable to take out private health insurance to cover eventualities where free medical attention is not, or is only partially, available. Leaflets giving information on the procedures you need to observe, both in the case of temporary spells and permanent residence abroad available from the Contributions Agency's International Services (tel: 0845 915 4811 or 44-191-225 4811 if calling from abroad).

CHILD BENEFIT WHILE WORKING ABROAD

There are various situations which, in different ways, affect your entitlement to receive child benefit while working abroad:

1. If you go abroad permanently, taking your children with you, your child benefits cease from the date of your departure. When you arrive in the new country you can only rely on that country's family benefit.
2. If you go to work in another EU country you will generally be insured under its social security legislation and so entitled to the local family allowances. If you are insured under another

EU scheme but leave your children behind in Great Britain, you may still be entitled to family allowances from the EU country in which you are insured. If you remain insured under the Great Britain scheme, child benefit may still be payable whether your children are in Great Britain or with you. If your children are not with you, you would have to maintain them by at least the weekly rate of child benefit after the first 56 days. If your children live with you but your spouse or partner is insured under another EU scheme, you will be entitled to local family allowances. However, you may be paid a 'supplement' equal to the difference between the local rate and the Great Britain rate of benefit if the Great Britain rate is higher.

3. If you have been sent abroad to work temporarily, for a period of not more than eight weeks, and you return within that time, benefit will continue to be paid whether or not you take your children with you. Child benefit orders cannot be cashed outside Great Britain, but you will be able to cash them when you return, provided each order is cashed within three months of the date stamped on it. After eight weeks of temporary absence, your eligibility for Great Britain child benefit ceases unless you happen to be in one of the reciprocal agreement countries.

4. You can also continue to be eligible for Great Britain child benefit, even after eight weeks of absence, if in the relevant tax year at least half your earnings from the employment which took you abroad are liable to United Kingdom income tax. However, in this case your entitlement cannot be decided until your tax liability has been assessed.

5. If a child is born abroad within eight weeks of the mother's departure from Great Britain and she is abroad only temporarily, child benefit may be paid from then until the end of the eight-week period of absence. If you wish to claim in these circumstances you should write to the DSS, Child Benefit Centre (Washington), PO Box 1, Newcastle upon Tyne NE88 1AA, quoting your child benefit number if you are already getting child benefit for another child.

6. Special rules exist in respect of serving members of the forces and civil servants; persons falling into these categories should consult their paying officer or Establishments Division.

Full details of these schemes, including the form CH 181(TO) which you have to fill in before your departure, are set out in leaflet CH 6, available from your local DSS office. Alternatively, you can get a copy by writing to DSS Information Division, Leaflet Unit, Block 4, Government Buildings, Honeypot Lane, Stanmore, Middlesex HA7 1AY.

UNEMPLOYMENT BENEFITS FOR JOB HUNTERS WITHIN THE EU

Under EU law you can go jobseeking for up to three months in most EU countries, provided you have been registered as unemployed in the UK for four weeks before departure. You are entitled to receive Jobseeker's Allowance on the day of departure and you actually register for work in the new country. While you are in the other country, you can continue drawing UK Jobseeker's Allowance via the employment services of the country you are in provided you follow their control procedures.

You should inform your local unemployment benefit office *in person* of your intention well in advance of your departure, and obtain from them leaflet UBL 22. The Pensions and Overseas Benefits Directorate of the Benefits Agency will then issue the authorisation form E303 to you if you are going to France, Greece, Portugal, Spain, Germany or Italy and there is enough time before your departure. Otherwise, it will be sent to your address there. If you are going to another EU country, the form will be sent to a liaison office in the country concerned. Regardless of which country you are going to, ask your local unemployment benefits office to issue you with a letter of introduction. You should give this – and form E303 if you have it – to the employment services when registering for work in another EU country.

In practice, many EU countries have blocked this progressive move by putting obstacles in the way over such matters as residence permits – France is particularly bad in this respect – because the UK is not alone among European Union countries in having an unemployment problem. The good news is that if you do succeed in getting a job in an EU country, in some states not only are wages and salaries higher but so also are unemployment benefits. If you are unlucky enough to lose your 'new' job after being insurably employed under the social security scheme of an EU country, your previous UK insurance may be taken into account to help you become eligible for unemployment benefits which are very much higher than those in the UK.

All Jobcentres now handle vacancies in the EU and can give further details on relevant legislation and social welfare provisions. The Employment Service issues a useful leaflet on these matters, called *Working Abroad*, as well as others detailing conditions in individual countries.

UK PENSION SCHEMES AND THE EXPATRIATE

UK pension schemes have been affected by changes in the state provisions introduced in July 1988. Many pension experts think that employees of companies contracted in to the state scheme, known as SERPS, might be better advised to set up a personal pension scheme which the new legislation now allows them to do, on an individual basis. The value of such a step would depend on a wide variety of circumstances, such as age, whether the expatriate has taxable income in the UK, and if the employer has a contracted out pension scheme, just how good its benefits are. The issues are very complicated and you should seek advice from a reputable financial management firm with experience of expatriate problems.

Checklist: Working abroad and National Insurance

1. Contact both the Contributions Agency and the Benefit Agency for relevant literature on working abroad and National Insurance contributions.
2. Consider paying voluntary contributions to maintain your benefits entitlement on your return and organise payment through direct debit from your bank or building society while you are away.
3. Check to see if you are still entitled to be paid Child Benefit.
4. If you are looking for work and claiming Jobseeker's Allowance, inform your local unemployment benefits office well in advance of your departure.
5. Take advice on your pension scheme arrangements while working abroad.

Part Three:

Preparing the Family

6 | Partner Issues

The success or failure of foreign assignments nowadays is more often than not affected by the family's willingness to relocate, and the pressures on an expatriate family should not be underestimated. Many families are organised around a dual-income couple with equal weight given to both careers. The problems of accommodating two careers, or for one partner to give up theirs for the sake of the other, are considerable. Furthermore, there is less willingness to send children to boarding school and many employees are accompanied by both partner and offspring to a new location. Creating a fulfilling experience for both partner and children is the key to a successful assignment and this chapter looks at some of the ways in which this may be achieved.

COMPANY ATTITUDES

Enlightened organisations have accepted that the days when the partner was a 'wife', and that a wife that did not work, are long gone. Unmarried and dual-earning couples are now frequently the case and, as such, the partner status has become an increasingly urgent problem to sort out. Many partners are unwilling to put their careers on hold. Furthermore, those that do will need help to turn the experience into a worthwhile venture if the employee is to complete the assignment.

It is perhaps no surprise that partners show reluctance to relocate. Relocation company ECA found that while 65 per cent of expatriates were accompanied by a partner on assignment, of the partners, 60 per cent had worked prior to the assignment but only 16 per cent worked during the assignment. It is quite reasonable to presume that a number of the 44 per cent who didn't work, chose not to; however, it is also safe to assume that many would have liked to work, but were not given the opportunity to do so. With this in mind, larger companies are beginning to recognise the need to provide support to partners. However, these are still a minority, for according to the ECA survey only 12 per cent of companies have established a uniform policy, and of that number, 35 per cent deal with partner careers on a case-by-case basis. Job searches, career counselling, network contacts and educational assistance are some of the ways in which these companies are trying to help partners. Table 6.1 shows the range of company assistance currently on offer or being considered by organisations.

However, companies with a long-established tradition of expatriation have also begun to develop strategies that see the partner included in the relocation process right from the very start, including the initial selection interview. The inclusion of the partner at this stage not only secures an understanding of his or her needs and expectations but gives a good indication of whether employees have thought through the impact a foreign assignment might have on their personal relationships.

Table 6.1   Assistance with partner careers

	Current practice (%)	Considering (%)
Networking contacts	50	10
Work permits	41	11
Education/training assistance	38	22
Career consultancy advice	33	18
Cost of career enhancement	25	12
Access to recruitment specialist	26	17
Arrange employment within company	24	10
Arrange employment with partner's company	6	3
Intra-company database/job swap	2	10

Source: ECA International

At the first interview we insist that they bring their partner with them. That has a number of messages. For a start, if an employee asks why their partner should attend, this immediately flashes a warning signal. Occasionally you get people who just haven't thought through the implications for their partner. In most cases, they have discussed it with their partner but have taken the view that 'it's my job, and I'll get it fixed up and find out what the implications are for you'. We turn it the other way round and say 'this is a deal between the two of you and us and it's only going to be as strong as the weakest of you. If we explain to you all the issues that may be involved, and you can discuss with equal amounts of information the implications for you, you can come to us together and raise your concerns and we will deal with them for you together'. We're talking to a team even though only one of them is likely to be working for us, particularly in a foreign assignment. The stresses and the pressures on the non-employee are potentially far greater.

John Thompson, PricewaterhouseCoopers

Employees will have the support and structure of the company to help settle in to their new location. The partner, on the other hand, might well be giving up a job, and certainly a social network, to move to a foreign location without any structure or obvious objective. Recruiters like John Thompson have recognised that it is a false economy not to try to help partners either to find a job or to have a local support network. Failed assignments are costly and many flounder on the trailing partner's desire to return home.

Elisabeth Marx writes about the problems faced by partners in _Breaking Through Culture Shock_ and suggests that the pressures are twofold. First, couples experience major problems and crises on international assignments because of the unique situation they find themselves in. Faced with the unpredictability of their situation and having to depend on each other, they are without their social network and normal social controls. Furthermore, Marx points to the fact that in most cases the female partner has to deal with the challenges of settling into a new place. These include organising schooling for the children, sorting out a home and the daily basics, and supporting a partner through the early stages of a new job. Additionally, she will have to try to tap into a social network for the children, and for her and her partner. Add to this the possible demands of her new job, for those who have found one, and one can see why enlightened companies are keen to involve partners from the earliest stage.

Professor Cary Cooper has written extensively about the pressures on dual-income families, and occupational stress. He believes that companies can avoid problems by communicating honestly and inclusively with couples: 'It would seem reasonable that the spouse should be given the "option" to get involved in the decision-making and information-sharing process concerning any move that may impinge on the family. At the moment, organisations are contracting with one element of the family unit, but making decisions which radically affect the unit as a whole. By operating in this way they often cause conflict between the individual and his/her family.' (Cooper and Lewis, *The Workplace Revolution*, Kogan Page).

FINDING WORK

The biggest problem for companies is in trying to find career opportunities for the partner in the new location. Apart from being able to find a suitable job to match up to the partner's skills in the new location, there are many parts of the world that will not allow couples to work on one work permit.

If you are a citizen of the European Union (ie live in Austria, Belgium, Denmark, Finland, France, Germany, Greece, Ireland, Italy, Luxembourg, The Netherlands, Portugal, Spain, Sweden or the United Kingdom) and you are being relocated within its borders, there are no such restrictions and partners are allowed to work without a permit.

Outside the European Union, however, work permits for EU citizens are hard to come by, as are permits for non-EU citizens to work in the European Union. In most cases work permits are provided only for the employee who has the backing of an international organisation and a specified job to go to. Dependants are generally allowed resident visas but the opportunity to work on their partner's permit is arbitrary and on the whole limited. For example, Australia allows dependants the right to work on an employee's permit, as does Sweden. Japan, on the other hand, allows part-time work. Islamic countries, such as Saudi Arabia, do not issue work permits to females unless they are in the teaching or nursing professions. Perhaps the most difficult country of all for which to obtain a work permit is the United States of America, which operates a rigorous immigration policy, unless the partner can show that he or she has unique and rare skills to offer.

Large companies are able to negotiate limited reciprocal arrangements on work permits with other countries, but these tend to be used up by employees. 'In some cases they can go with a joint work permit,' explains John Thompson, 'in other cases there is a real problem and virtually prohibitive because if you have an unmarried partner, for example, some countries will not give visas. They would not be recognised as a de facto spouse. In some cases we have to say, well, it won't work. As far as we are concerned their status is what it is and if they are going together as an established couple, provided the immigration authorities in the country we are dealing with recognise that, we will do so as well. But we have to look at the practicalities of what can be done.'

Given the difficulties, a few companies will try to find work within their own company for a partner with appropriate skills and relocate them in their own right. Others might begin communication with a partner's company to see if there are possibilities for relocation to the same destination within their existing organisation. However, both these, as seen by the ECA survey results, are the least favoured options. Barry Page from Arthur Andersen Consultants points to further problems, caused by the changing workforce profile, in trying to relocate working partners. 'I have come across organisations where the spouse or partner has a more senior position than the employee and that creates more problems. Also, one cannot presume that the spouse or partner is a female either.'

Many companies find it easier to help partners obtain work permits in their own right rather than to try to do so as a dependant, and to do this have set up network systems and recruitment search facilities to help look for new opportunities. For example, Shell International has set-up its OUTPOST Web site, www.outpost.expat.nl/sec, which provides information to partners who wish to work or develop their skills during and after expatriation. Likewise, ICI provides advice through a career consultancy agency for partners seeking jobs, and advice is given on academic and professional qualifications, and whether training is needed to pursue their career abroad. The company has also helped trailing partners to set up businesses. However, partners looking for work should also think about taking up some of the suggestions in Chapter 1, Job Opportunities, in their search for a job in their own right. Further useful Web sites are listed at the back of this book.

It is quite possible to look for work once relocated and in situ. However, work permit restrictions might, once again, cause problems and it is worth finding out the situation before leaving for your foreign destination.

FURTHER EDUCATION

If finding a job or obtaining a work permit proves too difficult, the time spent abroad might be a chance to explore other avenues. There are several options available to a trailing partner. For example, investigating educational opportunities in a new location could be one avenue for a trailing partner. Universities and business schools might offer an alternative structure and social network to a job. Furthermore, taking a local qualification might aid the process of finding a job in the new location. For example, INSEAD, the French Business School, provides a career service to holders of its MBA.

The Internet is also becoming an invaluable educational tool. There is an increasing number of distance learning courses available through the World Wide Web. As mentioned in Chapter 1, the Open University Business School is one institution that is using electronic means to fully explore educational potential and offers a range of six-month courses on a distance learning basis. Professionals might also use this opportunity to take post-graduate professional qualifications. Professional associations and regulatory bodies will advise you on the availability of distance learning courses. Non-professional education might also be available. For example, learning the language of your host country will provide both practical help and intellectual stimulus.

NETWORKING AND CONSIDERING THE CHILDREN

An invaluable aid to partners is the network of contacts than an employee's company can provide before expatriation. This is not just a way to find out what the location is really like but also provides invaluable contacts on arrival. Shell International has recognised the importance of this and has set up a worldwide information network 'Outpost' of Shell expatriate families, which is run by volunteer Shell partners and spouses. Likewise, PricewaterhouseCoopers encourages contact with expatriates already in location and tries to link up non-working partners.

Once again, the Internet has come into its own when considering the opportunities of contacting other expatriate partners. The plethora of Web sites for expat spouses is too numerous to mention here and is listed in the back of this book. However, apart from the Shell Spouse Centre at www.outpostexpat.nl/sec, there is also the *Electronic Telegraph's* expatriate Web site at www.telegraph.co.uk, The Expat Club at www.artinliving.com, Expat Resources for Spouses at www.thesun.org and Expat Forum at www.expat-forum.com. Numerous nationality-, location- and occupation-specific forums also exist on the Internet and, again, are listed at the back of the book. Furthermore, if your partner's company has not got an expat partner's Web site, it might also be a good time to enquire as to the possibilities of setting one up.

The focus of settling children in to a new country tends to be placed on schooling, and this will be dealt with in depth in the next chapter. However, it is also important to consider the effect that expatriation will have on their psychological and social development. Each child is, of course, uniquely different and will deal with new situations in his or her own way. For some children the opportunity to experience a new place and meet new people will be regarded as an adventure and will be welcomed. For others, it could be a profoundly disturbing experience, with family and friends disappearing from their daily lives. Older children will also present problems and before relocating it is worth considering how they might find living in a more restrictive or more liberal environment and what kind of freedoms they might expect in comparison to their home culture. Harsh punishments can be handed out for the use of 'soft' drugs and other such misdemeanours in many parts of the world. The example of the flogging of a US teenager for vandalism in Singapore should act as a warning. However, the advice remains consistent. As companies need to include partners in the decision-making process, so too children should be included in preparatory discussions and be given information about their new home. An inclusive process for the whole family might well ease some of the anxiety and stresses of relocation. Likewise, new technology might provide the answer to homesick children who can keep in contact with friends and family through the use of e-mail and the Internet. As in other situations, children can act as conductors for the emotional highs and lows of a family and if there is tension and anxiety surrounding the decision to relocate they are also likely to pick this up. Using the time before departure to investigate and research your destination with your children could be a useful exercise for the whole family.

USING YOUR INITIATIVE

No matter how supportive a company might be, in the end the trailing partner role is unlikely to be an easy one. Investigating all the possibilities and opportunities before you go is vital: whether it be job opportunities, further education or building a network of contacts to develop a social life. The last of these might also provide openings that will not become apparent until you have arrived in your new location, such as voluntary work or job opportunities. The stresses and strains on relationships should also be expected and a positive approach to the experience might help ease them. As with your partner's career change, relocation could add to your own career or life expectations by giving you international work experience and/or new skills – such as a language – and by opening new horizons. Having decided to make the move, a flexible approach will be the best way of ensuring that you are open to the opportunities available to you.

Checklist: Partner issues

1. Can you find work in the new location and are your qualifications recognised?
2. Can you work as a dependant or will you have to apply for a work permit in your own right?
3. Is your new location sympathetic to unmarried partners, same-sex partners and women who want to work – all of these can affect your chances of being granted a work permit?
4. Can your company or your partner's company find work within their organisation for you in the new location?
5. What are the educational possibilities in your new location and can your partner's employer help you identify them and/or training opportunities?
6. Does the company have a network for expat partners either on the Internet or through telephone communication?
7. If your company does not have a network for expats, are you in a position to start one yourself?
8. Talk to other expats about the host country's environment for children and give particular thought, if you have teenagers, as to what kind of social life they might be able to have.
9. Involve your children in finding out about the new destination through different media or by making contact with expat children already in situ.
10. Encourage your children to use communications technology to keep in touch with friends and family.

7 Your Children's Education

For those contemplating a job abroad, the issue of schooling cannot be taken lightly. Not only can an unsatisfactory educational solution prejudice a child's chance of achieving academic success, it can also create tensions that have an adverse effect on the home and working environment. In some cases it may lead to the premature termination of overseas contracts.

Educational options certainly demand careful thought and planning. Among the possibilities to be considered are:

1. A boarding school in the UK.
2. A day school in the UK (with guardianships/relatives).
3. An expatriate school abroad.
4. A company-sponsored school abroad.
5. A local national school abroad.
6. Home teaching abroad.

The ultimate choice will be determined by the age, ability and personality of your child, together with the quality of education available abroad and the expected duration of a contract. It will also be based on personal financial considerations and on the education support policy of the employer.

School fees (all, or a substantial part) may be paid by major international companies and organisations, and in some cases by governmental agencies. Whether such an allowance is used to contribute towards education at a UK boarding school or at a local fee-paying school will depend on local availability and the employer's policy. Some of these organisations employ trained staff to offer advice and support. They may also cover travelling expenses to and from the school in the UK, including air fares.

Smaller British companies may indicate that the salary they offer includes an unspecified sum towards the cost of schooling. Locally owned companies, particularly in developing countries, rarely provide an educational allowance.

MAINTAINING CONTINUITY

One factor that must be considered at the outset is that few organisations can be relied upon to give any help with school fees once the assignment abroad has been completed. On return to the UK many parents may find it difficult to finance boarding school fees from a lower, and often more heavily taxed, personal income. However, it can be disruptive to move your children from one school to another and particularly inadvisable at a sensitive stage in their schooling when they have begun a GCSE or A-level course. On the other hand, if you have chosen a school abroad with a curriculum that bears little or no resemblance to that followed in the UK, your child may find it hard to cover lost ground. When selecting a school it is crucial to look ahead and to make plans which will serve your child's best interest when your overseas contract comes to an end.

Most schools will go to considerable trouble to make arrangements to see prospective parents, often at short notice. Where possible take your child with you when you visit a school and listen to his or her comments. Whatever your personal feelings about education, it is essential that those of your child are fully respected. Many children have sensible views about what is best for their own development and, where necessary, they should be persuaded rather than instructed.

Your child may be eager to make the transition from state to private school and adapt well to a new environment. However, you should be aware that moving back to the state system can be difficult for ex-independent school pupils. These difficulties can also be encountered by children returning to a local school routine after the cultural diversity of an international educational environment.

The major problem for most children of expatriates is the lack of educational continuity, particularly when they are obliged to move from country to country, and school to school, every few years. If your child is to realise his or her potential you must try to provide educational stability. Much can be done to ease the process of transition by providing a new school with a detailed profile of your child. Reports, syllabus information, titles of books which he or she has been using and levels of attainment can enable a teacher to assist your child to settle happily into life in a new school with the minimum of disruption.

CONTINUED SCHOOLING IN THE UK

Many parents find it difficult to decide whether to send their child to a day or boarding school. For parents who are working overseas boarding is an obvious choice. Indeed, some parents may opt for a job abroad in order to finance their children's education at a boarding school.

How to find a boarding school

Selecting the most appropriate school for your child can be a time consuming and confusing process, but there are several organisations to help you make your choice.

The Independent Schools Information Service (ISIS), Grosvenor Gardens House, 35–37 Grosvenor Gardens, London SW1W 0BS (tel: 020 7798 1500, fax: 020 7798 1501, www.isis.org.uk) produces a number of helpful publications including *Choosing Your Independent School* (£12.95 including postage and packing). They also offer a comprehensive placement service (£350 + VAT), with reductions for siblings, and a consultancy service, which consists of an interview at the London office (£100 + VAT) or a telephone interview (£40 + VAT). A clearing house service is available to provide a shortlist of suitable schools, at a charge of £30 + VAT.

Advice is also available free of charge from Gabbitas Educational Consultants Ltd, Carrington House, 126–130 Regent Street, London W1R 6EE (tel: 020 7734 0161 or 020 7439 2071, fax: 020 7437 1764, www.gabbitas.co.uk). Gabbitas invites parents to tell them as much as possible about their child, their circumstances and the type of school they are looking for. On the basis of this information they are able to recommend a selection of suitable schools from a wide range of independent boarding and day schools. Shortlisted schools are asked to send parents a prospectus. It is then up to the parents to visit the schools personally. There is no charge for this service. Gabbitas also offers detailed guidance on education at all levels (a fee of £135 + VAT per hour is charged for such consultations). Experienced consultants deal with a range of educational issues, including options at 16+ and planning for higher education and career opportunities.

How to choose a boarding school

Having shortlisted several schools, either with or without the guidance of a professional organisation, parents are well advised to read the prospectus through carefully, and to prepare a checklist of questions in readiness for a visit to a school.

Many of the factors governing choice are self-evident and conclusions will be arrived at quickly. Access to an international airport, proximity to relatives, religious denomination, co-educational or single-sex, the academic aims of the school and the scale of fees are points which all parents will need to consider. Also important are:

☐ the academic record of the school;
☐ the qualifications and approach of the teaching staff;
☐ the staff/pupil ratio;
☐ the physical environment;
☐ the attitude to discipline;
☐ the quality of sports education;
☐ the range of information technology;
☐ the range of extra-curricular activities;
☐ the quality of pastoral care;
☐ costs;
☐ the numbers in the sixth form;
☐ the quality of careers counselling;
☐ contact with parents;
☐ the house system;
☐ school publications;
☐ references.

Entrance examination

To be admitted to an independent secondary school your child will normally be required to pass the school's entrance test or the Common Entrance examination, which is set for candidates of 11+, 12+ and 13+ (the appropriate examination is normally determined by the child's age on 1 September in the year of entry).

☐ At 11+ the subjects examined are English, mathematics, science and reasoning. Examinations take place in January and November.

☐ At 12+ candidates sit papers in English, mathematics, science and French (written and oral). Latin may be offered as an optional paper. Examinations take place in February/March and November.

☐ At 13+ the papers are English, mathematics, science, French (written and oral), history, geography and religious studies. English as an additional language, German, Spanish, Latin and Greek may be offered as optional papers. Examinations take place in February/March, June (for most candidates) and November. Candidates for boys' schools most commonly take the 13+ examination.

Each senior school sets its own entrance standards and is responsible for the assessment of papers. Some schools require candidates to sit their own independent examinations in addition, or as an alternative, to Common Entrance. The examinations are normally taken at the candidate's own school.

Children applying to boarding schools from abroad or from state schools will be in direct competition with those who have been tutored for the entrance examinations at UK prep schools. Many schools will take this fact into consideration when making their assessments. However, in some cases it may be necessary to arrange individual coaching in advance of the examination. Consultancy and assessment, as well as tuition, are available from members of the Association of Tutors, Sunnycroft, 63 King Edward Road, Northampton NN1 5LY; tel: 01604 624171. Supportive tuition or complete coverage can be provided for primary and secondary work, as well as some university-level work. Some services are available on a distance basis, and some as intensive, holiday-period schemes. Examination advice and preparation for particular exams, like the Common Entrance, is a particular expertise.

The syllabuses for each subject, and the examination papers, are set by the Independent Schools Examinations Board. Copies of syllabuses, past papers and information are available from: The Independent Schools Examinations Board, Jordan House, Christchurch Road, New Milton, Hants BH25 6QJ; tel: 01425 621111, fax: 01425 620044.

Scholarships

Many independent schools offer entrance scholarships to children of outstanding ability or potential. These may be based either on general academic standard or on particular strengths, notably musical, sporting or artistic. Individual schools will supply details on request.

A number of schools offer bursaries for means-tested families. Others make specific awards to the children of clergy and service families.

ISIS runs an advisory service on scholarships and bursaries for parents seeking general advice.

Insurance and financial planning

A growing number of financial service groups and independent financial advisers are able to offer school fee plans, with obvious benefits for those who are able to plan and save well in advance. For those with a more immediate requirement, loan schemes, both equity and non-equity based, are available. ISIS produce a useful leaflet called *School Fees*.

Many schools cooperate with insurance companies in schemes for the remission of school fees during unavoidable absence through illness. Other policies are available that guarantee the continued payment of fees in the event of a parent's death, disablement or redundancy before the completion of schooling.

Maintained boarding schools

Some local authorities run their own boarding schools or offer boarding facilities alongside day schools. Eighteen of these maintained schools have opted out and are now grant maintained (grant maintained schools will be given a new status under government plans but this should not affect the education provided). Although any child with a legal right to attend school in Britain may seek entry to any maintained school, some authorities give priority to local children, even for boarding places. As tuition is free at these schools and parents pay only for boarding, the overall costs are approximately a half to two-thirds of the cost of an independent school. Many pupils are from service families, or have parents who work for banks or government agencies abroad.

The Directory of Maintained Boarding Schools provides details of 38 schools which have boarding places. Copies may be obtained from The Boarding Schools Association, Ysgol Nant, Valley Road, Llanfairfechan, Gwynedd LL33 0ES, tel/fax: 01248 680542 or from the DfEE Publications Centre, PO Box 5050, Sudbury, Suffolk CO10 6ZQ (tel: 084560 22260, fax: 0845 6033360, www.dfee.gov.uk).

Local authority grants

Some education authorities are prepared to give grants to assist with boarding school fees when both parents are abroad and there are no places available in a state boarding school. Application should be made to the director of education or chief education officer for the area in the UK in which the family is normally resident.

Arrangements for your child

A boarding school accepts responsibility for the day-to-day welfare of its pupils in term-time, but overseas parents will naturally want assurance that their child is being cared for at all times, including short holiday periods and occasions when they may be in transit between school and home. There are a number of organisations that care for children in these circumstances.

Child supervision

Some boarding schools are able to send a school bus or driver to collect children from, and deliver them to, the nearest airport. Where this service is not available parents may wish to use a commercial escort service. These can be provided by:

☐ Universal Aunts Ltd, PO Box 304, London SW4 0NN (tel: 020 7498 8200, fax: 020 7622 1914) can arrange for children to be taken to and from school according to parents' instructions. They try to allot the same 'aunt' to a child so that a warm relationship is established. When required to do so they can also arrange for children to be accommodated for the night in the home of one of the aunts. Holiday accommodation is also available.

☐ Corona Worldwide, c/o The Commonwealth Institute, Kensington High Street, London W8 6NQ (tel/fax: 020 7610 4407) provide a dependants' (adults and children) escort service for members.

Finding a guardian

Most boarding schools require parents to appoint a local guardian for their child. Several organisations are able to offer a guardianship service for parents who do not wish to impose upon relations or family friends.

Guardianship schemes have developed in response to demands from parents and schools to cover welfare, education and finance. They are provided by, for example, the following organisations:

☐ Clarendon International Education, 41 Clarendon Square, Royal Leamington Spa, Warwickshire CV32 5Q2 (tel: 01926 316793, fax: 01926 883278, www.clarendon.uk.com).

☐ Guardians and Tutors, 131 Pomphlett Road, Plymstock, Plymouth PL6 7BU (tel: 01752 401942).

☐ Gabbitas Educational Consultants Ltd (address on page 60) run a comprehensive guardianship service which takes care of all aspects of education, welfare and finance.

☐ Joanella Slattery Associates (JSA), Gilpin, Station Road, Withyham, Hartfield, East Sussex TN7 4BT (tel: 01892 770585/0850 943106; fax: 01892 770120, e-mail: joanella@sol.com, www.cea.co.uk).

☐ GJW Education Services, Southcote, Coreway, Sidmouth EX10 9SD (tel: 01395 512300; fax: 01395 577271, e-mail: gjweaver@netcomuk.co.uk).

Day schools in the UK

If you feel that your child is unsuited to boarding school life, or that it would be too disruptive to move schools – for example, during the GCSE years – you may wish to consider a day place. Where relatives and friends are available to care for your child this arrangement can work smoothly, particularly when a child continues at his or her present school. Many older children are reluctant to leave their friends and interests behind, and are able to respond positively to a new degree of independence.

In some cases, where there are no relatives or friends to rely on and parents wish to avoid placing their child in lodgings, mothers stay behind with their children. Although this offers the child continuity it can cause strains in the marital relationship and may offset the financial benefits of the posting.

Few employers offer more than a token allowance for lodging if your child remains at a day school in the UK.

SCHOOLS ABROAD

Expatriate schools

Unlike other nations such as France, Germany, Japan or Switzerland, Britain provides no financial assistance for the creation and management of schools for British expatriates. This means that British parents moving abroad must expect to pay substantial school fees unless they choose to send their children to local national schools.

British schools

So-called 'British schools' abroad use English as the language of instruction and aim to follow a curriculum that corresponds to the National Curriculum. This is an advantage for children who will return to the UK system. The extent to which the schools are genuinely British in outlook will depend on the background of the staff and headteacher, and the influence of the local British community. Although a high percentage of British pupils usually attend these schools, they are open to pupils of different nationalities.

Most British schools are not government approved. However, a group of 26 schools in the EU are members of the Council of British Independent Schools in the European Communities (COBISEC), which is recognised by the Department for Education and Employment (DfEE). Like UK state schools, COBISEC schools receive regular inspections from the Office for Standards in Education (OFSTED). Advice is available from the COBISEC Secretariat, c/o Mrs S Melchers, Lucy's, Lucy's Hill, Hythe, Kent CT21 5ES; tel: 01303 260857.

A number of British schools are affiliated to UK professional educational associations, such as the Headmasters' and Headmistresses' Conference (HMC) and the Girls' Schools Association (GSA). Such links enable schools to keep abreast of educational developments taking place in the UK, and to share the benefits of staff development courses.

The European schools

The nine official European schools were set up by agreement among the member states of the EU to provide a multinational education almost exclusively for the children of staff employed in the institutions of the EU. The schools are situated in Brussels (2), Luxembourg, Mol (Belgium), Varese (Italy), Munich and Karlsruhe (Germany), Bergen (Holland) and Culham (UK). The European schools are day schools with a 4 to 19 age range. Pupils are organised in separate language sections and follow a common curriculum leading in the secondary school to the European Baccalaureate, the schools' own leaving examination. A tenth school is under construction in Brussels and should open in September 1999. Information about the schools is available from the European Schools Team at the DfEE (tel: 020 7925 5000).

American schools

American schools offer an American curriculum, but may be an option for British children because the language of instruction is English. It is important to remember that the educational approach will be quite different and that pupils will be prepared for American examinations at college entry level, such as the Standard Achievement Tests (SATs). To graduate from an American school a certain number of credits are required. Credit courses in the final two years of schooling may include Honours and Advanced Placement Sections which provide able students with special challenges. British universities are familiar with the entrance requirements of leading American universities and set similar entry requirements for applicants from American-style schools.

International schools

International schools are established in most capital cities of the world. They may be distinguished by the fact that they are independent of any state system and aim to educate children from a variety of nationalities.

Many are outstanding, offering intellectual pluralism and exceptional cultural variety – typically 50 to 60 different nationalities are represented in the student body. Some are members of international associations such as the United World Colleges and the European Council of International Schools (ECIS), others have headteachers in membership of the (British-based) Headmasters' and Headmistresses' Conference or the Girls' Schools Association.

In many respects they are as varied as their locations – large or small, monolingual, bilingual (using a foreign language as a medium of instruction for some subjects) or even multilingual (using more than one foreign language as a medium of instruction), traditional or emphatically modern. Some are subsidised by local governments, others are among the most costly schools in the world. Almost all are co-educational, and in the majority the language of instruction is English.

International schools may follow a standard US college preparatory programme or a standard GCSE or International GCSE (IGCSE) programme, or a combination of these. Although a number of schools also work towards national examinations such as the German Abitur or the Spanish Bachillerato, at sixth-form level many are now preparing for the diploma of the International Baccalaureate Organisation (IBO).

The International Baccalaureate (IB) is based on a two-year curriculum that maintains a balance between the sciences, the arts and languages. The programme is broader than A-levels as all students must offer one subject from each of six groups:

- ☐ Language A (first language)
- ☐ Language B (second language)
- ☐ Individuals and societies
- ☐ Experimental sciences
- ☐ Mathematics
- ☐ Electives (including art, music, IT).

Of the six subjects studied, three are taken at Higher level, and three at Standard level. This represents a deliberate compromise between the European emphasis on breadth and the British tradition of rigorous specialisation. In effect students offer three subjects to A-level equivalent standard and three subjects to a standard somewhat above GCSE. To be eligible for the award of the Diploma candidates must score a minimum of points and meet three additional requirements: submission of an extended essay; satisfactory completion of a Theory of Knowledge Course; and compulsory participation in a CAS programme (Creativity, Action, Service).

Students holding the IB Diploma have entered more than 700 universities throughout the world. All UK universities accept the IB as satisfying their general requirement for entrance. For further information contact: The International Baccalaureate Organisation, Curriculum and Assessment Centre, Peterson House, Fortran Road, St Mellons, Cardiff CF3 0LT (tel: 02920 774 000, fax: 02920 774 001, www.ibo.org).

Another worldwide school-leaving certificate, which has been available to English-medium schools throughout the world since 1986, is the Advanced Intermediate Certificate of Education (AICE). AICE is a 'group' certificate which is awarded on the basis of a broad and balanced curriculum of five full-credit courses or their equivalent. All candidates must take at least one course from three subject groups: mathematics and sciences; languages; and arts and humanities. The AICE curriculum, which is designed to be of worldwide relevance, offers a high degree of flexibility. As there are no compulsory subjects, student programmes may range from the highly specialised to the general. Most UK universities now accept AICE as an alternative to A-levels. AICE is administered by the University of Cambridge Local Examinations Syndicate (UCLES), 1 Hills Road, Cambridge CB1 2EU (tel: 01223 553311, fax: 01223 460278, www.ocr.org.uk).

How to find an overseas school

Help and advice on the selection of an overseas school can be provided by World-wide Education Service (WES) Ltd, Canada House, 272 Field End Road, Eastcote HA4 9NA (tel: 020 8582 0317/0318, fax: 020 8429 4838, www.wesworldwide.com). This company should not be confused with World-wide Education Service (Home School) Ltd, which is mentioned further on and is a completely separate entity.

For detailed information about the 400 international schools in membership of ECIS and brief details on 400 non-member schools, including enrolment, curriculum, fees, school premises, extra-curricular activities, staff details and school ownership, see *The International Schools Directory* (£35), which is available from John Catt, Great Glenham, Saxmundham, Suffolk IP17 2DH; tel: 01728 663666. The online version of the Directory can be found on the ECIS Web site on www.ecis.org.

How to choose a school abroad

When selecting a school abroad it may prove useful to consider the points raised earlier on choosing a UK boarding school. However, there are several additional factors which should be considered when evaluating overseas schools:

1. Many employers pay for families to visit the country before their projected move. This gives them the opportunity to visit the available schools (it is useful to obtain prospectuses beforehand) in person, and to consider the alternatives with existing expatriate parents and organised parents' groups which are attached to the schools. However, it is important to remember that other people may have standards which do not correspond to your own.

   In many instances expatriate schools become both a community and a social centre for expatriate families. This can be a great help for incoming families.

2. It is advisable to link house-hunting with the choice of school so that transportation problems can be considered in advance.

3. A rapid turnover of pupils can be expected in many schools as a reflection of the frequent movement of personnel by companies. However, this should not be the case with the majority of staff. As children may take time to adjust to new teaching styles it is important that there is continuity in the classroom.

4. It is important to establish how schools overseas are controlled. Many schools are run by boards composed of leading figures from the local community, including representatives from the parent body and the organisations which use the school. The latter may be relied upon to ensure that the facilities available to their employees are of a high standard.

5. Every effort should be made to meet the headteacher, who is responsible for the quality and organisation of the school. He or she will be able to tell you whether there is a waiting list for admission to the school and when you need to register your child. In some instances the waiting time for admission can be a full academic year. Other schools may be ready to accept pupils at almost any time.

6. Take time to consider the curriculum. How far does it correspond to the National Curriculum in the UK? How straightforward will it be for your child to transfer back to the UK? Try to establish how much support, both pastoral and academic, is

provided for individual children, to enable them to cope with the process of transition.

7. It is important to consider the type of report and record-keeping system which is in operation in the school. How much information will be available as a record of your child's achievement at the school? Pupil profiles are particularly essential for children who move from school to school frequently.

8. The language of instruction will be of key importance to your child. Find out what kind of English is used – whether it is American, British or non-mother-tongue English. How many children and staff do not have English as a first language? Are they likely to hinder your child's progress?

9. Expatriate schools are geared to accept pupils at any stage during the school year. However, the process of transition is generally easier when pupils begin school at the start of a new term.

10. If your company is not offering an educational allowance, do take account of costs. ECIS reports that in Paris full day fees can range from $10,000 in a junior school to $15,000 in a secondary school. In New York comparable figures are $10,000 at elementary level and $18,000 at secondary level, in Hong Kong from $7,000 to $10,000 and in Brazil from $10,000 to $16,000. In addition, some schools may require parents to pay a substantial registration fee.

Company-sponsored schools

Where difficulties arise in finding a suitable local school, companies may decide to open their own site-based school. The success of such enterprises will depend to a large extent on the quality of the teaching staff and the existence of educational support. Schools may be very small, and a group of children of different ages and ability will be taught in one class by a single teacher. In remote areas it can be difficult to attract suitably qual-ified staff and the spouses of on-site employees may be encouraged to take responsibility for classes.

Without external monitoring, company schools may lose touch with educational developments and offer a rather limited education. Regular contact with an outside source ensures that satisfactory educational standards are maintained.

Home School Teaching can set up and monitor small schools in isolated overseas locations, often with fewer than 20 pupils, for international companies or groups of parents. They also recruit teachers. Private family tutors can be arranged for a fee which is negotiated on an individual basis. Home School Teaching, Blagrove House, Blagrove Street, Reading RG1 1QA; tel: 0118 958 9993, fax: 0118 958 9994, e-mail: office@creshome.demon.co.uk, Web site: www.creshome.demon.co.uk.

Local national schools

Within Europe there are significant advantages to be gained in sending your child to a local national school, not least an opportunity to acquire proficiency in another language and to absorb a new culture. Although the standard of educational provision may vary there is no doubt that in some countries, such as France and Germany, it is excellent. However, a complete immersion in another language and culture is demanding and it will depend very much on the age and ability of the children as to how successfully they can adapt.

Learning the full range of school subjects in a new language can be exacting, particularly where no provision is made for extra language tuition. Parents who do not speak the necessary language themselves must remember that they will be able to offer little advice and assistance to their child, who may feel isolated as a result.

For those on short-term contracts it is important to consider how well such a schooling will prepare children for the next stage in a UK education. Certainly, a child working towards GCSE examinations could expect to be disadvantaged. The experience may also pose difficulties for younger children returning to the UK.

Transfer into and out of school systems in other parts of the world can also pose problems. Traditional teaching methods which rely on rote learning are still applied in many developing countries, where schools are frequently ill-equipped and crowded. As education is so highly prized as a route out of poverty, expatriates will not be encouraged to supplant a local child. However, where no alternative exists, parents may need to compensate for a restricted curriculum by providing supplementary lessons at home.

Differences in attitudes to schooling are particularly marked in countries where religious and political beliefs have shaped the curriculum. Even in other parts of the English-speaking world there are fundamental differences in approach. For example, in Australia formal schooling starts at 6 and secondary education at 12.

Home study

Occasionally parents are faced with the prospect of teaching their children themselves because no school is available locally. This is a demanding activity but can be very rewarding, especially for spouses who find that they are prevented by local laws from taking up employment.

An advantage of lessons given at home is that they can be designed to provide educational continuity, particularly where instruction follows a plan provided by your child's previous school or a recognised UK-based commercial 'home school service'. Home school requires the strong commitment and active participation of a parent, but offers continuous support with teaching difficulties as they arise.

The World-wide Education Service (Home School) Ltd (mentioned above) has been concerned with home teaching in the UK and overseas for over 100 years. It provides full courses, books, materials, teacher notes, lesson plans, timetables and monitoring procedures to enable parents to teach children aged 4 to 14 years, and to be involved in the assessment process. Each family is assigned a tutor who provides regular guidance and advice and can be contacted at any time. Specialist questions are referred to a team of WES Home School advisers. Tutors are available for personal interviews – for example, during home leave.

The WES Home School curriculum includes all core and foundation subjects specified by the National Curriculum so that children are able to fit back into a UK school with relative ease. WES also offers a Standard Assessment Testing Service based on the statutory SATS which occur in schools in England and Wales at the end of Key Stage 1 (Year 2, age 7 years), and Key Stage 2 (Year 6, age 11 years). The tests are administered by the teaching parent at home and returned to WES for marking by qualified and experienced teachers. In addition to finding out what levels their children have reached, advice on what they need to learn, or revise, in order to improved, is provided. At the same time, parent-teachers are strongly encouraged to relate their child's learning to the local environment. The benefit to the child of living in another country is stressed throughout the programmes. Although children educated at home can miss the social contact with their peers and a competitive school environment, WES Home School claim that they are often in advance of their contemporaries when they return to schools in Britain.

Increasing numbers of parents choose to teach older children at home. Structured correspondence courses, which require relatively little parental guidance, are available from Mercers College, 14 Baldock Street, Ware SG12 9DN; tel: 01920 465926, fax: 01920 484909. The needs of children of all ages are catered for, and courses aim to follow the National Curriculum. Programmes include reading and numeracy schemes for young children and preparation for the Common Entrance Examinations.

A broad range of courses is also offered which leads to the General Certificate of Secondary Education (GCSE) and the International General Certificate of Secondary Education (IGCSE). The IGCSE is a single-subject examination, but students can take the group examination, the International Certificate of Education (ICE), sitting seven subjects from six subject groups. Both examinations are administered by the University of Cambridge Local Examinations Syndicate (UCLES).

Many students also continue to take GCE O-levels; it is still possible to sit these overseas and they are a good introduction to A-level work. The college offers A-levels.

The National Extension College, 18 Brooklands Avenue, Cambridge CB2 2HN (tel: 01223 316644, fax: 01223 313586, www.nec.ac.uk), also offers correspondence courses leading to GCSE/IGCSE and A-level.

Support, advice and information for families contemplating home-based education as an alternative to schooling are available from Education Otherwise, PO Box 120, Leamington Spa CV32 7ER.

Checklist: Your children's education

1. Consider the options in relation to your child's age, ability and personality, and in relation to the quality of education in your new location.
2. Consider whether your organisation will contribute towards your child's education.
3. Does your host country's education system bear any resemblance to your native country's?
4. If you are considering using the independent sector, what are the financial implications, particularly when you return from your assignment?
5. If your child/children are to go to boarding school, what arrangements can be made for a local guardian?
6. What are the local alternatives and can you speak to other expat parents to find out what educational facilities are like in your new location?
7. Are the qualifications offered by your local national or international schools compatible with your domestic ones?
8. Can you team up with other expat families to provide a home teaching group?
9. If not, will your company provide support in setting up a company school?
10. If your child has special needs, contact support agencies for advice.

8 Health, Security and Welfare

HEALTH RISKS

Whether you are relocating to a new country by yourself or with your family, one of the most important pre-trip considerations is what health hazards might be encountered in your host country. You might feel that developed countries might not represent too many risks to a visitor. However, it is always advisable to seek expert advice, regardless of your destination. This advice should include information not only about local health risks but also about the health service and access to medical care in your host country. While the emphasis is on developing countries, travellers should also be aware that risks in non-Third World countries are still prevalent, for example the hepatitis virus in areas of Turkey, and a recent outbreak of diptheria in Russia.

A useful book that can be thoroughly recommended is *Travellers' Health* by Dr Richard Dawood (published by Oxford University Press). This provides detailed information and guidance on every conceivable medical area and is essential reading before departure.

The risks to children will also need to be identified. Some illnesses, such as gastroenteritis, present a far greater risk to children than to adults and it is essential that you arm yourself with information concerning symptoms and medical treatment, such as the administration of a fluid-replacement solution. You will also need to make sure that your child's immunisations are up to

MediCare International

Most schemes appear pretty similar on paper and you only see the difference when it's too late. Not with MediCare International, we offer quality healthcare at all levels – even covering maternity and routine dental care. MediCare International is one of the world's most comprehensive and respected healthcare companies.

MediCare International provides considerable expertise and excellent volume discounts to companies. This gives management the opportunity to provide the very best health cover for employees, including local nationals and their dependants. MediCare International also prides itself on caring for individuals, with benefits including all out-patient services, no age limit and annual cover of up to £1,000,000 per person.

Of course the most serious thing you can lose when abroad is your health, but it can still be very distressing to lose cash, credit cards, baggage etc. These are all protected by MediCare International's optional Trip Travel Insurance.

Yet it is only when you need to claim that the true colours of an insurance company shine through. MediCare International keeps its promises, ensuring claims are settled promptly. Plus, every member is issued with a membership card quoting details for emergency assistance. Proving you have the means to pay hospital bills could mean the difference between life and death.

Medical insurance when living, travelling or working abroad can and often is, an essential part of life. We understand your needs and our 24 hour 365 days a year Customer Service Centre is set up to deal with exactly these needs.

MediCare International *is* the business.

date and to identify any specific vaccines that may be required. Seek advice for babies under six months who are not able to have these immunisations.

Specialist organisations

Good general advice on health preparations before departure is available from the Web site of the Medical Advisory Service for Travellers Abroad (MASTA) at www.masta.org and is shown below:

☐ Make sure you are up to date with your immunisations such as tetanus and polio, and check which others you might need for your destination.

☐ Allow 6–8 weeks to undergo a full course of immunisation.

☐ Malaria tablets should be taken 1 week before entering a malaria area or 2–3 weeks before if taking Mefloquine.

☐ Find out what your blood group is to ensure prompt treatment in an emergency.

☐ Find out how you can contact emergency services in your new location.

☐ If you are taking medication, make sure that you have adequate supplies and make a note of the medicines you are taking and the dosage to inform a doctor in an emergency.

☐ Do not take any drugs to a Third World or developing country unless they are prescribed and labelled.

☐ Keep a record of your medical history and briefly note down the relevant details of treatment and medication.

☐ Note down any pills or medicine to which you are allergic.

MASTA also offers health briefs on 230 countries. Information can be obtained direct from MASTA on 020 7631 4408, and from their Traveller's Health Line on 0906 8224100 (charged at 60p per minute). A particular feature is a personalised health brief, combining a personal medical check-up with very up-to-date information on the country (or combination of countries) to be visited, from the MASTA database, which covers more than 250 countries and includes the latest data from the Foreign Office. Central billing for companies can be arranged to cover all their employees who travel abroad. One MASTA service particularly geared to the intending expatriate is a detailed health brief and an extensive individual health report on the country concerned.

Other organisations specialising in travel medicine are as follows:

☐ The Malaria Reference Laboratory at the London School of Hygiene and Tropical Medicine, which runs a helpline on 0891 600350 (charged at 50p per minute).

☐ The Travel Clinic, Hospital for Tropical Diseases, 4 St Pancras Way, London NW1 0PE, which offers preventative advice and has an extensive range of health products and immunisations available. For information, call their Healthline on 0839 337733 (charged at 50p per minute); to make an appointment, telephone 020 7388 9600.

☐ British Airways Travel Clinics, which form a network of 29 clinics nationwide, with an additional three in South Africa. Call 01276 685040 for details of your nearest clinic. Details are also available on the British Airways Web site: www.britishairways.com. The clinics offer a one-stop service, providing immunisation, health protection items such as mosquito nets and water purification tablets, and anti-malarial tablets. The British Airways Travel Clinics are affiliated to the Geneva-based international charity the Bloodcare Foundation, which can send screened and tested blood worldwide. Cover is available for individuals or families, or for a company, on a monthly or yearly basis.

There is, however, one major international health hazard that has come to the fore since earlier editions of this book: the problem of acquired immune deficiency syndrome (AIDS). It has reached epidemic proportions in some parts of Africa and other developing countries. It is no longer sufficient to warn expatriates against the dangers of promiscuity. People can become infected through transfusions of infected blood or treatment with instruments that have not been properly sterilised. Expatriates are now advised to contact the local British embassy or high commission, which keeps a register of reliable blood donors among the expatriate community. It is also inadvisable in many countries to attend local doctors' or dentists' clinics unless they are known to enforce the highest standards of hygiene. Medical kits should also be top of the packing list.

Organisations such as MASTA can advise on the appropriate contents.

Those working in Saudi Arabia should note that they will have to produce a doctor's certificate to show that they are HIV negative. It has been pointed out that this can raise problems when applying for medical insurance. Even the answer 'yes' to the question 'Have you ever been HIV tested?' can raise the suspicion that your lifestyle exposes you to the risk of AIDS. Thus, if you have been HIV tested in connection with an assignment to Saudi Arabia, you should point this out if the question arises on a medical insurance form.

An extremely useful leaflet, *Travellers Guide to Health*, which covers prevention and planning, emergency care and international health care agreements, and contains a copy of form E111 for free or reduced-cost emergency medical treatment in most European countries, can be obtained from your GP, or through the Health Literature Line on 0800 555 777. A comprehensive guide is available in the form of *Health Information for Overseas Travel* (published by The Stationery Office, £7.95, tel: 0870 6005522, www.tsonline.co.uk). This detailed work is primarily intended for reference by GPs, but serious travellers will find it most useful, as it provides a thorough guide to disease risk, immunisation and other hazards, as well as child-specific information.

EXPATRIATE MEDICAL INSURANCE

Most of the countries that expatriates go to do not operate a national health service like that of the UK. It comes as something of a shock to find oneself paying £50 or more for a routine visit to a doctor or dentist and the costs of hospitalisation can be such as to wipe out the savings of months, or even years. In places like the EU, South Africa, Australia or other developed Commonwealth countries there are established local methods of medical insurance, and in many cases the cost of this is included in the remuneration package. If not, it is certainly a matter which should be clarified while you are negotiating the job offer.

As far as OPEC and similar resource-rich economies are

concerned, some of these countries do have state medical schemes, and as a matter of fact their hospitals are, in many cases, better equipped than our increasingly rundown institutions. They are, however, established primarily for the benefit of local nationals, which means that the customs and culture of medical care are different from those which most westerners are used to. For this reason, most expatriates in those countries arrange for attention in private hospitals which, needless to say, tends to be very expensive indeed. Medical insurance for anyone going to these places is therefore essential and a number of plans have now been developed specifically for expatriates by MediCare International BUPA International PPP healthcare and Goodhealth Worldwide among others. Tables 8.1 and 8.2 detail the individuals premiums and benefits schedule of MediCare International's two level of International and Executive International Plan as of 2002. However, the insurance business is fiercely competitive; if you are paying your own insurance it is vital to ask your broker for a complete list of all the plans that are available, so that you can make a comparison between them. You will need to establish whether quoted premiums include or exclude insurance premium tax for an accurate comparison. It is also worth finding out how long companies take to settle claims.

It is important to be sure that the scheme covers medical attention irrespective of the circumstances which caused it to be necessary. A case has been reported where an expatriate was seriously injured by an assault while at home, only to discover that his medical insurance did not cover injuries sustained outside his workplace. Another point to watch, though it does not strictly speaking come under medical insurance, is personal accident cover and consequential loss of earnings. It is worth checking whether your cover extends to that eventuality.

It is also necessary, when it comes to making claims – and particularly when requesting repatriation for urgent treatment – that the local practitioner should be credible from the point of view of the insurers. It is a good idea to make yourself known to him or her at an early stage after your arrival and to notify your insurers about his or her identity. You should also carry the name of your insurers with you or at least keep it in some convenient place. Goodhealth Worldwide, PPP healthcare and MediCare International issue a

Table 8.1 MediCare International Health Plan Individual Premiums

For the purpose of this policy the following countries are deemed to be the Caribbean area:

Anguilla, Antigua, Aruba, Bahamas*, Barbados, Belize, Bermuda*, Bonaire, Cayman Islands, Costa Rica, Cuba, Curacao, Dominica, Dominican Republic, El Salvador, Grenada, Guadeloupe, Guatemala*, Haiti, Honduras, Jamaica, Martinique, Mexico*, Nicaragua, Panama, Puerto Rico, St. Lucia, St. Vincent, Trinidad and Tobago, Venezuèla, Virgin Islands.

*It is accepted that this country is not within the Caribbean region but for the purposes of underwriting is included in this category

Area 1 Worldwide excluding the USA, Canada and the Caribbean.

Premiums are per person

Age Band	International Plan (£ annual)	Executive International Plan (£ annual)
Child	327	477
18–25	496	746
26–29	588	896
30–34	643	969
35–39	742	1,125
40–44	828	1,248
45–49	881	1,327
50–54	1,159	1,738
55–59	1,477	2,210
60–64	1,890	2,830
65–69	2,831	4,258
70–74	3,843	5,788
75–79	4,572	6,886
80+	5,568	8,352

Area 2 Worldwide including the USA, Canada and the Caribbean.

Premiums are per person

Age Band	International Plan (£ annual)	Executive International Plan (£ annual)
Child	781	1,195
18–25	1,285	2,036
26–29	1,532	2,434
30–34	1,668	2,648
35–39	1,928	3,058
40–44	2,134	3,369
45–49	2,272	3,559
50–54	2,986	4,679
55–59	3,798	5,954
60–64	4,845	7,585
65–69	7,294	11,475
70–74	9,859	15,628
75–79	11,736	18,616
80+	14,361	22,460

Premiums for the Optional Trip Travel and Personal Accident benefits are as follows:

Trip Travel: £95 for the insured person or £145 fo the insured person and dependants.
Personal Accident: Administrative and clerical occupations: £66.50 per unit.
Non-hazardous manual occupations: £100.00 per unit

Table 8.2 MediCare International Health Plan Benefits Schedule

Benefits Schedule

Annual maximum aggregate £1,000,000. This is restricted to £100,000 for home country cover

	International Plan	Executive International Plan
INPATIENT AND DAYCARE		
Hospital services, including theatre, intensive care and nursing	Full Refund	Full Refund
Hospital Accommodation – for the cost of a single bedded room including meals for the patient	Full Refund	Full Refund
Parent Accommodation – for one parent accompanying an insured child aged 16 years or under	Full Refund	Full Refund
Surgeon and Anaesthetist Fees – for the reasonable and customary charges	Full Refund	Full Refund
Psychological and psychiatric disorders – for the reasonable and customary costs	Full Refund Subject to maximum 30 days	Full Refund Subject to maximum 30 days
Physician fees – for the reasonable and customary charges made by the treating physician for treatment during the admission	Full Refund	Full Refund
Hospital Cash Benefit – to be paid when treatment and accommodation is received free of charge	£25 per night	£25 per night
Local Ambulance Services – to take a patient to or between Hospitals	Full Refund	Full Refund
Emergency Medical Transportation – to take a patient who has a critical medical condition to the nearest Hospital. This benefit does not apply to: Maternity; Local Nationals in their Home Country	Full Refund	Full Refund
Nursing at Home	Full Refund, subject to maximum 26 weeks in any one policy year	Full Refund, subject to maximum 26 weeks in any one policy year
Accident & Emergency Services – performed in a Hospital casualty ward or emergency room immediately following an Accident	Full Refund	Full Refund
OUTPATIENT – all subject to a £25 excess per claim		
General medical practitioner fees – for the reasonable and customary costs	Covered for 3 months following discharge from hospital under direct order of a physician. Nil excess	Full Refund

	International Plan	Executive International Plan
Diagnostic tests, pathology, x-rays and physiotherapy	Covered for three months following discharge from hospital under direct order of a physician Nil excess	Full Refund
Specialist/Consultant Services – for the reasonable and customary costs	Covered for three months following discharge from hospital under direct order of a specialist or consultant Nil excess	Full Refund
Osteopathy and chiropractice – for treatment recommended and ordered by a Physician	Not Covered	Full Refund
Prescribed Drugs	Covered for three months following discharge from hospital under direct order of a physician Nil excess	Full Refund

OTHER BENEFITS

	International Plan	Executive International Plan
Oncologist fees, chemotherapy and radiotherapy	Full Refund	Full Refund
Computerised tomography and magnetic resonance imaging – for the reasonable and customary costs when medically required	Full Refund	Full Refund
Organ Transplantation – the cost of transplantation of kidney(s), heart or liver	Not Covered	Full Refund up to £100,000
Emergency Dental Treatment – for treatment to natural teeth following an accident to restore or replace or for immediate relief of pain provided within 48 hours following the accident	Full Refund up to £1,000	Full Refund up to £1,000
Routine Dental – only available where proof of regular six monthly check-ups available	Not covered	Full Refund subject to £30 excess and 20% co-insurance thereafter
Maternity Care	Not covered	Full Refund up to £5,000, subject to 20% co-insurance

Table 8.2 continued

	International Plan	Executive International Plan
Newborn children – for the costs from birth to 30 days following discharge of the child from hospital and subject to completion of an addition of dependant's form	Full Refund up to £5,000, subject to £100 excess and 50% co-insurance	Full Refund up to £5,000, subject to £100 excess and 50% co-insurance
Repatriation – the cost of the preparation and air transportation of the mortal remains of an insured person who dies outside the home country	Not covered	Full Refund up to £5,000
Local Burial – the costs of the preparation and Local Burial of the mortal remains of an insured person who dies outside the home country	Not covered	Full Refund up to £5,000

OPTIONAL BENEFITS

Trip Travel Insurance – for any number of trips up to 60 days	Baggage Cash & Credit Cards Cancellation/ Curtailment Delayed Travel Personal Public Liability	Up to £1,500 Up to £500 Up to £1,500 Up to £100 Up to £1,000,000
Personal Accident Cover for bodily injury arising out of –	Death Loss of one or more limbs. Irrecoverable loss of sight Permanent total disablement	Available in units of £50,000 to a maximum of £250,000

NOTES

Geographical Area – Any medical costs incurred outside the selected Geographical Area will be met for a maximum period of 30 days in any one insurance year, provided that the trip was not specifically made the purpose of obtaining medical treatment and the aggregate period spent outside the selected Geographical Area has not exceeded 30 days per insurance year and treatment commenced during that period.

Eligibility – all nationalities and their dependants are eligible to join other than citizens of the Containers of America resident in the Continents of America or persons subject to exchange controls or local insurance licensing regulations

Chronic conditions – cover is included for treatments required to treat chronic conditions

Please note, this is a schedule of benefits only. Please refer to the MediCare policy terms and conditions for full details.

card which provides a convenient *aide-mémoire*. They carry the policy number and also emergency contact numbers. Most international healthcare providers offer 24-hour customer service. An individual does not have to be in a medical emergency; one can call 24 hours a day, 365 days a year, to discuss a claim or membership entitlements or just to ask for advice. This is particularly useful for people moving farther afield, where the time zones may be very different.

Another firm which issues its clients with a card is International SOS Assistance, whose medical and security schemes enable the holder, or those looking after him or her, to call for medical assistance at six main centres throughout the world. They specialise in emergency medical evacuation to the nearest high-quality medical facility, repatriation and return of mortal remains. PPP, BUPA, Goodhealth Worldwide, Expacare, IPH, William Russell, Carecard International and other private insurers use these services. As they point out, it is only of limited use to have cover for repatriation unless it can be implemented easily. GESA Assistance provides a similar service to, among others, Falcon Healthcare.

Catering particularly for the retired expatriate, the Exeter Friendly Society does not automatically increase premium rates with advancing age, making their policies a good buy for the over-50s.

John Wason (Insurance Brokers) Ltd, founded by a former expatriate, offers a specialist 'Overseas Personal Insurance' scheme, which includes optional medical and personal accident/sickness cover worldwide. Levels of cover accord with 'units' purchased.

Finally, there is the possibility of free, or subsidised, local medical care courtesy of a reciprocal agreement with the UK health authorities. The EU and many other countries have such agreements, but the terms do vary. Form E111 is the required paperwork and can be obtained from your GP, or through the Health Literature Line on 0800 555 777. However, this scheme is no substitute for a good insurance policy.

Some of the questions you should ask about your medical cover are as follows:

1. Does the scheme cover all eventualities?
2. Are the scheme's benefits realistic in the light of local costs?

3. Can you make claims immediately or is there an initial indemnity period during which claims are disallowed? (Some insurers insist on this to protect themselves from claims caused by 'pre-existing medical conditions'.)
4. Is there a clause providing for emergency repatriation by air, or air ambulance, if suitable treatment is not available locally? If so, who decides what constitutes an emergency and/or adequate local treatment?
5. Is the insurer's nearest office accessible personally or by telephone?
6. What is the length of the insurer's settlement period for claims?
7. Is there a discount for members of professional or other associations?
8. Does the policy continue to apply, partly or fully, while you are back in the UK?
9. What is the insurer's attitude to AIDS and HIV tests?

PERSONAL SECURITY

There are overseas countries where crimes against persons, either for gain or to make political points, are a serious hazard. Countries where Islamic fundamentalism is on the increase are a case in point. Other places, notably in Africa and Latin America, qualify as high-risk locations in terms of personal safety, eg Colombia, Zimbabwe, Brazilian cities and Johannesburg. There are also corporate or national connections which may be the target of terrorists:

☐ Anything to do with Israel. It is still advisable to carry a separate passport if you have a visa for Israel but also travel to the Middle East.

☐ Employees of companies associated with pollution, nuclear waste and animal experiments.

☐ Nationals of countries that have recently been, or are currently, in serious dispute with countries in which an expatriate is living – or even its allies.

According to the international security consultants Merchants International Group (MIG), resident expatriates tend to be more at risk in these circumstances than visiting businessmen. However, the terrorist attacks on the World Trade Center in New York and the Pentagon in Washington of 11 September 2001 have brought to the forefront the constant risks from terrorism to which all business travellers are exposed, even in the most developed countries. MIG which speculates in the 'grey areas' of risk often associated with developing countries, is available for advice on these matters. For more information, visit the MIG Web site at www.merchantinternational.com. Since 11 September 2001 it seems less likely that the chances of winning the lottery jackpot are higher than that of being anywhere near a terrorist attack.

ACCIDENTS

Finally, it is worth sounding a note of warning. In many countries getting involved in legal action can be disastrous – even when it is over a minor incident. It is certainly worth researching your host country's attitude to such events and what kind of ethical stance it takes on such matters – including that of bribery. Check if your company has an ethical policy on such matters.

In some parts of the world it might be wise to hire a driver rather

Checklist: Health, security and welfare

1. Avoid daily routines, like taking the same route to work every day at a fixed time.
2. Remove bushes and thick vegetation around the entrance to your house or place of work – they could make a hiding place for criminals and people tend to be least vigilant as they approach familiar places.
3. If you think you are being followed, head immediately for a place where there are as many other people around as possible. Criminals prefer not to strike when there are witnesses about.
4. Report suspicious incidents to the police and encourage your family to be alert for them; for instance, 'students' coming to

your door to make unlikely-sounding surveys. If you get threatening telephone calls, report these to the police, also and try to remember any peculiarities of voice or accent, or any background noise that might give a hint as to where the call was made from.

5. Watch out for abandoned cars in the vicinity. These are sometimes dumped by criminals to test police vigilance.

6. Avoid conspicuous displays of affluence.

7. Try to have a room in your house to which you and your family can retreat if serious danger threatens. It should have good doors with stout locks, and windows that can be secured from the inside but which do not bar escape routes. If possible, get professional advice on how to prepare what is called a 'keep' in your house.

8. Using firearms as a form of self-defence is fraught with danger. You will nearly always be faced with more than one assailant and you have to be prepared to shoot to kill. That in itself is much less easy than it is made to look in the movies; furthermore, in some countries foreigners are always in the wrong in such circumstances.

9. The best form of defence and survival is to rehearse a plan of action in your mind in case you are attacked or in danger – and to stick to it if you can. The thing to avoid above all is panic, because that way you lose control of the situation.

than take the risk of getting involved in an accident yourself. It is important not to take any unnecessary risks, as many countries are unsympathetic to practices accepted as normal in other parts of the world, such as drinking alcohol or gambling.

9 | *Adjusting to Living and Working Abroad*

Living and working overseas can be extremely rewarding in personal, financial and career terms. It is also likely to herald a dramatic change of lifestyle. All expatriates, no matter to which country they are posted, have to make some adjustment to life overseas, and all members of an expatriate's family will be affected by the move, whether or not they venture abroad. If, as a married person, you go abroad 'on unaccompanied status', you and your family will have to make a number of adjustments to living separately. There is much to be gained in going abroad as a married couple, but in so doing you may be asking your spouse to give up a career and possible future chances of employment, disrupting your children's education, and removing your family from their normal sources of comfort and support (see Chapters 6 and 7).

For families who do decide to relocate together, a failure to adapt might mean having to terminate the contract early. Such unscheduled returns to the UK tend to cause considerable disturbance and hardship to all concerned. There is a high turnover rate among expatriates, so before you commit yourself and your family to working abroad it is important to discuss the likely consequences of the move with other members of your family.

CULTURE SHOCK

In contemplating a move overseas you have probably tried to imagine what it will be like. Most people think about the physical differences: the heat, the humidity, the dirt, etc, although they are rarely able to assess how these differences will affect their daily lives. How will working in 90 per cent humidity impair your effectiveness? Could you negotiate an important contract in an atmosphere more suited to the tropical house of your nearest botanical gardens? It is difficult to appreciate how much of the background to daily life is taken for granted; for example, drinking water from a tap, flicking a switch for light, pushing a button for instant entertainment. In underdeveloped countries many of these basics of everyday life either do not exist or function irregularly. While it is easy to imagine that things will be different, it is hard to envisage how this affects the quality of daily life and your sense of well-being.

But the differences that prove the greatest barrier to adjustment are the ones that cannot be seen and that are not normally even thought about. Despite regional differences in the UK most people have grown up with common experiences and expectations of how the world works. In any given situation, most people have a fairly clear idea of what is expected of them and what they expect of others. However, different nationalities do not necessarily share the same assumptions and expectations about life, or about how other people should behave. In Britain we share a common culture and, on the whole, common beliefs about what is right and proper. Other cultures, though, have quite different underlying values and beliefs, different expectations and concepts of 'normal behaviour'. Britain is nominally a Christian country, yet although much legislation and ordinary behaviour have their origins in Christian teaching, a relatively small proportion of the population would see Christianity as the driving force of British society.

By contrast, in Saudi Arabia, Islam underlies everything. It regulates the legal and political system and the conduct of all aspects of everyday life and is so perceived by its own nationals. It can be difficult to understand how other people operate; it is easy to assume that the motivations of others are understood, while misunderstanding them utterly. In Britain the ground rules of human behaviour can be taken for granted, but overseas they must be questioned and come to terms with. For example, in Malaysia it is not uncommon for expatriates to feel that their local subordinates are disloyal when, instead of discussing some decision with which they disagree, they simply choose to ignore it. Yet to the Malaysian it would be unpardonable to cause a superior to lose face by questioning him in public; far more polite simply to ignore what is considered to be a poor suggestion.

Even unconscious behaviour is open to misinterpretation. For example, in the UK an individual who avoids eye contact would usually be categorised (unconsciously) as shifty or guilty. In Nigeria the same individual would be seen as respectful, because to avoid eye contact with an older person is a mark of respect. The classic example of how the smallest physical cues are subject to different interpretations is one of distance. The British tend to feel comfortable standing two to three feet apart when chatting; the Saudis prefer to stand closer together. A Saudi and a Briton talking to each other will each unconsciously try to establish the distance at which each feels comfortable. The Briton will feel threatened when the Saudi edges nearer and the Saudi will feel rebuffed as the Briton sidles backwards. Neither will appreciate the impact of his or her unconscious behaviour on the other. This kind of disorientation is experienced constantly by the fledgling expatriate, causing many expatriates to respond aggressively when no hostility was intended.

The expatriate experiences considerable anxiety when faced unknowingly with the loss of minor cues: the familiar signs and symbols that are taken for granted in the UK but are open to different interpretations in the host country. This constant disorientation is unnerving and can cause considerable stress. The syndrome is so common that it has been given a name – culture shock.

Doctors have long recognised that changes in normal lifestyle can result in stress, and ultimately physical and mental illness. Change of home, change of friends, change of job, change of lifestyle, loss of or separation from the marital partner may all be experienced by the expatriate, who may be deprived of his or her traditional means of support and solace. A new job is always stressful, but when the job is in a new (and seemingly hostile) environment, the tensions are even greater. Symptoms associated with culture shock include heightened anxiety and worry, feelings of isolation and helplessness, and a poor performance at work. Most expatriates eventually settle down, more or less successfully, but there is a predictable cycle to the adjustment and three main stereotyped responses to adaptation.

First, there is the chauvinistic expatriate, whose response to his or her predicament is to try to create a mini encapsulated UK or 'Little England'. This expatriate's attempts to understand the local way of doing things, or local colleagues, are minimal. Faced with the difficulties of this new environment he or she retreats from what is perceived as a hostile host country and people. The blame for misunderstandings is never anything to do with him or her, but is always the fault of the 'stupid' locals. This expatriate falls into a trap of denigrating everything local and idealising everything from home, ultimately provoking real hostility from local counter-parts and making a reality of his or her view of him- or herself alone against the world. Local expatriate clubs are full of this kind of expatriate, who often indulges his or her aggression over more drinks than are healthy.

The chauvinistic expatriate is experiencing culture shock. He or she is disorientated by the environment and feels constantly at sea. The symptoms of this state are incessant complaining, glorification of the UK, alcoholic over-indulgence, marital difficulties and general aggression. At this stage the expatriate will find it hard to work with local colleagues or clients and will be permanently miserable. It is at this stage also that expatriates tend to terminate their contracts, prior to completion, with major repercussions for their families and their own careers. Fortunately for most expatriates, this is a passing stage and after their first home leave, when the realities of life in Britain are forced upon them, they manage to adapt successfully.

The second, much rarer, response is to 'go bush'. This expatriate eschews the company of his fellow expatriates, and tends to over-idealise all things local. He identifies totally with the host culture, which many of his local colleagues find both patronising and suspect.

The third and probably most appropriate response, but the most difficult to achieve, is that of the 'open-minded expatriate' who, without abandoning his or her own values, is able to accept the new culture and attempt to understand it. This involves under-standing how the host society's values are reflected in everyday behaviour. Decisions are made without the necessity for qualitative judgement. While differences are acknowledged, they are not categorised as better or worse.

If, prior to arriving abroad, you can come to terms with the idea that there are real cultural differences which need to be understood, you will find it much easier to adjust. These cultural differences affect work and home life. Often at work the differences are hidden because on the surface the work to be done is the same as at home, but local colleagues may have different ways of doing business and different attitudes to time and concepts of loyalty. Management styles may differ and motivation and discipline have quite different connotations. For example, many other nationalities find Western haste in business negotiations unpalatable; it is good manners and a useful way of assessing a business associate to chat seemingly inconsequentially before getting down to real negotiations. The Westerner considers it a waste of time, even insulting. In many parts of the world ethnic loyalty is a salient feature of everyday life, and a member of one tribe may be under an obligation to find jobs not only for his extended family, ie sons and daughters of aunts, uncles, cousins, and children of his father's other wives, but also for members of his own ethnic group. Outside the West, age is still considered to bestow authority and seniority, even at work. Social adjustment can also be difficult. Business is often conducted at social events; business entertaining at home may be the norm. Social life can be restricted, as in many areas expatriates make little attempt to get to know local people and mix almost entirely in expatriate circles. This can cause considerable pressure, as any minor upset at work or at home is common knowledge and long remembered.

The married expatriate living alone abroad often has the most difficulty in adjusting, both when working and when on leave. Single people often feel excluded from much social activity which revolves around the family. Single women suffer especially, as other expatriate women may resent or even fear them, and friendship with local colleagues can be misinterpreted. However, it is often the partners who bear the brunt of culture shock and have the greatest difficulty in adapting, as discussed in a previous chapter.

PREPARING YOURSELF FOR THE CHANGE

So how can you, as a prospective expatriate, prepare yourself and your family to make the appropriate adjustments? First, you and your family should try to find out as much as possible about the country before you accept the assignment, and preferably before you go to the job interview. Once you have accepted a job offer, some employers will give you a briefing of some description. Relatively few employers seem to appreciate that the cost of staff turnover, in money, time, effort and damage to relationships with their clients, merits an outlay on briefing expatriates and their families before their departure.

You will need to know something about your employer, the nature and responsibilities of your job, the terms and conditions of your contract and whether the benefits offered match the prevailing conditions in the country. You will want to learn about the country, its history, geography, climate, politics, economics, form of government, people and religion, etc. Much of this basic or factual information will be available in standard publications from the national embassies and tourist offices (although most countries naturally like to present a favourable picture of themselves). There are a number of specialised directories available in public reference libraries containing this information and some banks, such as HSBC, produce factual booklets. The DTI produce a vast range of publications aimed at business abroad, many of which contain information of value to intending expatriates. A full list is provided in the Export Publications Catalogue, available FOC from DTI Export Publications, Admail 528, London SW1W 8YT; tel: 020 7510 0171, fax: 020 7510 0197, as well as details of other services. Your local Government Office or Business Link is another source of information linked to the DTI. Corona Worldwide produces its own *Notes for Newcomers* which contains background on each country with advice on setting up home.

The financial problems of expatriate life, such as personal taxation, insurance, etc, and other aspects of interest to expatriates are covered in several magazines catering specifically for their needs, available on subscription:

☐ *Home and Away* (monthly; £75 for 6 issues, £120 for 12 issues), published by Expats International, 29 Lacon Road, East Dulwich, London SE22 9HE; tel: 020 8299 4986/7/8, fax: 020 8499 2484;

☐ *Nexus* (monthly), published by Expat Network, International House, 500 Purley Way, Croydon CR0 4NZ; tel: 020 8760 5100, fax: 020 8760 0469, e-mail: expatnetwork@demon.co.uk, Web site: www.expantnetwork.co.uk;

☐ *Resident Abroad*, published by FT Finance, and available via the Subscriptions Department, PO Box 387, Haywards Heath, West Sussex RH16 3GS; tel: 01444 445520, fax: 01444 445599 (Europe, £59 plus VAT at local rates; rest of the world, £69).

In addition, Expat Network offers a total support service for expatriates. It is a leading expatriate membership organisation which enjoys a firmly established reputation within the overseas recruitment sector. The expatriate community and the overseas employment market need a level of understanding which can only be achieved over time. Most things are different, from the way in which contracts are negotiated, the job search itself, the problems involved with tax, personal finances, currency, locations, social security, pensions, etc. Expat Network can offer advice for each and every eventuality. A number of services are offered. The monthly magazine *Nexus* deals with expatriate issues, offers in-depth industry features, contractual news and has a 12-page job supplement.

Some companies run their own; others use outside organisations. If your employer will not pay for you to attend a course, it would be worthwhile paying out of your own pocket. Ideally, both partners should attend, and children can also benefit.

Corona Worldwide runs one-day 'Living Overseas' briefings for men and women (price around £250) providing information and advice on living abroad and a one-to-one briefing, with a recent returner, on the country of your posting. Prices quoted are subject to revision. Emergency telephone and other briefings are also organised – fees for these can be obtained on request.

The Centre for International Briefing provides residential programmes and training for men and women taking up long-term appointments or short-term contracts abroad, and for home-based managers responsible for international personnel. Cultural and business briefings cover all major regions of the world, include all aspects of living and working, and allow a rapid transition to the destination country. Customised programmes provide training in international negotiation and communication skills, intercultural communication, international team-building and skill-transference in a foreign culture. Language tuition is also available, and the Centre's Language Plus programme combines intensive language and communication studies with business and cultural briefings. Details of programmes are available from the Customer Services Department, The Centre for International Briefing, Farnham Castle, Farnham GU9 0AG; tel: 01252 721194, fax: 01252 719277.

For expatriates going to Japan, China, Korea or other East Asian countries, individually prepared briefing and language sessions are available from East Asia Business Services at the University of Sheffield. Contact the Director, Dr John Bland, EABS, 317 Glossop Road, Sheffield S10 2HP; tel: 0114 222 8060, fax: 0114 272 8028, e-mail: EABS@Sheffield.ac.uk. These briefings are tailor-made and can be residential or in-company, according to the client's requirements. Family participation is encouraged. Sister organisations in destinations can provide further services. Briefings are modular and designed to provide new skills and practical knowledge. Sessions are conducted by business people with specific experience of the region.

The External Services Division of the School of Oriental and African Studies within the University of London provides a wide range of briefing and language services for business/government and private individuals. Open briefings on Japan and China are offered on a regular basis, including the two-day Japan Business Orientation Programme and the China Business Orientation Programme. Briefings may be integrated with language tuition if required and are offered on a tailor-made basis for most of the countries or regions of Asia and Africa. Details are available from the Co-ordinator, Ms Dzidra Stipnieks, SOAS External Services Division, University of London, Thornhaugh Street, Russell Square, London WC1H 0XG; tel: 020 7323 6396, fax: 020 7637 7355.

Going Places Expatriate Briefing, 84 Coombe Road, New Malden, Surrey KT3 4QS; tel: 020 8949 8811, provide tailored briefings to individuals or groups, in-house or in the home. Briefings last from three hours to a full day and cover preparation, living in-country, working in-country, coming home. Expertise is available on over 50 countries for both the working and accompanying partner. Guideline costs indicate £950 plus VAT per day per individual or couple; £100 a head thereafter. Going Places will provide its own facilities if more convenient.

These courses, and some employers, arrange for you to meet recently returned expatriates, and this is particularly useful if you can work out in advance, preferably in the form of a checklist, what you and your family really need to know. Such a checklist can also be helpful if you are offered, as has become increasingly common for senior positions, the possibility of a 'look-see' visit to the location in question.

Some expatriates have reported that the British Council are often helpful in terms of overcoming entry shock and giving advice and information about local amenities and activities.

LEARNING A LANGUAGE

A further aspect of learning about the host country is to master a few basic greetings in the local language. Even when it is not strictly necessary, familiarity with the sound of a language makes everything seem less strange and it is appreciated locally.

The traditional picture of the Englishman who expects all foreigners to speak English or hopes to get by with schoolboy French has disappeared. In the modern world of fast-moving communications, language proficiency is an essential tool. It is true that English is the world's leading language for business and commerce and is taught in most schools as the second language. But in many countries knowledge of the indigenous language is essential and often a prerequisite of employment. It is vital where a job involves contact with local people, particularly in administration or industry, where orders and instructions have to be given and understood. Even where a job is technical and does not involve direct communication, it is an advantage to be able to join in conversation and be more fully integrated with local society.

Anybody working in the EU should be proficient in French and/or German. In Spain and Latin America, Spanish is essential (except in Brazil, where Portuguese is spoken). In the Third World, and in the Middle East, knowledge of indigenous languages is not so essential but it is useful to speak Arabic or Swahili, particularly in more remote areas. So the best thing you can do if you are going to work overseas is to learn one or more languages or brush up on your existing knowledge.

The increasing demand for languages is being met in a number of ways. There is the 'do-it-yourself' approach which can include:

1. Learning at home, using Linguaphone courses or other self-study materials.
2. Hiring a private tutor. Try to find a native speaker, who is prepared to conduct most of the lessons in the foreign language rather than waste valuable time talking about the language in English.
3. Open learning courses at your local college of further education or university. Many have established 'drop in' centres where you have access to a language laboratory, and possibly also computer-assisted learning, with back-up from a tutor when you need it. This form of learning can be very effective for those whose time is limited and who need a flexible programme of study.

You may prefer to attend a language class, and these are run by most local authority adult education institutes and colleges. However, learning on the basis of one or two sessions a week is not the most effective way of getting to grips with a foreign language – you will make a lot more progress on a more intensive course.

Private language schools generally offer intensive or 'crash' courses. Be careful to check the bona fides of a course before you enrol. An example of the type of tuition available is Berlitz (UK) Ltd (9–13 Grosvenor Street, London W1A 3BZ; tel: 020 7915 0909, fax: 020 7915 0222), which offers language programmes to suit the linguistic needs for all in both the business and non-business fields. Berlitz offers crash courses, private lessons and semi-private courses for two to three people in most languages. The full-time Total Immersion® course lasts from one to six weeks for those wishing to improve their existing ability quickly. In-house courses for companies are also available.

Conrad Executive Language Training (15 King Street, London

WC2E 8HN; tel: 020 7240 0855, fax: 020 7240 0715), founded in 1974, is specifically geared towards meeting the linguistic needs of business people. Tuition is structured to suit both the schedule of each client and specific language requirements. Classes can be held at Conrad's Covent Garden centre, in-company or privately, after a thorough language evaluation and needs analysis. Conrad is registered to ISO 9000 by BSI. Courses available: the Crash Course (9 am–4 pm), suitable for all levels and held over five days (not necessarily consecutively); and the Extensive Course, also suitable for all levels, which can be taken between 8 am and 8 pm – classes last at least one hour and are at times to suit the client. Conrad also offers cross-cultural training programmes for groups and individuals for all countries, and the Corporate Group Course (ideal for companies requiring language training for a small group of executives who have the same objectives and similar background knowledge).

The European Centre is a language consultancy helping individuals, companies and other organisations to communicate more effectively in international markets. Winner of two national awards in 1996, it specialises in the design, management and delivery of language training programmes for business and vocational purposes. All the programmes are designed to meet individual or corporate needs, based on a language assessment and training needs analysis. Further details from Jonathan Smith, The European Centre, Peter House, St Peter's Square, Manchester M1 5AN; tel: 0161 281 8844, fax: 0161 281 8822, e-mail: training@evcentre.co.uk.

Fees at language schools are high, but there is general agreement that it is a worthwhile investment. Administrators of language schools sometimes complain that too few companies attach real importance to language proficiency and often leave it too late for effective action.

The Association of Language Excellence Centres (ALEC) is a professional body for providers of language training and related services for business. It aims to establish and maintain quality standards and help organisations and individuals to improve their performance in international markets, mergers and acquisitions with language training and consultancy geared to the needs of business, including: language training for business;

translation and interpreting; country, cultural and trade briefings; needs analysis and language audits. For details of LX Centres in your area or application for membership contact Karen Wilkinson at ALEC, Cowley House, Little College Street, London SW1P 3XS; tel: 020 7222 0666, fax: 020 7233 0335, e-mail: kwilkinson@westminster.com.

Other options include foreign cultural institutes, such as the Alliance Française or the Goethe Institut, which run well-established courses, and organisations running courses abroad (nothing can beat learning a language in the country where it is spoken). Courses abroad are advertised in *The Times* and *The Guardian*.

Further information and advice are available from CILT (the Centre for Information on Language Teaching and Research), 20 Bedfordbury, London WC2N 4LB; tel: 020 7379 5101, fax: 020 7379 5082. Written enquiries are preferred. At the same address is NATBLIS, the National Business Language Information Service (tel: 020 7379 5131, fax: 020 7379 5082), which provides information on business language training and on providers of business language services – training, cultural briefing, interpreting, and translation.

TAKE IT EASY

Once you arrive overseas you should take it easy, adjusting to climatic changes, as they will affect your physical and subsequently your mental state. Coping with so many new stimuli all at once is overpowering and you will need time to find your bearings. Tiredness and depression make it hard to react positively to your new situation. It is part of the adjustment cycle to feel frustrated and depressed, but if you can make the effort to understand the underlying cultural reasons for your frustration, you will be well on your way to adjusting successfully and enjoying your life abroad. After that you just have to cope with the culture shock of returning to the UK at the end of your tour.

Checklist: Adjusting to living and working abroad

1. Try and find out as much as possible about your host country –
   not just the physical conditions but about its culture, values and
   beliefs.
2. Become familiar with the ground rules for behaviour towards
   colleagues and with attitudes to age and gender.
3. Be aware of the symptoms of stress and culture shock.
4. If you experience culture shock, find someone to talk to, perhaps
   an experienced expatriate, and seek professional help for
   prolonged symptoms.
5. Use the Internet, public libraries and specialist services to find out
   as much information as possible about your new location.
6. Ask your employer to send you and your family on a briefing
   course before departure.
7. Try and learn the language of your host country – it will help you
   integrate into your local society.
8. Be aware that you might well experience culture shock on your
   return to your home country.

Part Four:

Making the Move

10 | *Moving Out*

WHAT TO TAKE AND REMOVAL

Whatever agonising variables you feed into your mental computer about what and what not to take, you will certainly find that in the end you are left with two basic choices – either to take very little other than clothes, books, favourite possessions and whatever small items you and your family need to feel at home, or to take virtually everything.

It clearly depends on where you are going, how long you are going for, and who you are going to work for. If you are taking up an appointment in a sophisticated European capital or in North America, obviously you will not need the same kind of things as you would in a developing country, say in Africa or Asia, where everything tends to be scarce and expensive. If you are going to a tropical country, or the Middle East, clothes and equipment will be very different from what you will need in a temperate or northern area.

As a rule, travelling reasonably light is the best course of action. Even if you are going to be away for a long time, it seldom pays to take large items of household equipment, such as sofas, beds or wardrobes; the cost of shipping bulky items is very high. In any case, it can take quite a long time to clear them through customs when they arrive, so you will either have to send them ahead or find yourself arriving in a new place without any furniture.

Such situations are apt to be inconvenient and will probably result in your having to buy some things simply to tide you over. Clothes, bedlinen, crockery, kitchen equipment and so forth are cheap to transport – shipping companies usually convey some baggage free of charge – and usually expensive to replace at the other end. Furthermore, these items lend themselves to being sent ahead, and you can usually make do, or borrow, in the meantime.

Antiques are always worth taking, since they are vastly expensive in most places outside the UK, but remember that old furniture and pictures can be sensitive to climatic change. Such problems may also exist with electronic equipment, and your CD player or food mixer may have to go through costly adaptations to fit in with foreign voltages. Records, tapes and musical instruments deteriorate in hot climates. There can also be problems over import controls, though most authorities have special dispensations for personal possessions.

As far as household equipment is concerned, much depends on the terms of your contract. Most commercial firms in developing countries will provide a fully furnished house or apartment (possibly also a car). Fully furnished means that everything, down to the last lampshade, is provided and you only need your personal effects. National governments and public corporations usually supply 'hard furnished' accommodation. Hard furnished is what it implies. Only the bare necessities such as tables and chairs and a bed are provided, and you will need to supply curtains, cushions, linen, loose covers, cutlery, crockery and kitchen gear. Often you can buy these things from an outgoing tenant or returning expatriate, but you have to be on the spot for this.

It is strongly recommended that where a couple are going out to a developing country the employee should travel out alone in advance, unless furnished accommodation is assured, and only send for the family when this has been fixed up. It may mean staying in a hotel or hostel for a time, but it is worth the inconvenience to be able to learn the ropes at first hand and decide what will be needed from home. Some companies arrange for both partners to go out in advance for a 'reconnaissance' visit.

In some cases, especially if the contract is a short-term one, in a difficult country, it is recommended that the employee should go out alone, leaving his or her family in the UK. This may sound heartless, but it does minimise the upheaval and avoids disrupting the children's education.

If you are going to a tropical country where conditions are difficult, you may not be able to buy such items as a deep freeze, food mixer, sewing machine, hairdryer and electric iron except in the main centres. A portable electric fan is useful if the house is not air conditioned. An electric kettle is a must and so is a torch. There may be power cuts, so stock up with candles.

If you have very young children with you, take pram, carrycot, pushchair and plenty of toys. Camping equipment, eg tents and sleeping bags, may be useful, and so may gardening tools, as many houses have quite large gardens. Take golf clubs, tennis rackets, photographic equipment, etc, since these leisure and luxury goods may be unobtainable or very expensive overseas, though this will again depend very much on where you go.

Stock up with cosmetics and toiletries, drugs and medicines since everything in this line is expensive and difficult to obtain. Find out the voltage and type of electric plug in use and, before you go if possible, check with the appliance manufacturer about any adaptations. A useful Web site address is www.kropla.com which is a comprehensive listing of worldwide electrical and telephone information and provides details of electric plugs and voltages used in different countries throughout the world.

Don't rely on somebody sending you something from home. Postage can be exorbitant, mails are slow and the contents liable to be pilfered. It may be possible to get your children, or your neighbour's children, to bring things out when they come on leave from school.

The best way to handle the question of actual removal is to consult one of the big removal firms. Overseas removal is not a job you should take on yourself, nor is it a good thing on which to try to save money. Moving abroad is a very different proposition from moving in this country and, in choosing your remover, it is better to ask for a good name than a good quote. The bigger removers are well informed about living conditions in overseas countries – check, though, that any printed literature they give you is fully up to date.

Removers are knowledgeable about what you can and should take with you, and most have agents at ports of entry who can help with the sometimes interminable business of clearing your belongings through customs. Another advantage of a 'name' remover is that they can generally get a better insurance deal than a smaller firm. You should, incidentally, increase your insurance to cover replacement costs at the other end. If you cannot get any specific information about this, an increase of 50 to 80 per cent over UK values will serve as a rough guideline.

An alternative to using one of the 'big names' is to contact one of the specialist consortia of overseas removal companies. These are made up of hand-picked, privately owned companies specialising in overseas removals. As a team, members provide the strength and capacity of a large international concern; individually they are able to provide a local, personal service that many customers prefer. All members conform to standards of service that are the same all over the world. So a remover operating out of the UK will provide the same level of service as his counterparts in Italy, for instance. Using the consortium method is rather like using a removal company with branch offices all over the world.

In the past there has been extensive publicity over the sudden demise of overseas removal companies, which – having received payment in advance – have left their customers' belongings either in the warehouse or, worse still, languishing in an overseas country. This usually resulted in families having to pay twice over for their household effects to be delivered, and many who could not afford to pay again had to abandon their belongings altogether.

Protection against this sort of disaster is now available through the Advance Payments Guarantee Scheme operated by the Overseas Group of the British Association of Removers. The Scheme provides that customers who have paid removal charges in advance to a firm participating in the Scheme are guaranteed that, in the event of the removal company ceasing to trade, their belongings will either be delivered at no further cost, or they will be refunded the cost of the removal charges.

It should not be assumed that all removers are in the Scheme. The safeguard provided by the Scheme is available only through members of the BAR Overseas Group. The guarantee is under-written by a mutual insurance company set up by the industry.

The British Association of Removers itself will be happy to supply readers with leaflets giving advice on moving abroad and brochures on the Advance Payments Guarantee Scheme. The Association also provides a list of companies participating in the Scheme. Readers should send a 9in × 4in sae to the British Association of Removers, 3 Churchill Court, 58 Station Road, North Harrow HA2 7SA (tel: 020 8861 3331, fax: 020 8861 3332).

Removal costs vary according to the distance to be covered, the method of transportation (land, sea or air), the terms of the arrangement (delivery to port or home, packed or unpacked) and a range of other factors. Customers should obtain *written* estimates from several companies. Beware of firms that quote on the basis of approximate measures. Be specific, understand exactly the terms of the arrangement and obtain a written agreement, so that you have what amounts to a contract with which to resist 'surcharges' imposed at the point of disembarkation.

Some people like to pack their own things. If so, it is best to use custom-made cardboard boxes, which are stout, light and can be banded to withstand rough handling and exposure. These generally come with movers' details, logo and grids in which details of the contents, origin and whether fragile or not, can be entered. It is essential to make a list of contents and advisable to see that your cases or boxes are readily identifiable for when you collect them at the other end. Smaller goods can be taken with you, up to the 20 kg allowable limit. Some things may be carried as hand luggage, depending on how full the plane is. But on all these points, be guided by the experts.

PETS

Pets often pose a problem. Some shipping companies and airlines require a bill of health from a veterinary surgeon. In all cases, before leaving the UK you should first obtain an export health certificate from the Ministry of Agriculture, Fisheries and Food. There are a number of specialist animal shipping services available. You will need to apply in good time beforehand to DEFRA for an information pack so that you can make the necessary arrangements. Changes to the quarantine rules are being discussed at the time of going to print. A document by the Department for Environment, Food and Rural Affairs has proposed that quarantine be replaced with a vaccination and electronic tagging procedure for animals being transported to and from rabies-free and EU countries. This change is unlikely to be put into effect until 2001. However, details can be found on the DEFRA Web site www.defra.gov.uk. In the meantime, pets still have to be placed in quarantine.

Checklist: Choice of removers

1. The remover should provide a free estimate and a written quote.
2. Does the quote specify *professional* packing under your general supervision?
3. How will fragile items, furniture and articles be packed?
4. What insurance cover is offered? If there is any excess (ie a minimum figure below which you will not be reimbursed), what is it?
5. Can the removers immediately provide the name and address of the port agents at your destination?
6. Will they deliver to your residence at the other end, or will you have to arrange clearance yourself? Check that the quotation specifies whether the goods will be delivered to residence or to port only.
7. What proportion of their current business is in overseas removals?

VAT

You will almost certainly find that some of the things you want are cheaper to buy here, even allowing for shipping charges. You should make sure that you take full advantage of the various VAT export schemes under which a UK resident going abroad can escape having to pay UK VAT altogether. There are two schemes, one for motor vehicles and one for other goods.

Motor vehicles

If you will be living outside the EU

You have to purchase your new vehicle from a dealer who operates the Personal Export Scheme. He or she will give you VAT Form 410 to fill in, which will require you to fulfil certain conditions. The relevant notes are found in VAT Notice 705. Motor cycles and motor caravans are also covered by this scheme.

☐ You must personally take delivery of the vehicle, and it must be used only by you, or someone else who is also leaving the EU and has your permission to use it.

☐ You have to take the vehicle abroad within 6 months of delivery, or within 12 months if you have lived outside the EU for more than 365 days in the previous two years, or more than 1,095 days in the previous six years.

☐ You and the car must remain outside the EU for at least 6 consecutive months.

Alternatively, the supplier can deliver the car directly to your destination, free of VAT. See VAT Notice 703.

If you will be living within the EU

You must complete Form VAT 411, supplied by the motor dealer.

☐ The vehicle must be new, and you must take it to your destination within two months of delivery. Cars must not have been driven for more than 1,864 miles in this time.

☐ You must declare the vehicle to the member state's fiscal authority.

After you have had the vehicle abroad for at least 12 months you may re-import it without paying VAT, provided you are either a diplomat, a member of an officially recognised international organisation, a member of NATO or returning UK Forces personnel or you can prove that the duty and tax have been paid. Otherwise you will have to pay VAT on the value of the vehicle at the time of re-importation. If you return to the UK within six months of the date of export, the full amount of VAT on the sale must be paid. If the vehicle is found to be in the UK after the date for its export shown on the registration document (ie six months from purchase date if you are leaving the EU, or two months otherwise), you will have to pay VAT in full and it will also be liable to forfeiture. This applies even if failure to export the vehicle is due to circumstances beyond your control (eg theft or destruction). Therefore, while the car is still in the UK, before export, it is essential to insure it for its full value, including potential VAT. Obviously, it is important to license, register and insure the vehicle if you will be using it in the UK before departure.

Other goods

If you have been in the EU for more than 365 days in the previous two years and are going to a final destination outside the EU for at least 12 consecutive months, you may buy goods using the Retail Export Scheme. At participating retailers, you must ask to complete VAT Form 435 at the time of purchase. To receive a refund equal to the amount of VAT you must get this form certified by a customs authority when the goods are exported – the goods must be delivered to your shipper or freight forwarder at your final point of departure from the EU. You cannot take delivery of them in this country. The refund is then paid by the retailer, not Customs and Excise. See VAT Notices 704 and 704/1. As there is a lot of documentation involved, you may find this procedure is not worth your while unless you are making fairly large purchases and only in one or two shops.

TAKING A CAR ABROAD

British people tend to prefer right-hand drive and will therefore consider buying their car here and taking it with them. First check at the embassy of the country you propose to live in that private car imports are permitted.

Probably the best way to plan this is to make a list of what you will want your car to do. The road surfaces may be worse than those you are used to, so you may consider taking a good second-hand car rather than a brand new one. You will not then be so worried about driving through very narrow streets. In some places drivers actually park by shunting the cars ahead and behind!

If you buy a new car in the UK before going abroad, you can use it here for six months, run it in and have your first service before you take it overseas. Check the servicing facilities in the area where you plan to live. It would be unwise to take a car abroad if the nearest dealer service is 70 miles away. This factor may well limit your choice.

A big car will be expensive with petrol and difficult to park. If you will be living in an apartment and there is no garage, the car will usually be left in the street and possibly for long periods at that. Consider carefully the security of your car and what you may have in it. Choose a model with locking wheel nuts and high-quality locks so that it is hard to get into without smashing the windows. Radio thefts are prevalent in some countries; therefore you may wish to consider a demountable radio.

Should you decide to take a small car to a hot country, always buy one with a sun roof because the smaller cars tend not to carry air conditioning.

People moving to Spain will often choose diesel cars because the fuel is half the price of petrol and easily available. Lead-free petrol is now available in many countries and you should check whether your engine will take this quality. Some engines need minor adaptation.

The other possibility is to hire a car in the UK. First check whether the hire company is happy with your destination and route. Restrictions depend on insurance cover for more out-of-the-way locations. You should also have the hirer provide you with proof of ownership – in this case form VE103a. Hirers are more than happy to do business with expatriates because of the length of hire and the fact that most are credit- and trustworthy. With regard to this latter point, it will be essential to pay by credit card.

Taking your existing car abroad

If you take the car you own at present abroad for longer than 12 months, this is regarded as a permanent export and the procedure is described in leaflet V526, obtainable from your local Vehicle Registration Office.

The following procedure applies to exports from England, Scotland, Wales and the Isles of Scilly only, not to Northern Ireland, the Isle of Man or the Channel Islands, where cars are registered separately.

Complete section 2 on the back of the Vehicle Registration Document, entering the proposed date of export, and send the document to your local Vehicle Registration Office or to the Driver and Vehicle Licensing Centre. This should be done well in advance of your departure.

You will receive back a Certificate of Export (V561) which in effect confirms your vehicle registration and replaces the vehicle registration document (V5). Some countries, however, are failing to recognise this certificate as a registration document, which can cause problems when you wish to re-register your vehicle in another country.

A different procedure applies in Northern Ireland, the Isle of Man and the Channel Islands, where vehicles are registered locally; it is necessary to register and license a car taken *to* these places for over 12 months as soon as the current British tax disc expires, if not before. The Certificate of Export mentioned above will still be necessary, although these authorities may accept the vehicle registration document for re-registration purposes.

Motoring services in Europe

The Alliance Internationale de Tourisme (AIT) has its headquarters in Geneva, and motoring clubs throughout Europe are affiliated to it, including the Royal Automobile Club and the Automobile Association. There is also the Federation Internationale de l'Automobile, based in Paris, of which the RAC is a member. These clubs provide a wide range of services to each other's members travelling abroad, so membership of one is worthwhile.

CUSTOMS

Regulations and procedures vary. Most customs authorities allow you to take in used things for your personal use and often let people, eg newly married couples, bring in new things duty free. Wherever possible keep receipts to show to the customs officials.

In most places, you are allowed to take in 'household and used personal effects', including refrigerators, radios, TV receivers and minor electrical appliances, but duties on new items of this kind are usually fairly steep. There are bans everywhere on guns, plants and drugs. Many Middle East and North African countries operate a boycott list, so do not take anything without checking the situation. Duty free wines, spirits and tobacco up to a certain amount – check with the airline – are normally allowed, except in most Middle East countries.

ESSENTIALS BEFORE YOU GO

There are certain things you must see about before you actually leave. There are obvious chores, like cancelling milk and papers, etc. Have a thorough medical check for yourself and your family before you go, including teeth and eyes. Some jobs, of course, depend on physical fitness. Make sure you have the necessary vaccination certificates and check the requirements. Most tropical countries need certificates against smallpox and possibly cholera and yellow fever; other vaccinations may be advisable. If you are going to the tropics you should contact your GP about anti-malarial precautions. For the most up-to-date advice on malaria in the region where you are going, you should contact the Malaria Reference Laboratory at the London School of Hygiene and Tropical Medicine.

In many countries it is advisable to include a rabies injection in your schedule of jabs for yourself and members of your family. You should also warn children of the perils of cuddling strange animals which may harbour other diseases in addition to the rabies threat.

Check that you have all your documents to hand – up-to-date passport, visas, cheque book, permits, health certificates, letter of appointment. Take spare passport photos – it is probably best for partners to have separate passports – and all your diplomas and references, even birth and marriage certificates. The appetite for documents is well-nigh insatiable in some countries!

Melancholy though it may sound, you should also make some provision for the unthinkable: instructions in the case of death, disablement or catastrophe while you are abroad. Contact your financial adviser or insurance company for more information.

If you have a reliable solicitor, you might also consider the possibility of giving him or her power of attorney. This is a simple legal transaction that essentially means that the person having that power can act in your stead. If you need a large sum of money to be sent out to you in a hurry, it is very useful to have a responsible person in the UK whom you can fax and who can raise the money from your bank. Likewise, if you have left your house in the hands of managing agents who are not doing their stuff, you need someone on the spot who can sort things out. Giving someone power of attorney obviously implies a high degree of trust, but there are occasions when it could save you the cost of a return fare home.

KEEPING YOUR VOTE WHILE LIVING ABROAD

On moving abroad, you retain your right to vote in UK and European parliamentary elections; however, there are a number of conditions of which you should be aware. To be eligible you must be a British citizen and satisfy *either* of two sets of conditions:

Set 1

- [ ] you have previously been on the electoral register for an address in the UK;
- [ ] you were living there on the qualifying date;*
- [ ] there are no more than 20 years between the qualifying dates for that register and the one on which you now wish to appear.

Set 2

- [ ] you last lived in the UK less than 20 years before the qualifying date for the register on which you wish to appear;
- [ ] you were too young to be on the electoral register, which was based on the last qualifying date before you left;
- [ ] a parent or guardian was on the electoral register for the address where you were living on that date;
- [ ] you are at least 18 years old, or will become 18 when the register comes into force.

You have to register every year on or before the qualifying date and you may continue to register while overseas for 20 years from the qualifying date for the last electoral register on which you appeared as a UK resident.

---

*The qualifying date in England, Scotland and Wales is 10 October each year and in Northern Ireland, 15 September. This is for the electoral register, which comes into force on 16 February of the following year and remains in force for 12 months from that date.

How to register

To register you must fill in an Overseas Elector's Declaration form RPF 37, which you can get from the nearest British consular or diplomatic mission. The following information will be required: your full name and overseas address, the UK address where you were last registered and the date you left the UK. The first-time overseas elector will have to find someone to support the declaration who is aged 18 or over, has a British passport and is a British citizen, is not living in the UK and who knows you but is not a close relative. First-time overseas electors who left the UK before they were old enough to register will also have to provide a copy of their full birth certificate and information about the parent or guardian on whose registration they are relying.

How to vote and remain registered

You do not have a postal vote. Instead you must appoint a proxy who will vote on your behalf. He or she must be a citizen of Britain, the Commonwealth or the Republic of Ireland, a UK resident, and willing and legally able to vote on your behalf. The application form for appointing a proxy is attached to the Overseas Elector's Declaration form. Your declaration, proxy application and, if required, birth certificate should be returned to the electoral registration officer for the area where you were last registered. The electoral registration officer will write to tell you whether you qualify as an overseas elector and will be included on the register: if you do not, he or she will explain why. You will be sent a reminder each year, and another declaration form will be enclosed with this.

REMOVAL NOTIFICATIONS

Don't forget to tell the following organisations that you are moving abroad:

Your bank.

Income Tax Office. Notify the Inland Revenue giving the exact date of departure.

Contributions Agency, International Services (for information on National Insurance Contributions and related health cover), Longbenton, Newcastle upon Tyne, NE98 1YX, or *The Benefits Agency, Pensions and Overseas Benefits Directorate* (for advice on benefits and related health cover), at Tyneview Park, Newcastle upon Tyne NE98 1BA. Include your full name, date of birth and UK NI or pension number, together with details of the country to which you are moving and the duration of your stay.

Vehicle licence. If you are taking your vehicle abroad for longer than a year this is regarded as a 'permanent export'. In this case you should return your existing (new-style) registration document to the Driver and Vehicle Licensing Centre, Swansea SA99 1AB, filling in the 'permanent export' section. Alternatively, you can apply to your local Vehicle Registration Office for the necessary forms.

Driving licence. You will probably want to retain your British driving licence. Some countries recognise it as valid and a list of those that do not is available from the RAC and the AA.

International Driving Permit. An International Driving Permit is obtainable from the RAC or AA (even if you are not a member) and is valid for one year. The licence is not valid in the country where it is issued so you must obtain it before leaving the UK. Most countries require residents to hold a local driving licence so check whether this is the case on taking up your new residence. Contact RAC Travel Services, PO Box 1500, Bristol BS99 2LH (telephone 0800 550055 for information), or any Automobile Association shop.

Motor insurance. Notify your insurers of the date of your departure – your insurance should be cancelled from that date and you should obtain a refund for the rest of the insurance period. Ask your insurance company for a letter outlining your no-claims record to show to your new insurer.

Life and other insurances. Notify the companies concerned or your insurance broker if you use one.

Council tax. Notify the town hall.

Dentist and optician. Let them know you are moving, as a matter of courtesy. It will save posting useless check-up reminders.

Private health insurance. Notify subscriber records department.

Gas. If you use it, notify your local gas supplier giving at least 48 _hours'_ notice. They will give you a standard form to fill in with details of the move and any current hire-purchase agreements. If appliances are to be removed they require as much notice as possible to arrange an appointment; there is a disconnection charge.

Electricity. Notify your local district office or showroom at least 48 _hours_ before moving. Arrangements are much the same as for gas.

Water. The local water board should also be notified at least 48 _hours_ before the move. Drain tanks and pipes if the house is to remain empty in winter.

Telephone. Notify your local telephone sales office as shown in the front of your directory at least _seven days_ before the move.

Libraries. Return books and give in tickets to be cancelled.

Professional advisers such as solicitors, accountants, stockbrokers, insurance brokers, etc. Make sure they have a forwarding address.

Stocks and shares. Write to the company registrar at the address on the last annual report or share certificates.

Organisations and clubs – any business, civic, social, cultural, sports or automobile club of which you are a member. For the AA write to Membership Subscriptions and Records, PO Box 50, Basingstoke, Hampshire RG21 2ED and for the RAC write to Membership Enquiries, PO Box 1500, Bristol BS99 2LH.

Credit card companies. Advise them that you are leaving the country.

Hire purchase and rental companies. Notify the office where repayments are made. You will need to settle your account.

Local business accounts – department stores, newsagents, dairy, baker, chemist, dry cleaner, laundry, motor service station.

Publications. Cancel postal subscriptions to newspapers, magazines, professional and trade journals, book and record clubs, etc.

National Health Service. Return your NHS card to the Family Health Services Authority for your area, giving your date of departure, or hand it in to the immigration officer at your point of departure.

Pension schemes. If you have a 'frozen' or paid-up pension from a previous employer notify the pension trust of your new address.

TV. If you have a rented set, make arrangements to return it.

Post Office. Notify day of departure and UK contact address.

Personal Giro. The Post Office have a special sae for this.

Premium Bonds – anything rather than join the sad list of unclaimed prizes! Contact Premium Bonds, National Savings, Blackpool FY3 9XR to check the current position, because in a few countries, Premium Bond holdings may contravene lottery laws.

Save As You Earn and National Savings Certificates. It is important to notify any permanent change of address. Advise the Savings and Certificates and SAYE Office, Durham DH99 1NS, quoting the contract number(s).

National Savings Bank. Notify at Glasgow G58 1SB.

National Savings Income Bonds. Notify Income Bonds, Blackpool FY3 9YP.

Your landlord. If you are a tenant, give the appropriate notice to quit.

Your tenants. If you are a landlord, that UK address you've organised will be needed.

Your employer. Give new address details, or a contact address, in writing.

Schools. Try to give your children's schools a term's notice that they will be leaving. If you wish your children's education to be continued in Britain, contact your local education authority or the Department for Education and Employment, Sanctuary Buildings, Great Smith Street, London SW1P 3BT, for advice, and see Chapter 7.

Make sure your *removers* have any temporary contact address and phone numbers for you, both in the UK and abroad, so that they can get in touch with you when the need arises. It is also useful for them if you can tell them when you expect to arrive in your new country.

Checklist: Moving out

1. Be practical about what to take and try to travel light.
2. Check what will be available in your new accommodation and consider whether it might be better for the working partner to go out ahead of the rest of the family.
3. Consult with a reputable removal firm with experience in overseas removal.
4. Increase your insurance to cover replacement costs at the other end.
5. If you have a pet, think about what will be the best arrangement in the long term. Quarantine regulations still exist but might be waived for specific countries by the time of your return.
6. Think carefully about whether or not you should take your car with you, as it might not be suitable for the terrain of your new home.
7. If you decide to take your car, obtain leaflet V562 from your local Vehicle Registration Office.
8. Have a thorough medical check-up before you leave.
9. Check that you have all your documents available and take spare passport photos.
10. Fill in an Overseas Elector's Declaration form RPF37 to keep your right to vote.

11 Settling In

You arrive, with or without your family, and may find you are not met at the airport. This is the first of many irritations which people going out to work for overseas governments may encounter. It does not usually happen with companies. You may have to stay in a hotel or hostel for a considerable time, so make sure in advance who is going to foot the bill. You will need money to meet such contingencies – and to pay for telephones and taxis to and from the airport.

Even if you are lucky enough to move into a house or apartment, you will find a bare larder. This is where any tins or packet foods you brought with you will come in useful. (In Jamaica, the Corona Worldwide branch will provide a loan of a 'basket' of essentials for people waiting for their baggage to be unloaded.)

One early need will be to fix up domestic help, if you want it. It is usually best to engage a house steward and/or any other servants on the personal recommendation of the previous occupant (you may inherit their staff) or a neighbour. Find out from the local labour office what the going rate is and negotiate accordingly, making it quite clear from the start what duties the staff will be expected to perform, eg in the kitchen, washing and housework. Living quarters are usually provided, but find out beforehand whether your steward plans to bring all his family and relatives to stay with him!

Both for insurance purposes and your own peace of mind, make proper security arrangements. Some people, either individually or in groups, employ nightwatchmen; others rely on dogs, or on special locks. The extent of pilfering and burglary in many African countries has grown alarmingly in recent years, so make sure your precautions are fully adequate. John Wason (Insurance Brokers) Ltd, founded by a former expatriate, offers a specialist Overseas Personal Insurance scheme, which includes home contents, belongings, money and personal liability, as well as optional medical and accident/sickness cover. It is claimed to be the only such policy available on a stand-alone basis, and as such would be useful for those in rented or company property.

At an early stage it is a good idea to see to all your requirements for banking and for obtaining work and residence permits, income tax coding, and the driving licence and test requirements where necessary. Find out also about health products and medical facilities, contributions to provident funds and subscriptions to clubs. Many employers pay for these.

Finally, keep a close eye on the health of young children, particularly on persistent tummy upsets and fevers. It is advisable always to use water you have sterilised yourself, not bottled water of unknown provenance.

There is also the question of preparation, other than physical, for your move. Do you know what the country you are going to is like? What facilities are there for shopping, leisure and entertainment? What is the climate like and what clothes will you need? Are there any pitfalls you should know about or any special behavioural dos and don'ts? Nowadays, overseas countries are very sensitive about foreigners understanding that their new patterns of government and economic development are not just pale imitations of the West.

The importance of getting properly briefed beforehand cannot be overestimated. This will not only save you from possible embarrassing situations – for example, if you don't know the rules about drinking in the Middle East – but will help you to decide what you need to take with you and give you some idea of the atmosphere in which you will work and live. Companies specialising in country-specific briefings are described in Chapter 9. Details can also be found in the Web site directory at the back of this book.

GOING THROUGH DIPLOMATIC CHANNELS

Expatriates who work for British companies or those from other Western countries in the developing or newly industrialised world can usually expect their employers to come to their aid in case of a political upheaval, or even if they get into personal difficulties – deserved or otherwise. Furthermore, they can expect their contracts of employment to be clear-cut and to conform to Western norms. Neither of these things is necessarily true if you work for a local employer, as is increasingly the case. The money is often better, but the risk is greater.

Some guidance on points to watch out for in taking up an appointment with a local employer in a developing country is given in the Employment Conditions Checklist in Chapter 2. Ultimately, though, you have no protection other than your own vigilance and UK diplomatic channels in the country concerned. They are generally very much criticised by expatriates as being ineffectual or indifferent, but the Foreign and Commonwealth Office claim this is because their role is not understood. For a start, they cannot intervene in contractual disputes, _unless_ a British subject is being discriminated against in comparison with other employees. They can, however, recommend you to a local lawyer who may be able to help you and they maintain carefully vetted lists of reliable legal firms. Best of all, they say, is to write to the British embassy or consulate nearest to your location before you leave the UK and ask them to put you in touch with someone who can give you a line on your prospective employer. Though UK diplomatic sources do keep track of known bad hats among employers, in the main they prefer such information to go through non-diplomatic channels, for obvious reasons.

The consular service of the Foreign Office is now very sensitive about the criticisms that have been made of it. If you fail to get an answer from the embassy or consulate you have contacted, or you are not satisfied with the service provided at a British embassy, high commission or consulate, you should write to: Head of Consular Division, Foreign & Commonwealth Office, 1 Palace Street, London SW1E 5HE; tel: 020 7238 4586, fax: 020 7238 4509.

Primarily, of course, the role of British diplomats is to protect British subjects from the consequences of political upheavals. For instance, they got them and their dependants out of Iran and Lebanon, though there seems to have been some, perhaps understandable, disarray in the advice given to expatriates in Kuwait following the Iraqi invasion in August 1990. They were less successful, also, in protecting expatriates from the reprisal arrests in Libya, but any expatriate who goes to a notoriously high-risk place like that must take into account the circumstances there before deciding to accept an appointment. Diplomats are also not able to protect you from the consequences if you break the law of the land you are in. At most they can visit you in prison, arrange for you to be properly represented legally and intercede discreetly for an amnesty for you. A UK or multinational company would, in such cases, arrange for you to be flown out on the first available plane, usually with the connivance of the authorities.

Whatever your feelings about the efficacy or otherwise of British diplomatic protection, you should register with the embassy or consulate as soon as possible after you arrive to work in any developing country. This means they can contact you if a sudden emergency arises, whether personal or political. It cannot do any harm; and if you wake up one morning to the sound of gunfire, as has happened to many an expatriate, you may be very glad that you took that precaution.

Foreign & Commonwealth Travel Advice is designed to help British travellers avoid trouble by providing succint and up-to-date information on threats to personal safety arising from political unrest, lawlessness, violence, natural disasters and epidemics. Some 650 notices are issued each year covering more than 130 countries. Notices are constantly renewed on the basis of information from our posts overseas. The full range of notices is available on BBC2 Ceefax pages 470 onwards, and on the FCO's Web site, along with a range of Consular Division publicity material, www.fco.gov.uk. The public can contact the Travel Advice Unit direct between 9.30 am and 4.00 pm Monday to Friday on 020 7238 4503/4504.

Other Consular Services information leaflets, including 'Checklist for Travellers', 'Backpackers and Independent Travellers' and 'British Consular Services Abroad' are widely distributed through travel agents, shipping and airlines, public libraries, Citizens Advice Bureaux and the UK Passport Agency, and can be obtained by faxing the Distribution Centre on 01444 246620.

READING MATTER

You may never have been much of a book buyer while living in the UK, but many expatriates report that not being able to get hold of books when they want them is an unexpected deprivation, especially in postings where other forms of entertainment, at any rate in English, are hard to come by.

Many places do, of course, have bookshops which stock some English titles, but the selection is often very limited (children's books are particularly hard to get) and prices are always much higher than the UK price shown tantalisingly on the jacket. You can, however, import your own books at standard London prices through the admirable Good Book Guide (24 Seward Street, London EC1V 3GB; 24-hour tel: 020 7490 9905, fax: 020 7490 9908, e-mail: enquiries@good-book-guide.co.uk) or order books on the Internet from Amazon.com. They are a mail order book service with a substantial trade among expatriates all over the world. You can choose your books from their monthly guide, for which there is a modest annual subscription, but they can also get any book in print for you, including paperbacks. There are also regular video and audio listings offering a wealth of entertainment: drama, documentary, comedy and children's programmes.

The choices in the guide are accompanied by brief, helpful notes written by outside experts (eg Chris Bonington on travel) and the selection of titles is broad, covering both high-brow literature and commercial best sellers, all chosen on merit alone. The subject areas are broad too, ranging through all kinds of interests. However, the Good Book Guide is not a book club – there is no obligation to buy. A free trial issue can be requested.

Payment is on a cash with order basis or by credit card and clear instructions are given with each issue of the guide on how to pay from anywhere in the world.

ENTERTAINMENT AND HOME COMFORTS

While your new home is likely to be a source of varied and new experiences, you might like to maintain some of the interests that you developed at home. The Internet can provide an invaluable link for this. Football fans can follow their team's progress through the season by logging on to both official and unofficial Web sites. Chat forums can also keep you in contact with fellow fans. The Internet might also be a way to find out if there are other expatriates or host-country fan clubs in your region, which could be a good way to meet people and set up a social network.

Using the Internet to keep informed with both world and local news is also a new innovation. Many radio and TV companies now use it to broadcast. For example, CNN, Reuters and the BBC all have news information. Furthermore, you can listen to some radio programmes through the Internet. The BBC has recently launched an audio online version of its news and entertainment programmes which can be found on the BBC site. National newspapers also use the Internet and some, such as *The Daily Telegraph*, publish the whole day's paper on their Web site. Furthermore, local newspapers are also setting up Web sites, so it is quite possible to keep in touch with your local news – including football reports, and local issues such as education and government. A listing of Web sites can be found at the back of this book.

Sending for goods through mail order catalogues can make up for deficiencies in local shops when working abroad. Although many companies that provide goods by mail order confine their activities to the UK and will not send goods abroad (no doubt because of potential payment problems), there is nothing to stop you making arrangements to get catalogues through UK friends or relatives and ordering through them. Expatriates with young children are reported to find the Mothercare catalogue very useful. Harrods and Fortnum & Mason will send goods anywhere in the world and you can pay by credit card. Harrods also operate worldwide accounts. However, e-commerce has also meant that receiving home comforts is no longer the complicated process it used to be and many large retail companies now have ordering facilities set up on their Web sites.

Checklist: Settling in

1. Try to organise domestic help as soon as possible and bring a few necessities with you.
2. Brief your domestic help as clearly as possible and identify duties from the start.
3. Make proper security arrangements and check that you have all your legal requirements for work, banking, medical help, etc.
4. Find out emergency numbers, including those of your consulate or embassy, and if you are relocating to a developing country, register with them as soon as possible.
5. Identify sources from where books and home comforts can be obtained, whether locally or internationally.
6. Seek out social networks through expatriate organisations, your employer or through the Internet.
7. If you have not used the Internet before, now is the time to try it out – it will be an invaluable source of information and support!

12 | Coming Home

Having completed a foreign assignment you might feel that your return home will be an uncomplicated affair. However, increasingly both companies and individuals are paying attention to the practical and psychological issues involved in repatriation. Not only do domestic issues, such as finding accommodation or dealing with tenants, need to be tackled, but career considerations and family issues need to be addressed. Furthermore, although you might feel confident about fitting back into professional and social networks, surprisingly some expatriates do experience a reverse culture shock on their return.

PERSONAL POSSESSIONS

If you are to reap the full benefit of a spell as a non-UK resident, planning for your return requires forethought and preparation, particularly in the matter of bringing back personal possessions. Price differentials between countries are no longer as great as they used to be, but there are still quite a number of places where, even taking freight into account, it is worth buying things like electronic or audiovisual equipment, even cars, locally and shipping them back home. In countries that operate exchange controls this may also be a possible way of taking out assets in the form of goods. But beware of the catch: unless you can show that an article has been used and owned for six months, you are liable for import duty – and VAT on top of that. It is no use asking an obliging vendor to provide backdated invoices, because if you are unlucky enough to come under investigation, custom officials check serial numbers as well as documents. Another thing to be aware of is that once your personal possessions, including cars, are imported without payment of import duty and VAT, they cannot be sold or disposed of within 12 months, or they become liable for both these taxes.

Even with well-used goods, you can be in for unforeseen costs unless you get your timing right. The problem is that possessions shipped back to the UK will not be released until their owner arrives home. You can get a relative to clear them on your behalf, but that person would be liable for provisional duty on their value which is only repaid when you yourself get back. It takes about a fortnight to clear goods through customs anyway, so you will need expert advice at the other end if you are to steer the difficult course between paying warehouse charges in the UK because the goods have arrived too soon, and finding yourself without the basic necessities of life because you have sent them off too late.

The most important thing, though, is that they should actually arrive. The cheapest form of shipping may not be the best. The right course of action is to find a local firm that has a reputable agent in the UK, and to make sure you get door-to-door insurance cover.

ACCOMMODATION

Providing you have gone through the correct tenancy arrangements, reclaiming your property should not be too complicated. However, be aware that if you return earlier than planned, and your tenants have time left on their agreement, you might have to find alternative accommodation for the outstanding tenancy period. In particular, under an Assured Shorthold Tenancy – unless your tenant agrees to move earlier – you will have to wait until the contract runs its course with two months' notice given after that period.

You should try and give the letting agents who are looking after your UK property at least three months' notice of your return, so that they can give due notice to the tenants. However, should you be unfortunate enough to come across a tenant who is unwilling to move on, it is possible to insure against legal and hotel costs.

FINDING A NEW JOB

Unless you have been sent out by a UK employer, the biggest problem in returning home can be in finding another job. Well before that point you should be sending your CV round to head-hunters who are always on the lookout for those with specialist qualifications. If you feel that you might have difficulty placing yourself on the job market on grounds of age or lack of specific skills, it may be worth consulting a career counsellor. They cannot 'find' you a job – and you should be wary of those who imply otherwise – but their advice, though not cheap, has been found to be a good investment by many mid-career jobseekers.

Returning employees are also faced with career dilemmas. The Arthur Andersen Survey reports that 21 per cent of companies expect their returning employee to initiate the search for their next position. Of those companies that do offer help, under 10 per cent begin to look for a position for the expatriate a year before return and approximately 40 per cent do so 6–12 months before the end of the assignment. Indeed, this is precisely what stops many employees taking on a foreign assignment in the first place: a lack of career opportunities on their return. Employees who are unable to return to their former job have a number of options available to them which are shown in Table 12.1.

Chapter 2 deals with this subject in some depth. However, it is worth repeating at this point that the issue of reintegration should be raised before taking on an assignment. An employer who values the skills that have been developed abroad will also be thinking about how best to utilise them on your return. Leaving this to chance, though, is not a good idea. At least a year before your return

Table 12.1 Post assignment options

Redundancy	50%
Re-assignment to another expatriate position	31%
Extension of current assignment	32%
Appointed 'special projects' in the home country	57%
Other	8%

Source: Arthur Andersen Expatriate Survey 1999

you should be entering into a dialogue with your employer about career opportunities for your return. If your company provides a mentor, he or she should also be able to help create a constructive dialogue and repatriation process.

If you are able to resettle back into your former job or one of equivalent status, it is also worth bearing in mind that time will have passed since you were last part of your home office team. Different faces, work practices and projects should be expected and it might take some time to readjust to your altered office environment.

The Arthur Andersen Survey found that a mere 11 per cent of respondents offered some form of post-repatriation support during the 12 months after return, and this tended to be with tax compliance rather than personal support. None of the respondents gave any form of help with readjustment to home-country living and working, which, as the report's author Barry Page comments, 'is interesting, since inability to re-adapt to home-country office culture is ranked as the most common reason given by returning expatriates for leaving their company following their repatriation'.

REVERSE CULTURE SHOCK

One of the most surprising aspects of returning home is the experience of reverse culture shock. Again, the passing of time needs to be taken into account. While you have been away things will have moved on in your home country and not only friends and family will have changed but your international experience will almost certainly have changed you as well. Your expectations might well have undergone a radical change abroad and coming home might mean that you, once again, have to re-adapt these to suit your circumstances. Much like any other major move, returning home requires a readjustment to new circumstances and time should be taken to absorb this process.

Fitting back into an office environment is one thing but it is also worth bearing in mind that partners and children might also experience difficulties settling back.

PREPARING THE FAMILY FOR RETURN

As with the move abroad, a trailing partner might well have to begin to search for another job on his or her return home. Beginning that search well in advance is well worth the time. Furthermore, enlightened companies are beginning to realise the need to provide information and support to enable partners to resettle. For example, Shell has 40 information centres worldwide providing information and support for partners. Children might also feel disorientated by returning home. Having to fit back into school and peer groups can be traumatic. Their experience of a different culture and returning to an unfamiliar environment might be disturbing for a period of time. Furthermore, they might not be able to return to their old school if places are scarce. Again, it is worth informing schools as early as possible about your return and to look for alternative arrangements should there be a lack of places. Children should be encouraged to keep in touch with home during a foreign assignment so that they are not completely out of step with changes on their return.

A foreign assignment is a fulfilling and life-enhancing experience. The re-adaption to home is part of that experience and its success or failure can affect the foreign experience in either a positive or negative way. Planning for your return is therefore a worthwhile process. Try and forewarn employers, tenants, schools and social contacts of your return well in advance. Keep your family in contact with friends and try and establish with your employer what the job opportunities there are likely to be on your return. Most important of all, try to be patient with the new situation. It might be home, but home can be also a 'foreign' place if you have spent some years away.

Checklist: Coming home

1. Think about what goods might be worth buying to bring home and purchase six months before returning.
2. Plan the shipment of possessions carefully to time with your return or look into warehousing arrangements.
3. Inform your letting agents as soon as possible of the date you are to return in order to give your tenants as much notice as possible.
4. Look into short-term rental arrangements if you are unable to move back into your property straight away.
5. Discuss with your employer well in advance what plans there are for you on your return – this should ideally take place 12 months before return. If you are returning without a job, contact head-hunters and agencies as early as possible.
6. Be prepared for reverse culture shock and give yourself time to become accustomed to changes in your home and work environment.
7. Contact schools in advance and make contact with your children's friends before returning home.
8. Contact partners' support centres run by your employer to identify career opportunities.

Part Five:

Country Profiles and Personal Taxation

Europe

WESTERN EUROPE

The following section gives information about European Union (EU) member states – Austria, Belgium, Denmark, Finland, France, Germany, Greece, Ireland, Italy, Luxembourg, The Netherlands, Norway, Portugal, Spain, Sweden and Switzerland. It does not cover the UK. More detailed information is provided on personal taxation for all countries except Italy, Portugal and Spain.

The European Union

The European Union is the world's largest single trading group, and the largest market. It accounts for just over one-fifth of the total global trade in goods. It is heavily dependent on international trade – more so than either the US or Japan. Increasingly, this trade is extending from manufactured goods to services: the fastest growing sectors are banking, insurance and telecommunications.

The Single Market, in force since 1993, allows unrestricted trade and free movement of capital and currency within the EU. Union citizens are entitled to travel, reside, study and work wherever they wish within the EU. Anyone is entitled to apply for a job and sign a contract of employment in another member state, without losing pension or health insurance entitlements acquired elsewhere in the EU. Monetary union in January 1999 saw the introduction of a new currency, the Euro. From January 2002 this replaced many of the local currencies.

The most important change so far this decade has been – in terms of employment – the right of any fully qualified professional from one EU or EEA state to be recognised as a member of the equivalent profession in another state without having to requalify (subject to a few safeguards). The rule applies to all professions to which access is in some way restricted by the state (or by Royal Charter in the UK) and which require at least three years' university-level education. This is creating many more opportunities for a whole range of professionals to work, set up businesses and offer services in other parts of the Union. Further details are given in the Department of Trade and Industry booklet, *Europe – Open for Professions*, available from DTI Business in Europe Hotline (0117 944 4888).

Other points that are worth noting are:

Passports and permits. A British citizen can work in EU countries without a work permit; all he or she needs is a valid passport showing that the holder is a British citizen.

Job opportunities. In general, skilled or highly skilled workers and those with professional qualifications or particular technical expertise will be able to find employment, but priority will usually be given to qualified nationals. The best opportunities are with multinationals or with British firms operating in other European countries (lists can usually be obtained from the British embassy in that country, although embassies *cannot* help people to find jobs). Details of job opportunities can be obtained from your local Jobcentre, which keeps in touch with the employment centres of EU countries about vacancies. Before you accept a job, it is important to know exactly what to expect in the way of terms and conditions. A useful leaflet entitled 'Working Abroad', as well as others detailing specific countries, are available from Jobcentres or the Overseas Placing Unit of the Employment Service. The DTI Business in Europe Hotline can also provide a number of useful publications.

Unemployment benefit. If you have been unemployed in the UK for four weeks, you can continue to draw unemployment benefit from the UK for up to three months while job hunting in the EU. You will need to sign on fortnightly at the local employment services office, and will receive the UK rate of benefit in the local currency.

However, in view of the fact that this is nowhere near enough to live on while job hunting, people who decide to prospect should make sure they have enough money to keep themselves during this period, or to get home at the end. Furthermore, many EU countries have made this right very difficult to exercise.

Driving licences. Newly qualified drivers are now issued with a pink EU driving licence. It is no longer necessary for drivers to exchange their old licence for a licence from their new country of residence within the EU.

AUSTRIA

The economy

Although Austria is self-sufficient in agricultural production, the economy is based on industry (steel, chemicals, transport equipment) and tourism. More than 80 per cent of trade is with other European countries, predominantly Germany. Consequently, Austria's entry into the European Union has enhanced these trade links.

Austria has also developed strong links with the emerging nations of Eastern Europe, particularly Hungary, where Austria is involved in a number of joint ventures, and also in Slovenia, Slovakia, and the Czech Republic. Many businesses undertaking work in Eastern Europe base themselves in Austria.

Working conditions

In general wages are higher in Austria than in the UK; for managers, up to 150 per cent more. The standard of living is therefore higher, but not by much. Taxation and social security payments are somewhat higher too, as is the cost of living – at least 15 per cent more. In most other respects, working life in Austria is similar to that in the rest of Western Europe. It is normal for managers and professionals to be granted up to 30 days paid vacation. A good knowledge of the German language is a basic requirement of any type of employment.

Useful information

Banking hours: 8.00 am to 12.30 pm and 1.30–3.00 pm, weekdays apart from Thursday 8.00 am to 12.30 pm and 1.30–5.30 pm. Closed Saturday and Sunday.

Shopping hours: 9.00 am to 6.00 pm Monday–Friday, 12.00–5.00 pm Saturday.

Electricity: 220 V, 50 Hz AC.

Driving: Speed limits are 50 km/h in built-up areas, 100 km/h on overland roads, and 130 km/h on motorways. International driving licence, third-party insurance and wearing of seat belts compulsory.

Education: Education is free and compulsory between the ages of 6 and 15. There are good facilities for secondary, technical and professional education. There are 12 state-maintained universities and six colleges of art.

Media: There are four national radio and two national television channels, together with 3 national and 12 regional daily newspapers.

Useful contacts:
British Embassy, Jauresgasse 12, 1030 Vienna, tel: (43) (1) 716130.
Austrian Embassy, 18 Belgrave Mews West, London SW1, tel: 020 7235 3731.
Austrian National Tourist Office, PO Box 2636, London W1A 2QB, tel: 020 7629 0461; www.austria-tourism.at; www.anto.com; www.salzburginfo.at/; www.info.wien.at/

PERSONAL TAXATION

Residence

An individual is resident in Austria if he or she has a 'domicile' (*Wohnsitz*) or 'customary place of abode' (*gewöhnlicher Aufenthalt*) in Austria. An individual is deemed to have a customary place of abode in Austria if he or she is physically present there for more than six months in any calendar year.

Resident individuals are subject to unlimited tax liability (*unbeschränkte Steuerpflicht*) on their worldwide income. Non-resident individuals are subject to tax only on certain Austrian-source income.

Taxation of personal income

Income tax is a progressive tax assessed on a calendar-year basis. Each individual is assessed separately and rates range from 21 per cent to 50 per cent (with intermediate rates of 31 per cent and 41 per cent). In 2002 taxable income not exceeding EUR 3,640 is taxed at 0 per cent; the 50 per cent band applies to taxable income in excess of EUR 50,870.

Certain types of income are taxed at reduced rates and some investment income is subject to a final withholding tax of 25 per cent. Income from one source may generally be offset by a loss from another source. In computing taxable income 'special expenses' (*Sonderausgaben*) and 'extraordinary charges' (*Aussergewöhnliche Belastungen*) may be deducted, subject to certain limitations. Certain tax credits (*Steuerabsetzbeträge*) are granted according to the taxpayer's personal circumstances.

Income from employment

Wages, salaries, bonuses, benefits-in-kind (accommodation, cars, loans, and so forth, but certain social facilities made available by the employer are explicitly tax exempt), expense allowances received (except for travel expenses up to certain amounts) and any other remuneration deriving from employment, and emoluments from statutory health insurance and pension plans are subject to salary tax withheld at source on a pay-as-you-earn basis after deduction of social security contributions. An employee's annual salary is usually paid in 14 parts consisting of 12 monthly payments plus a Christmas and a holiday bonus, as these extra payments are taxed at a favourable flat income tax rate of 6 per cent. Expenses exclusively incurred to generate income are tax deductible by filing a personal income tax return. A special concession for expatriates provides for certain simplifications of tax assessment.

Investment income

Dividends and interest

Dividends and interest on deposits with Austrian banks and on bonds derived from Austrian sources are subject to a 25 per cent withholding tax, for individuals considered as the final income tax payable with related expenses not being deductible.

Dividends from foreign sources are taxed at progressive rates (the ECJ is currently examining whether this rule is in breach of the EU treaty).

Income from real property

This income, net of related expenses, is taxed at progressive rates. There is no withholding tax on rents, nor is there is any imputed income from owner-occupation.

Taxes on capital

Capital gains

Private capital gains are generally exempt from tax. Income from the sale of private property is subject to tax as a speculative gain only if the period of ownership has not exceeded 10 years (in the case of real property, with exceptions for owner-occupied residences) or one year (for other assets). Moreover, capital gains arising on the sale of a privately held significant shareholding and unrealised capital gains on ceasing residence in Austria (exit charge in individuals) are taxed at half of the average income tax rate. A significant shareholding is one that at any time during the last five years has amounted to at least 1 per cent of the relevant company's capital.

Wealth tax

There is no wealth tax in Austria.

Double tax treaties

Austria has concluded over 50 tax treaties on income and capital, including treaties with the UK and the United States.

For further information on tax and social security, please contact:
Liza Papousek
Certified Tax Consultant
BDO Auxilia Treuhand GmbH
tel: +43 (01) 5 37 37 303; e mail: papousek@bdoauxilia.at

BELGIUM

The economy

During the latter part of the 1980s Belgium attracted wealth and investment out of all proportion to its size. At the crossroads of Europe, and host to the main EU institutions, Belgium has been well placed to attract investors.

Old industries have been restructured and small, hi-tech firms have been encouraged. The service sector now accounts for the majority of national income, with financial services making a major contribution. Nevertheless, Belgium is still very much a manufacturing country, and is one of the largest car exporters in the world.

Although fairly wealthy, Belgium's public debt is one of the highest in the developed world. Most of the leading economic indicators look good and Belgium is well placed to exploit its central position as the 'capital' of Europe.

Working conditions

EU nationals with valid passports are free to come and go, but they must register at the local town hall within eight days of arrival. A temporary residence permit, valid for three months, will be issued and can be extended for another three months if you have a job.

After this initial period of six months, a one-year permit can be obtained. Children must also be registered.

The level of managerial and executive salaries is higher than in the UK. An upper middle-ranked executive could expect to earn at least £55,000 a year. Increasingly, a company car would be provided in addition to the basic salary.

Useful information

Banking hours: 9.00 am to 3.30 or 4.00 pm Monday–Friday; banks close during the lunch-hour.

Postal service: Post office hours 9.00 am to 12.00 pm and 2.00–4.00 or 5.00 pm Monday–Friday.

Shopping hours: 10.00 am to 6.00 pm Monday–Saturday.

Electricity: 220 V, 50 Hz AC.

Driving: Speed limits are 50 km/h in built-up areas, 90 km/h on overland roads, and 120 km/h on motorways. Front and back seat belts compulsory, children under 12 prohibited from sitting in the front. Maximum blood alcohol level 0.5 g/l.

Transport: Distances are so short that most travel is done by train or car. Rail services are efficient and there is a good network of roads and autoroutes, with ring roads round the large towns. Urban transport in Brussels is adequate, but buses and trams get very crowded.

Health care: The health services are part of the general social security system, which is a very comprehensive one. Everyone has to belong to a *mutualité/mutualiteit* (sickness insurance fund). You have to pay for a visit to a doctor and for prescriptions but about 75 per cent of the cost of medical treatment may be reimbursed by the *mutualité*. Many hospitals and clinics are run by different denominational groups. People who are currently insured under the UK social security scheme should obtain the necessary forms for reciprocal treatment from the DSS before leaving the UK. An English-speaking medical helpline operates on 02 648 8000.

Education: Education, both primary and secondary, is free and compulsory for all Belgian children between 6 and 18. As well as the state schools there are many Catholic and independent schools in

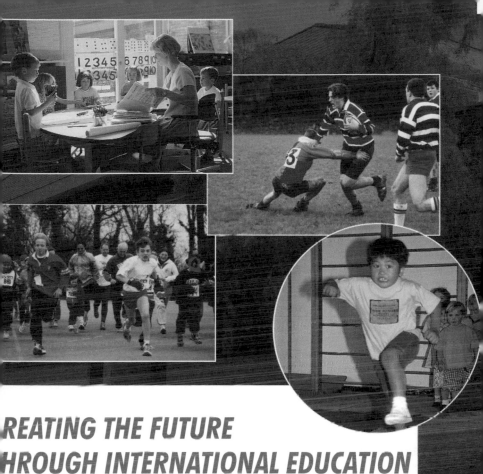

CREATING THE FUTURE
THROUGH INTERNATIONAL EDUCATION

At The British School of Brussels, your children will receive the finest all-round education available in the capital of Europe. Our Internationally recognised curriculum caters for pupils from 3-18 – and a long record of outstanding results at all levels confirms our academic excellence.

But that's not all.

BSB students enjoy working and playing in the safe environment of our beautiful campus surrounded by woods and lakes. They profit from our spacious modern facilities and generous staffing ratios for classroom and outdoor activities.

We make special provision for language tuition, and encourage initiative through independent learning. At the same time, individual support or small work groups meet the needs of those who require more concentrated help.

And of course, the opportunity to develop caring relationships in the dynamic multicultural BSB community offers an ideal start to the lives of tomorrow's world citizens.

To find out more, or to arrange a visit, contact:

Sue Bailey, Admissions Officer
The British School of Brussels
Leuvensesteenweg 19 - 3080 Tervuren
Tel : 00 32 2 766 04 30
Fax : 00 32 02 767 80 70
E-mail admissions@britishschool.be
www.britishschool.be

BSB
THE BRITISH SCHOOL OF BRUSSELS

GIVE THEM THE BSB ADVANTAGE

Brussels and elsewhere. There are a number of European and International Schools. The International School of Brussels takes in children from 3 to 18 in kindergarten, elementary and secondary schools and has over 1,000 boys and girls, the majority being from the USA. There is a smaller International School at Antwerp. The British School of Brussels, which is co-educational and follows the UK National Curriculum, has over 1,000 students aged 3 to 18. There is also a school in Antwerp offering a British curriculum. The small English Primary School in Brussels caters for children from 3 to 12. The St John's English-speaking school at Waterloo, near Brussels, caters for children between 3 and 19 and takes in boarders.

There are French- and Dutch-speaking 'free' universities at Leuven and Louvain-la-Neuve, state universities at Ghent and Liège and university centres at Antwerp, Mons and Diepenbeek. Education is free and standards are high.

Useful contacts:
British Embassy, Rue d'Arlon, 1040 Brussels, tel: 32 2 287 6211; www.british-embassy.be/
Belgium Embassy, 103 Eaton Square, London SW1, tel: 020 7470 3700.
Belgium Tourist Board, 31 Peper Street, London E14 9RW, tel: 020 7456 0045; www.visitbelgium.com/; www.belgique-tourisme.net

Expatriate information:
Expats in Brussels, www.expatsinbrussels.com/
Expatriates Guide to Belgium, www.netcat.co.uk/rob/be/bel-idx-shtml
Xpats.com, www.xpats.com/; www.expatriate-online.com

PERSONAL TAXATION

Residence

Like many countries, Belgium taxes on the basis of residence. In general individuals are considered to be resident in Belgium for tax purposes if they establish their 'domicile' (*domicile/domicilie*) or established place of residence or the centre of their wealth (*siège de fortune/zetel van fortuin*) – the centre of their vital and economic interest, such as bank account, mail, household – in Belgium. Physical presence is not conclusive.

In order to determine whether someone is resident in Belgium, factual circumstances have to be taken into account. However, in absence of any rebuttal, an individual is deemed to be resident if he or she is registered at the National Population Register.

Taxation of personal Income

Residents are subject to income tax on their worldwide income, divided into four categories:

☐ rental income from real (immovable) property;
☐ income from movable property (investment income);
☐ professional income;
☐ miscellaneous income.

The tax year is the calendar year. Rates of income tax are progressive and range from 25 per cent to 50 per cent (exclusive of the crisis surcharge and a communal surcharge). Income is assessed on a previous-year basis, so that income of the year 2002 is taxed in 2003 at 2003 tax rates. For 2002, single taxpayers are entitled to a tax-free minimum taxable income of EUR 5,480 and married couples to EUR 4,350 per spouse. Additional minima are available in respect of children and other dependants.

Income from Employment

Employment income (salary, benefits in kind, termination payments, and so forth) is fully taxable. However, employment income from a treaty country is exempt from tax for a Belgian resident, although it is added to taxable income when determining the rate of income tax to be applied to taxable income (this method is known as 'exemption with progression').

A tax credit of 50 per cent is available for employment income from a non-treaty country, provided that the income was taxed abroad, no matter at what rate.

Professional expenses are deductible, either on a lump-sum basis, or on the actual amount incurred, provided this can be substantiated. Employees can also benefit from a number of tax-free 'social benefits' (such as meal tickets, medical insurance and sick-pay arrangements), provided that the related requirements are met.

Expatriates temporarily residing in Belgium can benefit from a privileged tax régime, provided that a number of conditions are satisfied, allowing them to be taxed as if they were non-resident (on the basis of the number of working days spent in Belgium). Moreover, they benefit from a tax-free allowance up to a maximum of either BEF 1,200,000 (EUR 40,902) (if working in control or coordination offices or scientific research) or BEF 450,000 (EUR 11,155) if working elsewhere.

A system of withholding tax operates on earnings.

Investment income

Dividends and interest

Both domestic and foreign dividends received in Belgium are subject to a final withholding tax of 15 per cent or 25 per cent. As an alternative, taxpayers can elect for dividends to be included in income taxable at progressive rates where this is beneficial.

Domestic interest is subject to a final withholding tax of 15 per cent. As an alternative, taxpayers can elect for interest to be included in income taxable at progressive rates where this is beneficial.

Foreign dividends not received in Belgium, and foreign-source interest, although exempt, still need to be reported in the tax return.

Income from real property

Income from Belgian real property is always taxable in Belgium. The amount of taxable income from real property in Belgium is normally an imputed income based on its cadastral value (deemed rental value). This is the rule not only for owner-occupied property but also for let property, unless let to a business, in which case the actual rental income, as reduced by qualifying expenses, is taxable.

In the case of real property situated abroad, taxable income is the actual rent received, although a standard deduction of 40 per cent, on account of expenses, is allowed. Where the property is unlet, its rental value is used as the base for tax. Where the real property is situated in a treaty country, however, income is exempt (with progression – see above) from taxation in Belgium.

Taxes on capital

Capital gains

Capital gains on shares are generally exempt from taxation, as are all gains arising from the normal management of private property.

However, some gains (considered of a speculative nature) are taxable as miscellaneous income.

Wealth tax

There is no wealth tax in Belgium.

Double tax treaties

Belgium has concluded over 60 comprehensive treaties to avoid double taxation, among which are treaties with the UK and the US.

For further information on tax and social security, please contact:
Marc Verbeek
Tax Partner
BDO Belgium GIE
tel: (0032) 2778 0100; e-mail: marc.verbeek@bdo.be

DENMARK

The economy

Denmark is traditionally an agricultural country and nearly three-quarters of its land is still used for farming and horticulture although employing only 6 per cent of the workforce. Though reduced in area since the end of the war, agriculture is highly efficient and food and dairy produce account for about one-fifth of total exports. The UK is a long-established market: Danish bacon and butter are found on many British breakfast tables. There has been a marked shift of resources towards manufacturing, the most important industries being food processing, metal and electrical engineering, transport equipment, textiles and clothing, paper, furniture, glass and brewing. Firms are small scale; about two out of three manufacturers employ fewer than 50 workers. Standards of design, styling and craftsmanship are high. However, by far the greatest proportion of the population works in the service sector. Despite recent spending increases and a trading deficit, inflation remains low.

Working conditions

It is not easy for foreigners to find work in Denmark, despite the free movement of labour provisions of the EU. Work permits are required for non-EU nationals, and are rarely granted. Most Danes speak English, but it is difficult to find employment unless you have a good knowledge of Danish. Rented housing is scarce and people are advised to try to arrange accommodation beforehand. Foreigners must apply for a residence permit to stay in Denmark for more than three months. Enquiries about residence permits should be made in advance to the Danish Embassy in London, or in Copenhagen to the Directorate of Immigration, 53 Ryesgade, DK-2100 Copenhagen 1 (tel: 31 393100). Holders of the residence permit must also get a personal code number from Folkeregisteret, Dahlerupsgade 6, 1640 Copenhagen.

The level of management salaries is appreciably higher than in the UK but deductions for tax and social security are higher too. However, the base rate of tax has been lowered to align it more with other EU countries.

The Danes have a good record of stable labour relations and co-operation between employers and unions. They have one of the lowest strike records in Europe.

The system of social security provides full cover against sickness, accident, retirement and other contingencies.

Useful information

Banking hours: 9.30 am to 4.00 pm Monday–Wednesday and Friday, 9.30 am to 6.00 pm Thursday. Unibank in Zealand, Mon and Lolland-Falster and Copenhagen 10.00 am to 5.00 pm.

Shopping hours: 9.00 or 10.00 am to 6.00 or 7.00 pm Monday–Thursday, 9.00 or 10.00 am to 7.00 or 8.00 pm Friday, and 9.00 or 10.00 am to 1.00 or 2.00 pm Saturday. Alcohol not sold after 8.00 pm.

Driving: Driving is on the right, and the roads are good. As in other Nordic countries, there are strict regulations against drinking and driving.

Transport: Copenhagen has an international airport (Kastrup) with frequent flights to European cities and to internal centres. Rail transport is efficient and reasonably priced – there are numerous concessions for families travelling together although public transport is expensive.

Health care: The standard of medical treatment in Denmark is high. Health services have recently been remodelled on British NHS lines, with the emphasis on group practice and preventive medicine. Hospital treatment is free. Charges for doctors' visits and prescriptions are refundable.

Education: Education is compulsory from the ages of 7 to 17. English is taught in all schools. In Copenhagen there is an International School for 4–19 year olds with an international/US curriculum; Rygaards School at Hellerup offers a UK curriculum for the age range 5–16.

Directory enquiries: 118.

Emergency services: 112.

Useful contacts:
British Embassy, Kastelvej 36–40, 2100 Copenhagen O, tel: 35 44 52 00; www.britishembassy.dk/
Danish Embassy, 55 Sloane Street, London SW1, tel: 020 7235 1255.
Danish Tourist Board: www.denmark.dt.dk; www.visitdenmark.com/

Expatriate information:
www.zitech.dk/userwebs/zn7ccc0846/briteuro.htm
AmericaWomen's Club in Aarhus, www.home8.inet.ck/bonnie/awcaa

PERSONAL TAXATION

Residence

An individual is resident in Denmark for tax purposes if he or she either has his or her principal residence (home) in Denmark, or spends at least six consecutive months (ignoring short breaks away) in Denmark.

Individuals who are resident are liable to income tax on their worldwide income, non-residents are liable on their Danish-source income only.

Taxation of personal income

For the purposes of the income tax on individuals, income is classified into three categories:

☐ personal income (including income from employment);
☐ capital income (including interest income, income from real property and certain capital gains);
☐ share income (dividends from Danish and certain foreign companies and certain capital gains).

Taxable income is subject to national income taxes and two levels of local income tax. There are four kinds of national income tax (basic income tax (*bundskat*); surtax (*mellemskat*); supertax (*topskat*) and dividend tax (*udbytteskat*). Local income tax is levied by counties (*amtskommunerne*) and districts (*kommunerne*) on the same base as national basic income tax.

Personal allowances, some given by way of a tax credit, are available to taxpayers according to their personal circumstances.

Income from employment

Domestic earnings from employment, whether in cash or in kind, are taxable in Denmark whether or not the employee is resident there. Employment income with a foreign source is taxable in Denmark only if the employee is resident.

Payments to an employee of expenses for travel, entertainment or any other service to be performed on behalf of the employer are taxable only to the extent that they are not actually expended in the performance of the service. Special rules apply for free housing and free use of a car or telephone provided by the employer. Some work-related benefits-in-kind of a value less than DKK 4,600 (2002) are exempt.

Employment income is taxed as personal income at rates of up to 59 per cent (this is the statutory maximum, inclusive of local income taxes).

Investment income

Dividends and interest

Taxable investment income for a resident includes interest, gains on certain securities, profits from gains on the sale of shares owned for less than three years, and gains on property other than owner-occupied property. Gains on owner-occupied property are normally exempt.

Such income, if the net income is positive (if it exceeds deductible expenses and losses) is taxed as capital income at rates of up to 59 per cent. Negative net capital income (the excess of allowable losses and expenses over capital income) is not recognised for supertax or dividend tax and consequently has a tax value of approximately 33 per cent.

Dividends received from both domestic and foreign companies and taxable gains on shares owned for more than three years are taxed as share income. Dividends from domestic companies are paid under deduction of 28% withholding tax. This tax is final provided that the individual's total share income for the year does not exceed DKK 39,700 (2002). Share income in excess of this amount is taxed at the higher rate of dividend tax, which is 43 per cent. Special rules may apply for dividends from foreign companies and gains on shares in such companies.

Income from real property

Income from real property is included in capital income, taxable at rates of up to 59 per cent. There is no imputation of income to owner occupiers but they are subject to a property tax.

Taxes on capital

Capital gains

See under 'investment income' above.

Wealth tax

There is no wealth tax in Denmark.

Double tax treaties

Denmark has concluded comprehensive tax treaties with approximately 75 countries including the UK and the United States.

For further information on tax and social security, please contact:
Hans-Henrik Nilausen
Tax Manager
BDO ScanRevision Statsautoriseret
tel: +45 (39) 155320; e-mail: hhn@bdo.dk

FINLAND

The economy

Finland is a highly industrialised country. Forestry, which used to represent a large part of Finnish exports, now accounts for 31 per cent of the total. Metal engineering, particularly electronics such as mobile phones, and shipbuilding, now constitute 50 per cent. Finnish glass, ceramics and furniture enjoy high international reputations. Other important industries are chemicals, pharmaceuticals, foodstuffs and electronic equipment.

The economy has been adversely affected by the collapse of trade with Russia. In the early 1980s, trade with the former Soviet

Union accounted for 20 per cent of exports; in 1997, this was down to 5 per cent.

Working conditions

In general, wages are higher in Finland than in the UK. Tax and social security deductions, however, are much greater, as are other living expenses, so that the net result is likely to be a standard of living equal to, or perhaps less than, that in the UK. On average, the cost of living in Finland is about 20 per cent more than the UK. Working hours are roughly the same. Holiday entitlement is greater. Although English is widely understood, at the very least a working knowledge of Swedish would be useful.

Useful information

Electricity: 230 V.

Driving: Speed limits are 50 km/h in built-up areas, 80 km/h on overland roads, 100–120 km/h on motorways. Seat belts compulsory.

Transport: The road network is comprehensive and of good quality in the south of the country. Traffic drives on the right. Cars cost about the same as at home, but servicing is cheaper. It is better to adopt a flexible approach to transportation. The state railway system is comprehensive, efficient and popular. Public transport is cheap, as are taxis. Finland also has one of the densest and cheapest domestic airline networks in Europe. Finnair operates to 20 internal airports, the northernmost being about 130 miles north of the Arctic Circle! In addition, there is a comprehensive range of international and domestic ferry services operating on the Baltic and the numerous inland lakes.

Education: State-provided education is co-educational, free and compulsory from 7–16 years. There are 21 universities or schools of similar level.

Directory enquiries: 118.

Emergency services: 112, police 10022.

Media: Four national television channels. Newspapers, books, plays and films appear in both Swedish and Finnish. There are a large number of newspapers to choose from.

Useful contacts:
British Embassy, Itainen Puistotie 17, 00 140 Helsinki, tel: 358 9 2286 5100; www.ukembassy.fi/
Finnish Embassy, 38 Chesham Place, London SW1, tel: 020 7235 9531.
Finnish Tourist Board, 3rd Floor, 30–35 Pall Mall, London SW1Y 5LP, tel: 020 7839 4048; www.mek.fi or www.thekingroad.com

PERSONAL TAXATION

Residence

Finland taxes individuals on the basis of residence. An individual is regarded as resident in Finland if he or she has his or her main abode in Finland or if he or she stays in Finland for a continuous period of more than six months. The stay in Finland may be regarded as continuous in spite of a temporary absence from the country.

Taxation of personal income

Residents of Finland are subject to income tax on their worldwide income whereas non-residents are liable in respect of income from Finnish sources only.

Income tax is charged at two levels – national and local. National income tax is levied at progressive rates on an individual's earned income; local income tax is levied at a flat rate on a similar tax base (except for some deductions that operate at the national level only and others only at the local level). Investment income is subject to national income tax only, at a flat rate of 29 per cent. The rate of local tax is set by each local authority in advance for the coming tax year.

The tax year is the calendar year. In the year 2001, the highest marginal national rate of income tax is 37 per cent. Rates of local income tax range from 15 per cent to 19.75 per cent. Personal allowances are available to taxpayers depending on their personal circumstances. Some allowances apply only at the national level; others only at the local level (including an earned-income allowance).

Individuals who are members of the Evangelical Lutheran Church or the Orthodox Church are additionally subject to church tax, set locally by the respective church's parochial body. Church tax is levied on the base for local income tax, at a flat rate of between 1 per cent and 2 per cent.

Income from employment

All forms of remuneration from employment are taxable. This includes salaries, bonuses, lump-sum allowances, and benefits in kind. Allowable deductions from employment income include home-to-work commuting (subject to a maximum of FIM 28,000 (EUR 4,709) and subscriptions to trade unions or professional associations. For other expenses, a standard deduction is available. In 2001, the amount of this deduction is FIM 2,700 (EUR 455).

A system of withholding on account of national and local income tax and church tax operates on earnings.

Non-resident employees are subject to a withholding tax at a flat rate of 35 per cent on their Finnish earnings

Special rule for expatriate experts

Expatriates working in Finland on a short-term basis may be treated as non-resident and hence liable to income tax at a flat rate of 35 per cent on their Finnish employment income if certain conditions are satisfied. These are as follows:

☐ the individual becomes resident in Finland at the beginning of the relevant period of employment;

☐ the pecuniary salary for this employment is at least FIM 35,000 or EUR 5,800 a month during the total period of employment in Finland;

☐ the individual's duties in Finland require special expertise;

☐ the employee is not a Finnish national and he or she has not been a resident of Finland in the five years preceding the year in which the employment begins.

A taxpayer can be regarded as a foreign expert for a maximum period of 24 months.

Investment income

Investment income is liable to national income tax at a flat rate of 29 per cent and is exempt from local income tax. Dividends from Finnish companies listed on the main list of the Helsinki stock exchange are paid with an imputation tax credit of 29/71 of the dividend, so individuals have no further liability in respect of dividend income. Non-residents suffer withholding tax at 29 per cent on dividends and royalties, subject to the contrary provisions of a tax treaty. Interest is generally tax-exempt for non-residents.

Taxes on capital

Capital gains

Capital gains on private assets are treated as investment income and subject to tax at 29 per cent. The taxable capital gain is computed by deducting the acquisition costs and costs of sale from the sale proceeds. In the case of real property, a minimum deduction of 20 per cent (where the property has been held for less than 10 years) or 50 per cent (for property held for 10 years or more) is available. Full exemption is granted, subject to certain conditions, to gains from the disposal of the taxpayer's main residence.

Wealth tax

Individuals resident in Finland are subject to wealth tax on their worldwide net wealth in excess of FIM 1,000,000 (EUR 168,188). The marginal tax rate is 0.9 per cent. Non-residents are taxable at 0.9 per cent on their Finnish *situs* assets in excess of FIM 800,000 (EUR 134,550).

Double tax treaties

Finland has a network of some 60 comprehensive double tax agreements, covering the UK and the United States among others, in the area of income and capital taxation. Finland has also concluded double taxation treaties on inheritances with some countries (for example, with the USA).

For further information on tax and social security, please contact:
Andre Kumlander
BDO International Liaison Partner
BDO Finland OY
tel: +358 94780812; e-mail: andre.kumlander@bdo.fi

FRANCE

The economy

The French economy withstood the worst effects of the US-led downturn in 2001, but unemployment remains stubbornly high at 9 per cent while GDP growth is not forecast to exceed 1.5 per cent in 2002/2003. Although France is one of the largest industrial powers in the world, it is the world's second largest agricultural exporter. Foreign companies now account for 27 per cent of manufacturing output and 30 per cent of exports.

France is well off for natural resources, with coal, natural gas, iron ore, potash, bauxite and fluorspar. However, despite an ambitious nuclear power programme, a steep rise in the price of oil could still wreak havoc. Trade is primarily with EU countries, headed by Germany, with the UK as its third largest export market. Principal exports are food, wine and dairy produce, petroleum products, metals, steels, chemicals, cars, non-ferrous metals, and a wide range of consumer goods. Fashion and luxury items, and tourism, are also important sources of revenue.

Industry is fairly evenly dispersed, though Greater Paris has the largest and most heterogeneous concentration and some areas, such as Brittany and the south-west, are under-industrialised. Textiles, coal and steel have declined but new technologically advanced and science-based industries, such as chemicals, electronics and nuclear engineering, have been developed particularly in the Lyon–Grenoble region.

Agriculture, largely dominated by small family farms, is still of major importance and influence, even though the numbers working on the land have steadily fallen and there has been a drift to the towns and cities.

Working conditions

European Union citizens do not require work permits but after three months must apply for residence permits from the town hall or police, which can prove difficult to obtain without a job. This is valid for five years, or the length of your contract if this is less than 12 months. The 39-hour week is standard. French workers are entitled by law to five weeks' annual leave. There are 11 public holidays. Many firms and offices are shut for much of August.

The level of managerial salaries is around 30 to 40 per cent higher than in the UK. Employers' contributions to social security are among the highest in Europe, but direct taxation is relatively low. Secretarial salaries are much the same as in the UK.

Most wages are fixed by collective bargaining at national level. Equal pay is theoretically obligatory – the gap between men's and women's pay is narrower than in most EU countries. There is also a minimum legal wage. Given the current economic problems, these areas are under a great deal of pressure for change.

Many fringe benefits are provided and most employers have to contribute to housing and welfare. The practice of a 13-month bonus is widespread and most manual workers are now paid monthly, instead of fortnightly, and enjoy staff status. French workers attach as much importance to social security and fringe benefits as to money wages.

Useful information

Banking hours: 9.00 am to 4.30 pm weekdays (closed afternoon before a public holiday), some closed on Saturdays. Closed for lunch 1.00–3.00 pm in provinces.

Post office: 8.00 am to 7.00 pm weekdays, 8.00 am to 12.00 pm Saturdays.

Shopping hours: 10.00 am to 7.00 pm Monday to Saturday, closed 1.00–3.00 pm and all day Monday outside Paris.

Electricity: 220 V (may vary).

Driving: Driving is on the right. Paris is congested and parking difficult, but the traffic flows. If you take your own car, you are obliged to have it fitted with seat belts back and front; yellow headlamps are no longer compulsory for motor vehicles.

Transport: The main centres are linked by internal airways and there are airports at Lyon, Marseille, Nice, Bordeaux, Strasbourg and Toulouse, as well as two in Paris: Charles de Gaulle and Orly. The railway network is highly efficient, with a number of express and TGV (260 km/h) trains. Fares are cheaper than in the UK. Direct rail link with the UK is via the Channel Tunnel. The roads are good and there is a network of motorways, on which tolls are payable. These can be expensive on a long journey.

Health care: There is a reciprocal health agreement with the UK. Medical attention is expensive but 75 per cent of the fees for doctors and dentists working within the French sickness insurance scheme can be reimbursed. A proportion of the cost of prescriptions can be refunded (40–70 per cent), as well as outpatient hospital treatment (80 per cent) although this system is under review, and may face cuts. Private treatment is costly. There is a British hospital in Paris, the Hertford, and a more expensive American one.

Education: Some expatriate parents send their children to local schools, which are of a high educational standard and where they can acquire a good knowledge of French. There is free compulsory education from 6 to 16 and below that age there are many crèches and nursery schools. Secondary education is in two cycles, from 11 to 15 and from 15 to 18. Those who complete the second cycle can take the Baccalauréat examination before proceeding to university or institutes of technology. American and British schools in Paris cater for children of diplomats and businessmen. The British School of Paris is geared to the UK system; it takes pupils from 4 to 18 and offers boarding facilities.

Directory enquiries: 12.

Emergency services: police 17, fire 18, ambulance 15.

Media: Most provincial regions have their own newspapers, but some Paris papers, such as *Le Figaro* and *Le Monde*, circulate nationally. There is a wide range of weeklies, the best known being *Paris Match* and *L'Express*. TV is state controlled with limited advertising, though cable and satellite facilities are expanding rapidly. There are one state, four commercial and a number of local private radio stations.

Useful contacts:
British Embassy, 35 Rue du Faubourg, St Honore, 75383 Paris, Cedex 08, tel: 44 51 31 00; www.amb-grandebretagne.fr/
French Consulate General, 21 Cromwell Road, London SW7, tel: 020 7838 2000.
French Tourist Office, www.franceguide.com/touristboard
www.maison-de-la-france.fr

Country information:
www.paris-anglo.com/
www.partisfranceguide.com
www.intro-france-usa.org
www.iway.Fr/parisAnglofiles/

Further information: Living and Working in France, by Genevieve Brame (published by Kogan Page at £12.99), provides in-depth information for expatriates living in France; www.kogan-page.co.uk.

PERSONAL TAXATION

Residence

France taxes individuals on the basis of residence. An individual is considered to be resident in France if any one of the following four criteria is met:

- ☐ the individual's permanent home is in France;
- ☐ the individual's principal place of sojourn, regardless of the permanence or otherwise of the available living accommodation, is in France;
- ☐ The individual carries out an occupation or employment in France, unless this is subsidiary to a main occupation carried out elsewhere;

☐ the individual's centre of economic interests (main investments and their management) or main source of income is in France.

A French resident will be subject to French tax on worldwide income whereas a non-resident will be subject to French tax on French-source income only.

Taxation of personal income

Individuals are subject to income tax on their annual taxable income. Taxable income is expenses and reliefs. The categories of income are:

☐ business (trading) income;
☐ professional income;
☐ income from real property;
☐ employment income;
☐ financial income and income from securities;
☐ agricultural income.

The tax year for income tax purposes is the calendar year, and the yearly taxable income is determined for the whole household, that is, husband, wife and dependent children. Income tax is levied at progressive rates, the maximum rate for 2002 (2001 income) being 52.75 per cent, to which miscellaneous social taxes must be added (different from social security taxes) amounting up to 10 per cent in 2002 applicable on certain income (investment income, rental income and so forth).

Income from employment

Employment income includes all benefits in cash or in kind received by an individual. Professional expenses are deductible, with taxpayers choosing between a standard deduction of 10 per cent or a deduction of actual professional expenses. There is also a special relief of 20 per cent of net employment income. Pensions are taxed in the same way as employment income. The 10 per cent and 20 per cent standard deductions are limited to EUR 12,229 and EUR 22,380 respectively (2001 income).

There is no deduction of tax at source (pay as you earn) from employment remuneration in France, except in the case of non-resident employees, from whose earnings tax at a maximum rate of 25 per cent may be deducted.

Investment income

Dividends and interest

Share dividends and bond interest from French sources are subject to income tax only if their amount exceeds EUR 2,400 for a married couple or EUR 1,200 for unmarried individuals (2001 income), and only if taxable income does not exceed EUR 92,646, if married or EUR 46,343, if unmarried.

Income from real property

Rental income from real property is subject to tax at progressive rates. There is no withholding tax on rents, nor is income imputed to owner-occupiers.

Taxes on capital

Capital gains

Taxable capital gains fall into one of two main classes: 'real property' and 'shares and securities'.

Provided that the gain is a 'long-term capital gain', it is computed net of an allowance of 5 per cent for each year of ownership after the first two. As a consequence, property gains are completely exempt after 22 years of ownership. The purchase price is increased by an inflation coefficient. Once the gain is computed, it is subject to top-slicing relief. One-fifth of the net gain is added to net taxable income as the top slice, and the resulting additional tax multiplied by five to arrive at the total income tax due.

Short-term gains are gains on property held for no more than two years. Here, there is no top slicing and income tax is payable on the gross gain (without adjusting the purchase price for inflation).

Capital gains on securities are taxed at a flat rate of 26 per cent (including social security surcharges). For gains of the year 2001, there is no tax if the total sale proceeds from shares and securities do not exceed EUR 7,623 in the year, and EUR 7,650 for 2002.

Wealth tax

A net wealth tax (*impôt de solidarité sur la fortune*) is levied on individuals whose net wealth exceeds a certain threshold. For 2001, this was set at FRF 4,700,000 (EUR 720,000) (measured at 1 January 2001).

Non-residents are also liable to net wealth tax, but only on certain assets situated in France. Their financial investments are specifically exempted.

Double tax treaties

France has signed tax treaties with more than 100 countries, including the UK and the United States.

For further information on tax and social security, please contact:
Jacques Dubarry
BDO Gendrot
tel: +33 (0) 1 41 12 13 32; email: jdubarry@bdo-gendrot.fr

GERMANY

The economy

Since reunification the German economy has shown strongly diverging trends: while the West was booming, the East was struggling to adapt to a market economy. Monetary union, which preceded the political union of the two Germanies, immediately created enormous pressures in the East – ailing industries were exposed to the full blast of competition from advanced Western countries.

Germany's wealth, originally based on coal, steel and heavy engineering, is now founded on a broad spread of modern industries, including petrochemicals, artificial fibres, electric and electronic equipment, machinery, machine tools, scientific instruments and cars. New industrial development has been particularly noticeable in the south.

For many years the West German economy has relied on migrant labour – particularly from Turkey, Greece, Yugoslavia and Italy – and has also had a liberal policy towards refugees, both from the East and from the Third World (1.6 million in 1996). The presence of large numbers of foreigners has created tensions in German society, exacerbated by the influx of refugees from Eastern Europe.

Working conditions

British and other EEA nationals are free to enter and move about the country; if you intend to stay for more than three months you will need a residence permit, valid for five years, from the Foreign Nationals authority at the local town hall or area administration centre.

At managerial level, the Germans do considerably better than the British. Secretarial and skilled worker salaries are slightly higher than in the UK. The cost of living is lower in Germany than in the UK. The British Chamber of Commerce publishes annual surveys of salaries and fringe benefits.

The standard working week is 36–40 hours for five days in many cases. There is a minimum of 25–30 days' holiday, plus 10–13 public holidays.

Wages and salaries are determined by collective bargains which usually have the force of law. There are separate arrangements for senior executives (*leitende Angestellte*). Individual contracts are usually for an indefinite period and terminated by written notice, with compensation according to age and length of service.

There is a long-established and comprehensive system of social security, with benefits related to earnings. Employers may provide, by law or by custom, additional benefits, eg 13-month bonus and group/performance bonuses, and help towards housing, meals, transport and recreation.

Useful information

Banking hours: 8.30 am to 1.00 pm, 2.30–4.00 pm weekdays.

Shopping hours: 9.00 am to 8.00 pm weekdays, 9.00 am to 4.00 pm Saturday; closed Sunday and public holidays. Hairdressers and restaurants closed Mondays.

Driving: Speed limits are 50 km/h in built-up areas, 100 km/h on overland roads, and 130 km/h on motorways; cars with trailers 80 km/h. Driving is on the right. Breakdown emergency number 01 8022 22.

Transport: There is a highly sophisticated network of air, rail and road transport, serving all parts of the country. All major cities are linked by motorways (*Autobahnen*).

Health care: Medical treatment is of a high standard and most costs are met through insurance funds. Charges are made for dentistry, medicine, drugs and medical aids. Refunds are possible if you exchange your Form E111 for a *Krankenschein* certificate issued by the German health insurance companies through the Local Sickness Fund.

Education: Education is compulsory from 6 to 18 (including three years at a vocational school on a part-time basis). A monthly fee is charged for nursery education between the ages of 3 and 6. The standard is high and thorough, and many expatriate parents send their children to local schools. Others want their children to continue education in the UK. There are International Schools at Dusseldorf, Frankfurt, Hamburg and Munich. The British Embassy runs a preparatory school in Bonn for children from 4 to 13. Fees vary, so it is necessary to check. Schools for the children of British military personnel sometimes admit children of civilians.

Emergency services: 110, fire 112.

Useful contacts:

British Embassy, Friedrich-Ebert-Allee 77, D-53113 Bonn, tel: 49 228 9167 0; www.britischebotschaft.de/

German Embassy, 23 Belgrave Square, London SW1, tel: 020 7824 1300.

German National Tourist Board, PO Box 2965, London W1A 3TN, tel: 0891 6001000; www.germany-tourism.de/

Expatriate information:
www.pagematic.net/
www.german-way.com/
www.german/expat.html

Further information: The Bundesverwaltungsamt publishes a brochure *Merkblatt 119*, covering in detail aspects of living conditions, household costs, price index on consumer goods, housing costs, labour law, education, driving licences, etc. The publication can be ordered from Öffentliche Auskunftsstelle für Auslandtätige, Grosse Bleichen 23, 2 Stock, D-20354 Hamburg (cover charge DM20.00).

PERSONAL TAXATION

Residence

An individual is considered to be resident in Germany for tax purposes if that individual has a permanent home or 'domicile' (*Wohnsitz*) or habitual abode (*gewohnlicher Aufenthalt*) in Germany. A permanent home is a house or apartment in Germany that the individual maintains under circumstances that imply that the stay is other than temporary. If no place of residence is maintained a continuous stay in Germany for more than six months will lead to the assumption of a habitual abode from the beginning of this period. Short interruptions are ignored.

Taxation of personal income

An individual who is resident in Germany is subject to tax on his or her worldwide income unless exempt under the provisions of a double tax treaty. Non-residents are subject to tax only on certain categories of income from German sources.

German residents are subject to income tax on seven categories of income, which are as follows:

☐ income from employment;
☐ income from a business or trade;
☐ professional income;

☐ income from capital investment;
☐ agricultural and forestry income;
☐ rental and royalty income;
☐ other income (including capital gains).

Taxable income from employment or capital investment and other income is computed by reducing the gross income by related expenses in accordance with the cash receipts and disbursements method.

A variety of allowances are available depending on the taxpayer's individual circumstances.

The tax year for income tax purposes is the calendar year. Income tax is levied at continuously progressive rates. Tax liability starts at a yearly taxable income of EUR 7,235 for a single person and EUR 14,471 for married couples (jointly assessed) in 2002 at a rate of 19.9 per cent. The maximum rate is 48.5 per cent on a taxable income in excess of EUR 55,008 (single persons) or EUR 110,016 (married couples). The maximum tax rate will drop to 47 per cent in 2003 and to 42 per cent in 2005.

Additionally, a solidarity surcharge (*Solidaritätszuschlag*) of 5.5 per cent is levied on the income tax due. Members of a recognised faith community are required to pay a church tax at a rate of 8 per cent or 9 per cent of their income tax payable, depending on their state (*Land*) of residence within Germany.

Income from employment

This includes all benefits in cash and in kind received by an individual, such as salaries, bonuses, reimbursements of tax, private use of company car, cost-of-living allowances, and so forth.

Employees may deduct all expenses incurred in acquiring and maintaining income, in some cases subject to limitations. For example, commuting expenses, moving expenses, and expenses for working tools are all deductible. A standard deduction of EUR 1,044 (2002) is available for employment income, but the full amount of itemised expenses may be claimed if they exceed this amount.

A system of deduction of tax at source (salary tax – *Lohnsteuer*) from employment income operates in Germany.

Investment income

Resident individuals are liable to German tax on their worldwide investment income, including dividends and interest. From 1 January 2002, the new 'half-income method' generally applies to dividend income. Under this method, only one-half of the dividend received is taxable income; the remainder is exempt. By the same token, only 50 per cent of the related expenses are deductible.

For investment income a standard annual deduction of EUR 1,601 (single persons) or EUR 3,202 (married couples) is available (2002 figures).

Rental income from real property is subject to income tax at progressive rates. In computing taxable income, the taxpayer may deduct depreciation, related loan interest and other related expenditure. There is no withholding tax on rental income and no imputed income from owner occupation.

Taxes on capital

Capital gains

Capital gains fall under the category of other income. Gains realised by the sale of private assets are generally not taxable if the time between acquisition and sale amounts to more than 10 years for real property and more than 12 months in the case of other assets, mainly shares and securities. However, gains from the disposal of a significant shareholding (of 1 per cent or more) are taxable whatever the ownership period.

Wealth tax

There is no wealth tax in Germany.

Double tax treaties

Germany has concluded over 70 comprehensive double tax treaties, including those with the UK and the United States.

For further information on tax and social security, please contact:
Karin Fiedler
Senior Tax Manager
BDO Deutsche Warentreuhand Aktiengesellschaft
tel: +49 (69) 95 94 1255; e-mail: Karin.Fiedler@bdo.de
or
Wolfgang Kloster
Senior Tax Manager
tel: +49 (30) 88 57 22–0; e-mail: Wolfgang.Kloster@bdo.de

GREECE

The economy

In the past few years, Greek economic policy has focused on gradually meeting the convergence criteria for joining the European
Monetary Union. Policy makers aim at Greece joining the EMU by
2001 at the latest, one year before the common currency (Euro) is
introduced in physical form. Real GDP growth has been significant
in the last four years. In the last few years, Greek growth rates have
been among the highest in the EU. Of more importance is the fact
that the high rates of growth are accompanied by even higher
investment growth rates which, on average, are more than twice as
high as the corresponding EU rates over the 1994–97 period.

The Greek economy was traditionally based on agriculture, with
small-scale farming predominating, except in a few areas in the north.
In common with all developing countries, there has been a steady
shift towards industry, and although agriculture still employs nearly
19 per cent of the labour force, it accounts for 11.16 per cent of GDP.

In manufacturing, which accounts for 21.35 per cent of GDP,
Greece's performance is hampered by the proliferation of small,
traditional, low-tech firms, often run as family businesses. Food,
drink and tobacco processing, textiles, chemicals, metal manufacture and engineering are the most important sectors.

The government's major concern has been to combat inflation,
which is now down to 5 per cent. Wages and earnings, though well
below the general EU level, have risen progressively but there is
still a large public debt, and a vibrant black economy.

Personal finance and taxation

The level of executive salaries is around 50 per cent lower than in the more prosperous northern EU countries but these are improving. Income tax is raised progressively on taxable income, against which allowances tend to be fairly generous. The top rate of tax is 45 per cent. On an average executive salary tax and social security payments would be around 30 per cent. Tax is deducted monthly, and the final balance is adjusted annually.

Working conditions

The EU provisions about free mobility of labour apply in Greece. You can freely take up employment, or enter the country to look for work, but you will need to register with the police (or the Alien's Department Office if you are in Athens) within eight days. You will need a residence permit for a stay of longer than three months. Greek bureaucracy is fairly intimidating, and can appear chaotic.

Job prospects for foreigners are slim at present, the best being with British firms with branches or subsidiaries in Greece or with multinational companies, especially in technological fields or in tourism. It is not very easy to find work and priority is given to Greek nationals. Military service is compulsory for men over 19.

Working hours are as in any hot country. In the summer (April to October) these are from 8.00 am to 2.00 pm and from 5.00 pm to 8.00 pm. Meals are eaten late and many people take a siesta in the afternoon.

There are 11 public holidays, including religious holidays. Annual leave is a minimum of four weeks after one year of service.

Useful information

Electricity: 220 V, 50 Hz AC.

Driving: Speed limits are 50 km/h in residential areas and 100–120 km/h on motorways. International driving licence required.

Transport: Transport is on the whole efficient and reliable and you can choose between air, rail, sea or bus. Most international air flights are based on Athens, and there are also regular services to and from

Salonika. Domestic airlines serving some 30 towns and islands are operated from Athens by Olympic Airways. The railways are efficient and serve the main centres north and south of Athens. Long-distance coach and bus services provide a means of seeing the country and many shipping routes connect the mainland with the islands. Taxis and cars can be hired, though car hire can be expensive. ELPA, the equivalent of our AA, runs a national road assistance service. Like all European cities, Athens has its traffic problems. The main roads in Greece are good, but conditions on local roads can be difficult, especially in the mountains. Cars are expensive. A Toyota Carina costs around Dr 6,250,500.

Health care: Doctor and hospital treatment within the Greek national health system is free, but you will have to pay 25 per cent of prescription charges. If you are in a remote area, you can reclaim a proportion of private medical expenses.

Education: Public education is provided free of charge from nursery to university level, and is compulsory between ages 6 and 15. Because of language difficulties, expatriate parents tend to send their children to schools in the UK or, if they can get in, to an International School. The British Embassy school, St Catherine's, in Athens is a preparatory school for British children of 3 to 13 years. The American Community School caters for boys and girls from 4 to 18. The fees vary according to age. Campion School in Athens offers education in English and enters pupils for GCSE and A-level examinations.

Emergency services: police 100, fire 199, hospitals 106.

Useful contacts:
British Embassy, 1 Ploutarchou Street, 106 75 Athens, tel: (30) (1) 7272 600; www.british-embassy.gr/
Greek Embassy, tel: 020 7 734 5997.
Greek Tourist Board, 4 Conduit Street, London W1R 0DJ, tel: 020 7734 5996; www.greece.org.hellas/root/html

Expat information: Americans Abroad, Greece, www.geocities.com/Athens/7243/

Business contacts: www. business.hol.gr/

REPUBLIC OF IRELAND (EIRE)

The economy

Although industry has expanded greatly since Ireland's entry to the EEC in 1973, the economy is still built predominantly on agriculture. Over 13 per cent of the workforce are employed in this sector. Main crops are wheat, barley and potatoes, and the produce of arable farming provides major exports.

Membership of the EU has been advantageous to the Irish, who have benefited from heavy farming subsidies. The EU has also encouraged the development of manufacturing industries, such as food processing, electronics and textiles. The government is also keen to provide incentives to business in all spheres, eg the current tax breaks for movie making. Tourism is the most important part of the service sector and, in recent years, has provided substantial revenue.

A chronic power shortage has recently been transformed by the discovery of natural gas fields off the south coast, although there is still a need to import coal and oil. Although inflation is very low, unemployment and the public debt remain uncomfortably high.

Working conditions

British and EU citizens do not need work permits. The Irish work an average of 40.2 hours per week. Agencies and Jobcentres are more common ways to look for jobs than through the press. The Irish language is *not* a prerequisite for most jobs, although teaching and some civil service jobs are notable exceptions. The normal holiday allowance is four to six weeks per annum. The gap between men's and women's salaries is similar to the rest of Europe, but closing.

Useful information

Banking hours: 10.00 am to 4.00 pm Monday–Friday, except Thursday 10.00 am to 5.00 pm.

Shopping hours: 9.00 am to 5.30 pm; many supermarkets stay open until 8.30 pm, Monday–Saturday. Lunch break in business is usually 12.30–1.30 pm.

Electricity: 220 V, 50 Hz AC.

Transport: Public transport prices compare with those in the UK. Urban bus routes are extensive and are now much improved. Season tickets are good value. One overground urban railway line (DART) services Dublin and runs north–south along the coast. There is an inexpensive, extensive and frequent coach service to all parts of the country. Trains are more expensive, but still cheaper than in the UK.

Ireland's roads have been vastly improved over the last decade with new motorways and road widening. There are international airports in Dublin, Cork, Shannon and Knock.

Health care: Medical care is provided free of charge in public hospitals to all persons who are resident, or are likely to be resident in Ireland for at least 12 months. Out-patient services (eg visits to a GP) are generally private, except for those on social welfare, but exemptions and relief are available. A high percentage of the populace have health insurance.

Education: At both primary and secondary levels most schools are run by church groups (Roman Catholic or other), although largely state funded. Admission is usually possible for members of other religions. Primary education is generally free, and also most secondary education, although many church-run schools (especially in Dublin) charge fees to supplement their state funding; from IR£1,000 and IR£1,500 for non-boarders. Two schools with experience in schooling for expatriate children are Blackrock College, Dublin (12–18) and Newman College, Dublin (15–18).

Media: There are four national newspapers; the *Irish Independent* and *The Irish Times* are the most popular. There are also evening and Sunday papers. Ireland has three national TV stations and national and local radio stations.

Emergency services: 999 (police, fire, ambulance).

Useful contacts:
British Embassy, 29 Merrion Road, Ballsbridge, Dublin 4, tel: 205 3742.
Irish Embassy, 17 Grosvenor Place, London SW1, tel: 020 7235 2171.
Irish Tourist Board, Info Service, PO Box 273, Dublin 8, tel: 353 1602 4000, www.ireland.travel.ie; www.dubchamber.ie/

PERSONAL TAXATION

Residence

Liability to Irish tax (and all references to 'Ireland' in the foregoing should be read as referring to the Republic of Ireland) is determined by the residence, 'ordinary residence' and domicile status of the individual. Subject to certain exceptions, Irish residents are liable to tax on their worldwide income and gains, whereas non-residents are liable to tax only on income and gains derived from sources within Ireland.

Residence status for Irish tax purposes is determined solely by the number of days in which an individual is present in Ireland during a given tax year. From 1 January 2002 the Irish tax year coincides with the calendar year (previously, the tax year has run from 6 April to 5 April).

An individual will be regarded as resident in Ireland for a particular tax year if he or she spends 183 days or more in Ireland for any purpose in that tax year or if he or she spends 280 days or more in Ireland for any purpose over a period of two consecutive tax years.

In the latter case, the individual is regarded as resident in Ireland from the beginning of the second tax year.

An individual who is resident in Ireland for three consecutive tax years will be regarded as 'ordinarily resident' for Irish tax purposes from year four onwards. Conversely, a person will not cease to be regarded as ordinarily resident until he or she has been non-resident for three consecutive tax years.

Domicile is a concept of general law and denotes the place where a person has his or her permanent home. It is distinct from legal nationality and from tax residence. Individuals coming to Ireland from abroad for a temporary purpose, and without any fixed intention of remaining permanently, will continue to be regarded as domiciled abroad.

Taxation of personal income

An individual is subject to income tax on his or her aggregate income from one or more sources, known as 'Schedules', one of which is subdivided into 'Cases'. Income from employment is classified as Schedule E; most investment income falls under Schedule D Cases III and IV or Schedule F. Income from Irish real property is assessed under Schedule D Case V.

Once income has been computed under the rules of each Schedule, it is aggregated and the individual's total income is then subject to tax at progressive rates (of which there are only two). Personal allowances available according to a taxpayer's personal circumstances are given by way of tax credits.

For the tax year 2002 the rates of income tax are 20 per cent and 42 per cent. Husband and wife are assessed jointly, but may opt for assessment as single persons where this is advantageous.

Income from employment

In general, any income derived from an employment with an Irish employer is fully liable to Irish tax. Income derived from an employment held with a foreign employer is also liable to Irish tax if the duties are carried out in Ireland, unless the income is exempted by the provisions of a tax treaty, or qualifies for the favourable basis of taxation known as the 'remittance basis'.

The remittance basis applies to individuals who are not domiciled in Ireland or to Irish citizens who are not ordinarily resident. Under that basis, foreign employment income (excluding UK-sourced income) is taxable only to the extent that it is remitted to (brought into) Ireland.

In order for the remittance basis on employment earnings to apply, both the contract and the paypoint must be located outside Ireland or the UK. For this reason, it is generally beneficial, where individuals are assigned to Ireland by a foreign employer, that they be retained on the foreign payroll.

Taxable income from employment includes salaries, bonuses, gains from share options, directors' remuneration, termination payments, benefits-in-kind and all other forms of remuneration from that employment, unless specifically exempt.

Expenses may be deducted only where they are 'wholly, necessarily and exclusively' incurred in carrying out the duties of the employment. A system of withholding tax on the pay-as-you-earn basis operates to deduct tax and social insurance contributions from employees' earnings. It is designed to deduct the full and correct amount by the end of the tax-year.

Investment income

Irish residents are liable to tax on their worldwide income, including investment income. However, persons who are resident, but not domiciled or not ordinarily resident in Ireland are taxable only on foreign (non-Irish and non-UK) investment income to the extent that such income is remitted to Ireland.

Dividends and interest

Deposit interest paid by Irish banks and financial institutions to Irish residents is subject to deduction of tax at source, currently at the rate of 20 per cent. There is no further income tax liability on such income. Interest income from foreign sources received by Irish residents is liable to tax at the recipient's marginal (top) tax rate.

Dividend income is liable to income tax at the individual's marginal tax rate. Dividends paid by Irish companies suffer withholding tax at the standard rate of tax, currently 20 per cent. This is allowed as a credit against the ultimate tax liability.

Encashment tax, currently at the rate of 20 per cent, applies on the encashment of foreign dividends by Irish financial institutions. This is allowed as a credit against the final income tax liability.

Income from real property

For a resident and domiciled taxpayer, rental income from real property, worldwide, is taxable, net of related expenses, as part of total income. For non-domiciliaries or those not ordinarily resident, see above. Income from Irish-situated real property will always be subject to Irish income tax.

Withholding tax of 20 per cent is deductible from Irish property rents paid to non-residents.

Taxes on capital

Capital gains

Capital gains tax is charged on gains realised from the disposal of assets, currently at the rate of 20 per cent. The taxable amount is generally the difference between the acquisition and sale prices. Relief is given for inflation through indexation of acquisition cost.

Irish residents are liable to capital gains tax on their worldwide gains. Persons who are resident but not domiciled are fully liable in respect of gains from Irish and UK assets, and on foreign gains to the extent that such gains are remitted to Ireland.

Wealth tax

There is no wealth tax in Ireland.

For further information on tax and social security, please contact:
Pat O'Brien
Senior Manager
BDO Simpson Xavier
tel: + 353 (1) 617 0176; e-mail: pobrien@bdosx.ie

Double tax treaties

Ireland has an extensive network of double taxation agreements, currently covering 39 countries, including the UK and the US.

ITALY

The economy

The Italian economy has been growing strongly in recent years but has recently hit recession. The lira has suffered massive devaluation since withdrawal from the ERM.

Italy has few mineral resources, apart from scattered deposits of sulphur, iron ore, zinc and lead, and is therefore dependent on overseas trade. There are, however, significant gas and oil fields which are being exploited, and Italy provides over a quarter of the

world's mercury. Its main exports are machinery, cars, metal manufactures, iron and steel products, artificial fibres, knitwear and
hosiery, and a wide range of luxury and semi-luxury items,
including food and wine of which Italy is now a bigger exporter
than France. Tourism, of course, is a major revenue producer and is
one of the country's largest industries.

Industry is unevenly distributed. The northern triangle –
Milan, Turin and Genoa – produces about one-fifth of the national
output and incomes are well above the national average. There
has been a steady migration of labour from the impoverished
south, both to the more prosperous north and to other EU countries. Successive governments have aimed at developing the
'mezzogiorno' but, despite government and EU aid, the south
has remained relatively poor.

Personal finance and taxation

Managerial and executive salaries are on a par with most EU countries. Income tax rates in Italy begin at 10 per cent and rise to a
maximum of 51 per cent. There are also local taxes, including a
property tax of 4–6 per cent. Italy, however, is where tax avoidance
devices flourish and you should certainly seek qualified advice on
your position if you are going there on a salary at the usual expatriate level. VAT (IVA) is 19 per cent.

Working conditions

Citizens of EU countries can enter Italy freely to look for and take
up a job; they do not need work permits, but you will need a residence permit. Register with the local police within seven days of
arrival. It is also necessary to obtain a tax number which will be
asked for when registering a car, buying a flat or getting a job.

The 40-hour, five-day week has become the general standard
(overtime is rare). Salaries are sometimes paid in 14–16 instal-
ments. Most collective agreements provide for four weeks' paid
leave for wage and salary earners. There are also 10 public
holidays. There is a growing trend towards accumulating public
holidays for summer vacations, so as to minimise disruption. Most
towns also have a holiday on the feast day of their patron saint,

and there are a number of half-day holidays. Employers have to face many additional charges, including a 13-month or Christmas bonus; assistance towards housing, transport and canteens; children's nurseries and kindergartens. Most of these concessions, which are negotiated, are common among the larger enterprises, and, in the case of smaller firms, often arranged through consortia. Some firms have savings plans. There are works' committees in firms employing more than 40 workers. The trade union movement is divided on political and religious lines. It is likely that many of these benefits will be reduced as the government continues its economic reorganisation.

Useful information

Banking hours: 8.00 or 8.30 am to 1.30 pm and 2.30 or 3.00–4.00 pm Monday–Friday.

Post office: 8.00 am to 1.30 or 2.00 pm Monday–Friday, 8.00–11.45 am Saturday.

Shopping hours: Vary from region to region, 8.30 am to 12.30 pm, 3.30 or 4.00–7.00 or 7.30 pm Monday to Saturday; usually closed Monday morning.

Driving: Speed limits are 50 km/h in urban areas, 90 km/h on secondary and local roads, 110 km/h on main roads outside urban areas, and 130 km/h on motorways. Front and back seat belts compulsory.

Transport: Rail fares are lower than in Britain, but some main-line trains require supplementary payments. The main cities are served by a network of toll motorways (*autostrada*), and other highways are in good condition.

Health care: The national health service covers the whole of the employed working population, including registered foreigners. Private treatment is expensive but most foreigners prefer it. Italy has the highest doctor/patient ratio in Europe. A number of hospitals are run by the Church.

Education: There are American and English schools in Rome and Milan. These schools, inspected by HM Inspectors of Schools, include St George's English School, Rome; The New School, Rome;

Sir James Henderson British School, Milan; and the International School, Milan. State schooling is free (although parents buy books and stationery) and most private schools are Roman Catholic day schools.

Emergency services: 113, carabinieri 112, fire 115.

Useful contacts:
British Embassy, Via XX Settembre 80a, I-100187 Roma Rm, tel: 39 06 4220 0001, www.britain.it/
Italian Embassy, 14 Three Kings Yard, London W1, tel: 020 7312 2200.
Italian State Tourist Board, 1 Princess Street, London W1Y 8AY, tel: 020 7408 1254; www.enit.it
Italian Tourist Web Guide, www.itwg.com/

LUXEMBOURG

The economy

Luxembourg has maintained its position as one of the richest countries in Europe. Its central location within the EU and a liberal fiscal climate have attracted a large service sector there, particularly in international banking and finance. To some extent this has compensated for the decline in manufacturing. Both inflation and unemployment are low. Thirty-four per cent of the population are foreigners attracted by employment prospects.

Working conditions

Gross pay is 50 to 100 per cent higher than in the UK at senior levels; many enjoy company fringe benefits (eg car, house).

Procedure for permits is as throughout the EU. A good knowledge of French and German would be valuable as both languages are widely used in business, although English is widely spoken. A knowledge of the Luxembourg dialect may be required for some jobs. All salaries and wages are tied to the cost of living index. The 40-hour week is standard.

Holidays are 25 days for all workers plus 10 public holidays. Most workers receive an end-of-year bonus. Salaried staff sometimes receive extra bonuses.

Useful information

Electricity: 220 V, 50 Hz AC.

Transport: The airport, which is only 4 miles from Luxembourg City, is served by regular British Airways and Luxair flights from Heathrow and Stansted.

Health care: Medical facilities are of a high standard but costly, although social security reimburses most bills. Some doctors have been trained in the UK: many speak English.

Education: There are three schools in Luxembourg which cater for non-national children and are English speaking. The Ecole Européenne is intended for children of EU and ECSC personnel, but is open to others.

Media: Two daily newspapers and a weekly English-language newspaper, *The Luxembourg News.*

Useful contacts:

British Embassy, 14 Boulevard Roosevelt, L-2450 Luxembourg, tel: 352 22 98 64; www.luxembourg.co.uk

Luxembourg Embassy, 27 Wilton Crescent, London SW1, tel: 020 7235 6961.

Luxembourg National Tourist Office, 122 Regent Street, London W1R 5FE, tel: 020 7434 2800, www.luxembourg.co.uk; www.etat.lu/tourism

PERSONAL TAXATION

Residence

An individual is resident in Luxembourg for tax purposes if that individual has either his permanent place of residence (*domicile fiscal/Wohnsitz*) or habitual place of abode in Luxembourg.

A permanent place of residence can be any form of living accommodation, provided that the individual has the use of it for a prolonged period and intends to keep it. A habitual place of abode (*séjour habituel/gewöhnlicher Aufenthalt*) in Luxembourg is deemed to exist if an individual is physically present in Luxembourg for a continuous period of six months, ignoring short absences on holiday.

Taxation of personal income

A resident is liable to Luxembourg income tax on his or her worldwide income; a non-resident is liable solely on income arising in Luxembourg. Income tax is imposed at progressive rates on the aggregate taxable income of an individual from one or more of eight distinct sources, of which income from employment is one.

The top marginal rate of income tax, inclusive of the 2.5 per cent surcharge on behalf of the unemployment fund, is 38.95 per cent, chargeable in 2002 on the balance of taxable income over EUR 34,500). Joint assessment of husband and wife (provided that they are both resident and living together) is mandatory. There are personal allowances available for certain classes of individual (blind, senior citizen, single parent and so forth) but relief for family circumstances is largely given by classifying taxpayers into three classes, depending on their marital status and existence of dependants. The rates of income tax are applied differently to these three classes.

The tax year is the calendar year.

Income from employment

All forms of income from employment, including salaries, wages, bonuses, travel allowances and benefits in kind, are taxable. Reimbursements of expenses incurred on the employer's behalf are generally tax free, as are payments for use of the employee's own car for business purposes, within certain limits.

A minimum standard deduction of EUR 540 is available for non-reimbursed expenses, regardless of the actual amount incurred. An additional deduction is granted for the cost of commuting between home and the place of work, computed according to set rules. Where the employee uses his or her own car on business and does not receive an allowance from the employer for this purpose, he or she may claim a further deduction. Actual expenditure incurred in obtaining and maintaining employment income is fully deductible if substantiated.

Salary tax in the form of deductions from earnings is withheld by employers and pension providers.

Investment income

Dividends and interest

Dividends from both Luxembourg and foreign companies are generally included in taxable income. However, one-half of dividends received by an individual from fully taxable Luxembourg and EU companies and companies resident in a treaty-partner country is exempt from income tax. Generally, withholding tax of 20 per cent is deducted from one-half of the amount of the dividend. This withholding tax is creditable against the individual's final liability. Where foreign dividends have been subject to withholding tax, the grossed-up dividend, inclusive of the withholding tax, is included in taxable income, and the foreign withholding tax may be claimed as a tax credit.

Interest received is taxable, and there is no withholding tax in most cases.

In addition to the half-exemption for Luxembourg dividends, the first EUR 1,500 (EUR 3,000 for married couples) of aggregate dividends and interest is tax exempt.

Income from real property

Rental income net of relevant expenses is taxable. Owner-occupiers are deemed to receive rental income, based on the assessed rental value of their property. The amount of this imputed income is 4 per cent of the first EUR 3,800 of rental value, plus 6 per cent of the remainder. Mortgage interest on a loan to acquire the property or build an extension may be deducted from this imputed income.

Taxation of capital

Capital gains

Gains on the sale of land and buildings are generally taxable as income. If the property has been held for more than two years, the gain is computed by comparing the proceeds with the indexed cost of acquisition. Gains from the sale of the taxpayer's principal residence are exempt.

Gains from the sale of significant shareholdings are also taxable, as are gains from all other assets disposed of within six months of acquisition. There is a maximum rate of 19.475 per cent on gains from assets held for more than six months (or real property held for more than two years). An exemption is available for the first EUR 50,000 of gains realised in any 10-year period. The comparable exemption for married couples is EUR 100,000.

Wealth tax

There is an annual wealth tax of 0.5 per cent on an individual's net assets as at 1 January. Real property is valued at a capitalised rental value generally well below market value. Liabilities are deductible, and there are a number of reliefs. Residents are liable on their worldwide assets; non-residents on assets situated in Luxembourg.

Double tax treaties

Luxembourg has concluded over 40 countries, including the UK and the United States.

For further information on tax and social security, please contact:
Guy Hornick
Partner
BDO Compagnie Fiduciaire SA
tel: 45 123 330; e-mail: guy.hornick@bdo-cf.lux

THE NETHERLANDS

The economy

The traditional image of The Netherlands as a land of bulbs, windmills and wooden shoes is perpetuated for the sake of tourists but, in fact, its modern industrial basis and rapid economic growth have placed The Netherlands in the forefront of European Union economies. Industry accounts for nearly one-third of both the national income and the working population.

It has no natural resources, apart from natural gas and salt in the east. The Netherlands is thus highly dependent on foreign trade and experiences recurrent balance of trade problems. The Netherlands is dependent on overseas suppliers for oil, but has stepped up its natural gas production to counteract this. Trading, banking and shipping businesses are of particular importance to the economy.

Agriculture, though its percentage contribution to GNP has fallen relative to industry, is still important and very efficient. Production continues to rise, with cattle and dairy products, fruit, vegetables and flowers as its principal products.

The main industries include electrical and mechanical engineering, textiles and clothing, steel, shipbuilding, processed foods and chemicals, with diamonds and furs in the luxury range. Oil refining and the petrochemicals sector dominate the Rotterdam area. The electrical and electronics industries are highly sophisticated and produce computers, telecommunications equipment and precision instruments. Coal mining, after being progressively run down, has ceased completely.

That the Dutch are internationally minded is shown in their industrial structures. The multinationals include Philips, the electrical giant, Unilever, Shell and other major oil companies. Joint German/Dutch enterprises have been set up in some sectors. Foreign investment is welcomed, particularly in the development areas in the north-east and south. The UK heads the list of foreign investors, with the United States second. Many of the large British companies have Dutch subsidiaries.

Traditionally a free trade/free enterprise economy, the state role is limited to setting a favourable climate for growth and investment.

Working conditions

Executive salaries are about 30 per cent higher than in the UK; secretarial salaries are roughly comparable.

A legal minimum wage is fixed for all workers aged 23 to 65 and is reviewed at least once a year in the light of movements in average earnings and the cost of living index. Apart from this, wages are determined by collective agreements – the practice of plant agreements has grown with the increase in the size of firms.

Collective agreements usually lay down procedures for dealing with disputes and provide for reference to arbitration boards in the event of failure to settle. The country has been relatively strike free.

Most contracts are written and provide for a two-month trial period. Dismissals and resignations come under government supervision; length of notice is governed by the terms of individual contracts and length of service – for managers the notice period is usually three months. In most industries the 40-hour week has become standard.

Workers are entitled to three weeks' paid holiday and most get more through collective bargaining. Five weeks is normal for managerial staff.

Useful information

Banking hours: 9.00 am to 5.30 pm Monday–Saturday.

Shopping hours: 11.00 am or 12.00 pm to 5.00 pm Monday, 9.00 am to 5.30 or 6.00 pm Tuesday–Friday.

Electricity: 220 V, 50 Hz AC.

Transport: Internal and urban transport is very efficient. Frequent train services link the main centres and there are country-wide bus services. The roads are good and not over-congested. Nearly everybody in Holland cycles and there are special cycle paths on the main roads.

Health care: The Dutch health service is based on a mixture of compulsory and voluntary schemes. The compulsory scheme covers about 70 per cent of the population. Private medical treatment is expensive. The Dutch are healthy, and have the longest life expectancy of any EU nationals. There is a reciprocal health agreement with the UK.

Education: Education is free (though some schools may request a voluntary contribution) and compulsory from 5 to 16, with part-time schooling for a further year.

The British School in The Netherlands is in the vicinity of the Hague and provides for children between 3 and 18 years. The fees compare favourably with other International Schools in The Netherlands.

There is a British Primary School in Amsterdam and a number of other International and American Schools in the major cities – details of these can be obtained from ECIS and COBISEC.

Useful Contacts:

British Embassy, Lange Voorhout 10, 2514 ED, The Hague, tel: 31 70 427 0427.

Dutch Embassy, 38 Hyde Park Gate, London SW7, tel: 020 7590 3200.

Netherlands Board of Tourism, 18 Buckingham Gate, London SW1, tel: 0906 871 7777, www.goholland.com

PERSONAL TAXATION

Residence

In The Netherlands the concept of residence is based on objective facts and circumstances. Court rulings indicate that the place where the spouse and children live is the main criterion for the determination of residence to a greater extent than physical presence.

A resident of The Netherlands is subject to Netherlands income tax on his or her worldwide income. A non-resident is liable to income tax on certain Netherlands source income.

Qualifying non-residents (largely those resident in other EU member states and countries having a tax treaty with The Netherlands containing an exchange of information article) may choose to be treated as resident taxpayers. In that case their worldwide income would become taxable in The Netherlands (subject to the provisions of his or her country's tax treaty with The Netherlands).

Taxation of personal income

Netherlands residents are liable to Netherlands income tax on their worldwide income. For this purpose, from 1 January 2001, income is placed into one of three 'boxes':

- ☐ Box 1: taxable income from employment, self-employment and imputed income from owner-occupation. Box 1 income is subject to progressive rates of tax of up to 52 per cent.
- ☐ Box 2: taxable income from a substantial (business) interest. In general, a 'substantial interest' refers to a shareholding of at

least 5 per cent in a company with share capital. Income taxable in box 2 includes dividends and capital gains, as well as other forms of income from such interests, except loan interest (taxable in Box 1). Box 2 income is taxable at a flat rate of 25 per cent.

☐ Box 3: taxable income from savings and investments. Investments include a taxpayer's second and further residences and let property. Actual income from assets in this category is ignored. Instead, all assets are deemed to yield a fixed income of 4 per cent and this fixed income is then taxed at a flat rate of 30 per cent. In effect, Box 3 income tax is a net wealth tax, at a flat rate of 1.2 per cent.

Non-resident individuals are subject to income tax on certain Netherlands-source income, at the rate appropriate to the relevant box.

The tax year for income tax purposes is the calendar year. A variety of tax credits are available, according to the taxpayer's personal circumstances, to set against the total income tax liability. Taxpayers are assessed to income tax separately, regardless of their marital status, but individuals living together as life partners (if unmarried, they must be registered as living together) are entitled to allocate Box 1, Box 2 and Box 3 assets between themselves as they choose and may claim certain additional tax credits. Non-residents are not generally entitled to these credits.

Income from employment

Income from employment includes all remuneration whether in cash or in kind. As far as expenses are concerned, neither the previous standard deduction nor deductions for specific expenses are any longer deductible. Reimbursements by employers of expenses incurred by employees on their behalf are tax free, however. A commuting deduction may be claimed for travel to work by public transport and there is a tax credit available to employees (a maximum NLG 2,027 (EUR 920) in 2001).

A system of deduction of tax at source (salary tax – *loonbelasting*) operates on earnings from employment.

The '30 per cent ruling' for expatriate employees

If certain requirements are met, Netherlands employers may grant expatriate employees a special tax-exempt allowance of 30 per cent of salary. Foreign employees resident in The Netherlands may nevertheless elect to be treated as non-resident for tax purposes. However, the election has effect in respect of Box 2 and Box 3 income only. With respect to these Boxes, the employee will be liable to tax on Netherlands-source income only. The election has no effect for Box 1 income so that income from employment, for example, will remain taxable on a worldwide basis as for residents proper.

Investment income

Dividends and interest

Investment income falls into either Box 2 or Box 3; in certain circumstances (see above) into Box 1. Dividends from significant shareholdings (5 per cent or more, generally) are taxable under Box 2 at a flat rate of 25 per cent.

Actual income from non-significant shareholdings and deposit interest generally is no longer taken into account for income tax purposes. Such income is tax free, but the taxpayer is subject to Box 3 income tax of 30 per cent on the deemed income (4 per cent) from the underlying assets.

Income from real property

Real property available for letting is a Box 3 asset, i.e. the taxpayer is taxable not on the actual rental income but at 30 per cent on the imputed income (4 per cent of their value). Mortgage and other debt is deductible in ascertaining the taxable value of the property.

The treatment of owner-occupied residences is twofold. The taxpayer's principal residence ('first home') is treated as a Box 1 asset. That is to say, the taxpayer is imputed with an amount of income (at a maximum rate of 0.8 per cent; maximum deemed income in 2001 NLG 17,189 (EUR 7,800)) proportional to the market value of the property with vacant possession. Mortgage interest is deductible.

Second and further homes are treated as Box 3 assets. The imputed amount of income is therefore 4 per cent of the value of each property (net of mortgage debt and secured loans), taxable at the flat Box 3 rate of 30 per cent.

Taxes on capital

Capital gains

Generally, private capital gains are exempt. However, capital gains on the sale of assets that belong to a business (Box 1) or capital gains that have arisen on the sale of Box 2 assets are taxable as income at the rates appropriate to those boxes (up to 52 per cent for Box 1 or at 25 per cent for Box 2).

Wealth tax

There is no longer a wealth tax in The Netherlands. It was abolished with effect from 1 January 2001.

Double tax treaties

The Netherlands has concluded over 65 comprehensive double tax treaties, including treaties with the UK and the United States.

For further information on tax and social security, please contact:
Armand Lahaije
Tax Manager
BDO Walgemoed CampsObers
tel: +31 10–24 24 624; e-mail: armand.lahaije@bdo.nl
or
Hans Noordermeer
Tax Partner
tel: +31 10–24 24 600; e-mail: hans.noordermeer@bdo.nl

NORWAY

The economy

The exploitation of oil deposits in the North Sea revolutionised Norway's economy and transformed its entire industrial and social structure. Thousands of workers left their traditional occupations in farms, fisheries and forests to find work in the rapidly developing oil sector, leading to severe pressure on housing and other social resources.

The government, anxious to avoid too much disruption and the development of a 'gold rush' mentality, proceeded cautiously, limiting rates of production and exploitation, and taking care of the pollution and preservation aspects. It participates in operations, through its ownership of Statoil and heavy taxation of companies. Norway is now the biggest oil producer in Western Europe, accounting for 40 per cent of its exports.

Oil apart, Norway is rich in mineral resources and has taken advantage of its cheap and abundant water power (which meets virtually all electricity requirements) to develop modern electro-metallurgical and electro-chemical industries.

Consumer and service industries have developed, eg food and fish processing, clothing and textiles, but half the nation's food still has to be imported. Two-thirds of the population are engaged in service industries – predominantly connected with oil, shipping and tourism.

The state plans and regulates economic development. The steel industry is dominated by the state-owned concern in the far north. In some cases, the state is the majority shareholder, but most manu-facturing, eg shipbuilding, is in the hands of private enterprise. The government welcomes regulated foreign investment, offering special incentives for underdeveloped and underpopulated areas.

Sweden is Norway's major trading partner, but trade with other EU countries – particularly the UK, Germany and Denmark – makes an important contribution.

Working conditions

In general, salaries are higher than in the UK, but so are deductions, and this is combined with a high cost of living.

The normal working week is 37½ hours and overtime is limited. All employees have four weeks' annual leave, and there are up to 10 public holidays. Industry contributes towards a jointly managed training fund.

EEA nationals

The EEA (European Economic Area) Agreement secures nationals of the EU and EFTA countries the freedom of movement and establishment throughout the area. Under the provisions of the Agreement you may stay in Norway for a period of three months to seek employment provided you are financially self-supporting. Should you succeed in finding work during this period, you must apply in person for a residence permit at the nearest police station, taking with you your national passport, two photographs and a 'Confirmation of Employment' from your employer. You may, however, commence work before a formal residence permit has been granted.

Nationals of other countries

A general ban on immigration has been in force in Norway since 1975. An exemption is most unlikely to be granted unless you have special skills which local job applicants do not possess. If you have received an offer of employment in Norway due to the demand for your qualifications you must apply for a work and residence permit through the Embassy which will transmit your application to the Norwegian immigration authorities. The time required to process the application is normally at least three months.

Useful information

Shopping hours: 9.00 am to 5.00 pm Monday–Friday, except Thursday 9.00 am to 7 pm, 10.00 am to 3.00 or 4.00 pm Saturday.

Electricity: 220 V.

Driving: Foreigners must be particularly aware of Norway's very strict 'drink and drive' laws. Anyone caught driving with more than 0.5 per 1000 ml alcohol in their blood must reckon with an almost automatic prison sentence plus suspension of their licence for at least a year. An alcohol concentration between 0.2 and 0.5 might also trigger substantial penalty.

Transport: Scattered settlements, and the country's topography, used to make transport and communications difficult. Regular shipping services serve the coastal towns throughout the year. There are regular sea/rail links within Norway and with Europe, and Norway cooperates with Sweden and Denmark in SAS, which operates regular air services internally and externally.

Emergency services: 112 police, 110 fire, 113 ambulance.

Media: TV entertainment includes Sky as well as several Norwegian TV channels, with Swedish TV in the east.

Useful contacts:

British Embassy, Thomas Heftyesgate 8, 0244 Oslo, tel: 47 2313 2700; www.home.sol.no/~embassy

Norwegian Embassy, 25 Belgrave Square, London SW1, tel: 020 7591 5500.

Norwegian Tourist Board, 5th Floor, Charles House, 5 Regent Street, London SW1Y 4LR, tel: 020 7839 6255, www.norway.org. uk/travel.htm; www.visitnorway.com

PERSONAL TAXATION

Residence

An individual is deemed to be resident upon arrival if he or she intends to stay, or actually stays, at least six months in Norway. Residence ceases upon emigration from Norway or upon a temporary stay abroad of more than four years. A temporary stay of at least one year terminates residence, provided that the individual can prove tax liability as a resident of the jurisdiction in which he or she is now present. New rules may apply from 2002.

A resident individual is subject to tax in Norway on worldwide income. A non-resident is taxable on certain Norwegian-source income only, such as from employment exercised in Norway.

Taxation of personal income

Taxable income of an individual is divided into two categories: general income (*alminnelig inntekt*) and personal income (*personinntekt*). These categories are not mutually exclusive. Personal income is income derived by an individual from his or her personal efforts. It consists of income from employment; income from self-employment; and the imputed income of a working shareholder in a limited company or a working partner in a partnership.

General income is all income and capital gains from whatever source, reduced by allowable deductions and allowances. It includes personal income (except for the imputed income of a working shareholder or partner).

Whereas personal income is assessed gross, general income is reduced by deductible allowances, such as interest payments, a standard employment deduction (see below); certain travel expenses, expenses for child care and so forth.

The income tax year is the calendar year. A personal allowance of NOK 28,800 (or NOK 57,600 for married couples assessed jointly; both figures applied in 2001) is available as a reduction of general income.

General income is liable to a flat rate of tax of 28 per cent. Personal income, in addition to its inclusion in the general-income base, is also liable to surtax at two rates: an initial rate of 13.5 per cent and a higher rate of 19.5 per cent. Surtax is payable only where personal income exceeds NOK 289,000 (or NOK 342,000 for married couples assessed jointly).

Income from employment

Income from employment includes salaries, wages, benefits in kind, director's remuneration, pensions, termination payments and so forth. A standard 22 per cent deduction (minimum NOK 4,000; maximum NOK 40,300) may be claimed regardless of the actual level of deductible expenses. Where deductible expenses exceed the standard deduction, they may be claimed on an itemised basis.

Expatriates on a temporary assignment in Norway of no more than four years' duration may claim a special deduction of 15 per cent, in addition to the standard deduction, pension contributions and the personal allowance. Most allowances are reduced *pro rata* where liability to tax does not extend over 12 months.

There is a withholding system on earnings.

The maximum combined income tax on income from employment was 55.3 per cent in 2001.

Investment income

Dividends and interest

Individuals receive a tax credit of 28 per cent, which is equal to the general tax rate. This entails that there will not be any liability to pay tax on dividends received from Norwegian companies. Dividends received from abroad are subject to 28 per cent tax.

Interest income is also classed as general income, liable to tax at 28 per cent. There is no withholding tax on interest.

Income from real property

Rental income from real property is ordinary income, liable to tax at 28 per cent on the gross income less deductible related expenses (such as interest and maintenance).

Owner-occupiers have an imputed income based on the value of the property.

Taxes on capital

Most disposals of assets give rise to a taxable capital gain, although there are important exemptions (subject to certain conditions) for the taxpayer's own residence and holiday homes. Capital gains are taxed as ordinary income.

Wealth tax

Resident individuals are subject to tax on their worldwide wealth. Non-residents are subject to wealth tax on the value of assets of a business in Norway and on immovable and tangible movable property located in Norway. Wealth tax is levied at a rate of 1.1 per cent.

Double tax treaties

Norway has a relatively wide treaty network, with over 70 countries, including the UK and the United States.

For further information on tax and social security, please contact:
Hilde Stansby
BDO Revico
tel: +47 22 47 86 00; e-mail: hildes@bdo.ro

PORTUGAL

The economy

Portugal has a population of around 10 million, many of whom are engaged in agriculture and fishing. Industry is 'low tech' and labour intensive. The biggest single sector is services (including public administration) which accounts for nearly 50 per cent of the working population. This probably explains Portugal's relatively low rate of unemployment and reflects a political situation in which various slightly right-of-centre governments have had to make economic sacrifices in the interests of political stability.

Personal finance and tax

Portuguese nationals are poorly paid by international standards. Expatriates could expect to be paid about 25 per cent more than the equivalent rate for the job in the UK.

Income tax is self-assessed annually and varies from 15 to 40 per cent. There is a local tax, and VAT varies from 5 to 30 per cent.

Useful information

Banking hours: 8.30 am to 3.00 pm Monday–Friday.

Post office: 8.30 am to 6.30 pm Monday–Friday.

Shopping hours: 9.00 am to 7.00 pm Monday–Friday, 9.00 am to 1.00 pm Saturday.

Electricity: 220 V.

Health care: Hospital treatment and essential medicine are free, but you will have to pay half the cost of non-essential prescribed medicines. There is a small charge for treatment by a doctor.

Education: There is a sizeable British community in Portugal, a couple of British schools and a British Hospital in Lisbon. Portuguese is essential in most areas.

Emergency services: 112.

Directory enquiries: 118.

Useful contacts:
British Embassy, Rua de Sao Bernado 33, 1249-082 Lisboa, tel: 351 1 392 4000.
Portuguese Embassy, 11 Belgrave Square, London SW1, tel: 020 7235 5331.

Tourist information:
www.nervo.com/pt/
www.portugal-info.nex/
www.ua.pt.turismo/

SPAIN

The economy

Although inflation is low, it is coupled with a high growth rate and high unemployment. The immediate economic prospect is not very good, though the country has the resources to emerge from its present difficulties. Spain has a large and successful agricultural sector and plentiful mineral resources. Tourism is a major industry. Important manufactures include cars, ships, steel and chemicals.

Personal finance and taxation

The principal jobs available for expatriates in Spain relate to employment with a multinational firm. Here international salary standards apply and prospective expatriates at executive levels should earn at least as much as in the UK, plus removal and other disturbance costs.

Spain is no tax haven, and income tax rates go up as high as 56 per cent. Taxes are levied at two levels: national and local. National taxes include corporate income tax, personal income tax, VAT, wealth tax, inheritance and gift tax. Local taxes are: property taxes, municipal gains tax, and various licence fees. Taxes are payable yearly, on 31 December.

Liability for income tax depends on residence (irrespective of whether a person has a work permit or residence permit); an individual is regarded as a resident if he or she is physically present in Spain for at least 183 days in the year. Residents pay tax on their worldwide income. A typical expatriate employee with a dependent spouse would pay 30–40 per cent of gross salary in tax and social security contributions. VAT (IVA) ranges from 6 to 33 per cent.

Working conditions

Working conditions in Spain increasingly resemble those in other European countries, with city offices abandoning the siesta. The normal working week is 40 hours, and overtime (paid at least 175 per cent of normal rates) cannot be forced. Annual leave is 30 days, plus 12 public holidays.

Useful information

Banking hours: 9.00 am to 2.00 pm Monday–Friday, 9.00 am to 1.00 pm Saturday (except in the summer).

Shopping hours: 10.00 am to 8.00 pm, closed between 1.00 and 4.00 pm, Monday–Friday.

Electricity: 220 or 225 V AC.

Health care: Under the social security system, hospital and medical treatment is free, and 40 per cent of prescription charges are covered, but you will have to pay for dental work other than extractions. About 40 per cent of hospitals are private.

Education: State education, compulsory between ages 6 and 14, is free; private education (much of it run by the Catholic Church) is not as expensive as in other countries. There are estimated to be at least a quarter of a million British residents in Spain and these have created a market for private English-speaking schools, which exist in most of the main cities – Madrid, Barcelona and along the east and south coasts and in the Balearic and Canary Islands. Up-to-date information on fees can be obtained from Mr A Muñoz, Legal Adviser, National Association of British Schools in Spain, Avenida Ciudad de Barcelona 110, Esc. 3a, 5oD, 28007 Madrid.

Emergency services: 112, police 91.

Useful contacts:
British Embassy, Callde de Fernando el Santo 16, 28010 Madrid, tel: 3491 700 8200.
Spanish Embassy, 66 Ciltern Street, London W1, tel: 020 7486 0101.
Instituto Cervantes, 102 Eaton Square, London SW1W 9AN, tel: 0171 253 0324.
Labour Office of the Spanish Embassy, 20 Peel Street, London W8 7PD, tel: 0171 221 0098.
Spanish Tourist Office, 22–23 Manchester Square, London W1M 5AP, tel: 020 7486 8077, www.uk.tourspain.es

SWEDEN

The economy

Sweden is one of the world's most prosperous and politically stable countries, rich in natural resources and with a highly diversified manufacturing sector, particularly strong in engineering. Its economy is mainly private. The standard of management is probably the highest in Europe, and the emphasis is on technologically advanced and science-based industry. Sweden suffered from the recession. Unemployment in 1995 was up to 8.3 per cent (the highest recorded level since the war). Recovery is now under way.

The government encourages foreign investment and offers special incentives for its northern and western development areas. UK companies are second to those of the United States, both in number and in the total of employees. Immigrant workers represent about 5 per cent of the labour force, over 50 per cent coming from other Nordic countries which form a common labour market.

Working conditions

Sweden became a member of the EU on 1 January 1995, so residence and work permits are no longer required. Although Sweden has been, and still is, short of skilled workers, it adopts a cautious attitude towards the employment of foreigners. As in Norway, there are openings for people who possess exceptional technical qualifications. Most British people work in a managerial or specialist capacity in a subsidiary or branch of a UK company.

The 40-hour, five-day week is standard, though hours may be slightly shorter for salaried staff. Opportunities for overtime are limited. Swedish workers are entitled to five weeks' annual holiday with up to 12 public holidays. (There is no substitute day if the holiday falls on a Saturday or Sunday.) Periods of notice according to age and length of service are laid down by law in agreements. Employer–employee relationships are highly egalitarian both in practice and in terms of legislation. Possibly for this reason, industrial disputes are rare.

Many employers provide subsidised canteens and contribute towards transport, holidays, health and leisure facilities. They are obliged in certain circumstances to provide language teaching, as well as housing, for immigrants. They bear a heavy proportion of contributions towards social security and pensions.

Useful information

Banking hours: 9.30 am to 3.30 pm Monday–Friday.

Post office: 9.30 am to 6.00 pm Monday–Friday, 10.00 am to 1.00 pm Saturday.

Driving: The Swedes drive on the right. The roads are mainly good and there are some motorways between the main cities in the south. UK and international driving licences are accepted; after two years you must obtain a Swedish licence. The main car manufacturers are Volvo and Saab. A Ford Escort would cost Kr127,700 approximately. If you import a car from the UK it must pass the very strict Swedish roadworthiness examination, which includes tough exhaust emission tests. It can be very expensive to bring a car up to the required standard if it fails. Seat belts are compulsory and the laws on drinking and driving are very strict.

Transport: Public transport is clean, efficient and universally available.

Health care: The level of health care is high, and charges are generally modest (free to the under-16s). There is a fee of Kr 120 for a visit to the doctor; house calls cost Kr 170. Specialist consultation is up to Kr 180. Emergency hospital admission is Kr 180–250 but once you are admitted to hospital your treatment is free. Medication for hospital patients is free, but outpatients and those who are prescribed medicines by their GP must pay prescription charges. The dental service is subsidised, and is free for children up to 18.

Education: State education is free, and of a high standard. A third of pre-school children go to nursery schools run by the communities. Children of foreign residents have special courses in the Swedish language if they attend Swedish schools. There is an International School in Stockholm for children from 4 to 15. The syllabus is American up to junior high-school level.

Emergency services: 112.

Directory enquiries: 07975.

Useful contacts:

British Embassy, Skarpogatan 6–8, Box 27819, 115 93 Stockholm, tel: 468 671 9000; www.british-embassy.com/

Swedish Embassy, 11 Montagu Place, London W1, tel: 020 7724 2101.

Swedish Travel and Tourism Council, 11 Montagu Place, London W1H 2AL, tel: 020 7879 5600; www.gosweden.org; www.cityguide-se/; www.visit-sweden.com

Expatriate information: www.heml.passgen.se/seanon/

PERSONAL TAXATION

Residence

An individual is resident in Sweden if he or she has a 'real dwelling and home' (*egentliga bo och hemvist*) in Sweden. A continuous stay of six months establishes a habitual abode (*stadigvarande vistelse*) in

Sweden, which also makes the individual resident, in this case from the first day. If the stay stretches over two years, the individual is resident in both years.

As soon as an individual satisfies one of the above criteria, he or she is considered resident in Sweden from that date. The residence of an individual and liability to Swedish tax on current income is determined under the same basic rules in the year of departure as for any other, including the year of arrival.

A resident is taxable in Sweden on worldwide income. A nonresident is liable to tax on certain Swedish-source income only. An individual will be taxed in Sweden on worldwide income until the day he or she departs from the country and ceases to be resident.

Taxation of personal income

Income tax in Sweden is levied at both the national level and the local level. National income tax (*statlig inkomstskatt*) is payable on earned income and investment income ('income from capital') whereas local income tax (*kommunalskatt*) is payable on earned income only.

The tax year is the calendar year. All taxpayers receive a personal allowance (*grundavdrag*) to deduct from their earned income for both national income tax and local income tax. The rate of local income tax, which is a single rate in every case, varies from one local authority area to another in a range from 26 per cent to 35 per cent (approximately). National income tax on earned income is charged at two rates. In the year 2001, the first SEK 138,400 of taxable earned income over SEK 252,000 is taxed at 20 per cent, and the balance at 25 per cent.

Income from employment

All remuneration that an employee receives from his or her own labour is regarded as taxable income from employment. Benefits in kind are generally valued at market value. Some benefits – such as meals, an employer-provided car and beneficial loans – are valued according to a standard rate.

As a general rule, income from employment is taxed on a cash basis. Deferred remuneration would not normally be taxable until receipt. An executive about to become a resident of Sweden should consider whether it would be preferable to arrange to receive any previously deferred remuneration prior to entry into Sweden. There is no special treatment for termination or redundancy payments. Generally, only expenses absolutely necessary in the course of employment are deductible, but these include home-to-work commut- ing (within prescribed limits). There is no standard deduction. A withholding mechanism operates on earnings from employment. Non-resident employees' earnings are subject to withholding tax at 25 per cent. If an individual is non-resident by virtue of staying in Sweden for no more than 183 days in a 12-month period, his or her earnings from employment in Sweden are free of tax if borne by a foreign employer without a permanent establishment in Sweden.

Investment income

All investment income is liable to national income tax at a flat rate of 30 per cent. There is no local income tax on investment income.

Dividends from Swedish companies are fully taxable without a tax credit. Where a closely held company makes a distribution to a shareholder who has, or members whose family have, actively worked for the company at any time in the preceding five years, the dividend may be classed as earned income, to the extent that it represents an 'excess yield' from the company.

Taxes on capital

Capital gains

In principle, gains on all types of asset are subject to tax. Capital gains made by an individual are taxable as investment income, but where they arise in the course of a business, they are treated as earned income. However, gains from immovable property and shares are invariably taxed as investment income.

As with dividends, a proportion of gains from the disposal of shares in a closely held company may be deemed to be earned income.

Wealth tax

Resident individuals are subject to wealth tax on their worldwide assets. Non-residents are taxable in respect only of their real property situated in Sweden. The rate of wealth tax is 1.5 per cent on net wealth in excess of SEK 1,000,000 (SEK 1,500,000 for spouses assessed jointly).

Double tax treaties

Sweden has concluded double tax treaties with approximately 80 countries, including the UK and the United States.

For further information on tax and social security, please contact:
Pether Rombo
Tax Partner
BDO AB
tel: +46 (0) 31 704 1318; e-mail: Pether.Rombo@BDO.se

SWITZERLAND

The economy

Switzerland is prosperous commercially, and the main cities are leading European banking and commercial centres. Agriculture is efficient and economic progress has been sufficient to attract large numbers of migrant workers, particularly from Italy. Apart from tourism and banking (crucial 'invisibles' which help to offset the visible trade deficit), Switzerland's main manufactured exports are machines and metal products, chemicals and pharmaceuticals, electrical goods, precision instruments, textiles, clothing and watches. Its main markets are the EU and the United States.

Working conditions

Managerial salaries are among the world's highest.

The Swiss government is at present reluctant to grant visas to foreign workers, and has imposed numerical limits on long- and short-term labour permits. In general, long-term permits are available only to people with special skills or qualifications who have been offered a position by a Swiss employer. Unsolicited applications are, therefore, not encouraged and have little or no chance of success. Similarly, the government has reduced the number of seasonal permits covering periods of nine months or less and annual work permits.

It is clear, therefore, that the best chance of long-term employment is with a British or American firm, or international agency with offices in Switzerland. Once you have obtained a position with a Swiss employer, or UK company based in Switzerland, your prospective employer must obtain the labour and residence permits you need. On entering the country you will need to produce a valid passport and an 'assurance of residence permit' or a visa from the Swiss consulate and an employment contract.

Useful information

Banking hours: 8.00 am to 4.30 pm Monday–Friday.

Post office: 7.30 or 8.00 am to 12.00 pm and 1.30 or 2.00–6.00 pm Monday–Friday, 7.30 or 8.00–11.00 am Saturday.

Shopping hours: 8.15 am to 6.30 pm Monday–Friday, 8.15 am to 4.00 pm Saturday.

Electricity: 220 V, 50 Hz AC.

Health care: Switzerland is, in general, a healthy place to live; however the incidence of AIDS in the country is among the highest in Europe. Expatriates are strongly advised, in their own interest, to join a health insurance scheme from the very beginning. You should seek information from your employer on this point. The insurance should comprise not only medical and hospital treatment but also adequate sickness benefit, since employees have only a limited claim to payment of wages in the event of illness. Most people in Switzerland are insured against illness and accidents through various kinds of insurance scheme. The most popular ones, the so-called *Krankenkassen*, try to exert control over physicians' fees. For private patients and patients covered by other types of insurance, physicians usually charge more, according to income. Specialists, as a rule, charge significantly more than general practitioners.

Social insurance agreements between Switzerland and various other countries make it easier to join specific health insurance schemes and in certain circumstances shorten the waiting period. Under some agreements, moreover, the Swiss employer is required to make sure that an employee coming from the country concerned is insured for medical care (doctor and hospital) and, if not, to take out adequate insurance for him or her; the employer can deduct the contributions for this from the employee's wages. In cases of doubt enquiries should be addressed to the appropriate consulate.

Useful contacts:
British Embassy, Thunstrasse 50, 3005 Berne, tel: 41 31 359 7700.
Swiss Embassy, 16–18 Montague Place, London W1, tel: 020 7616 6000.
Swiss Tourist Board, Swiss Centre, Swiss Court, London W1V 8EE, tel: 020 7734 1921, www.switzerlandtourism.ch/

Tourist information:
www.swisstin.com; www.about.ch/; www.schweizferien.ch/ (good links page)

PERSONAL TAXATION

Residence

The extent to which an individual is liable to Swiss federal, cantonal and communal income tax depends on the individual's residence status. Residence status generally begins with the date of arrival and ends on the day of departure.

An individual is considered resident where that individual has a home where he or she intends to dwell or has a place of abode (a presence of 30 days, combined with a gainful activity, or 90 days without a gainful activity are sufficient to establish a place of abode in Switzerland).

A resident is liable to tax on worldwide income and net wealth, with the exception of foreign real estate and income thereof.

Taxation of personal income

In Switzerland, tax jurisdiction is shared between the federation and the cantons. Each of the 26 cantons levies income and wealth taxes according to its own tax laws. Although the cantonal tax laws have been harmonised to a large extent, the tax rates vary widely from canton to canton. The rate of income tax is inclusive of a church tax (for the Protestant, Evangelic, Roman Catholic and the Christian Catholic Churches), which is calculated as a percentage of the cantonal/communal rate. In addition to federal and cantonal taxes, taxes on income are also levied by the communes (local authorities) in each canton. These communal taxes are usually a straight percentage of the cantonal tax, but that percentage varies from one commune to another.

All tax rates (federal, cantonal and communal) are progressive rates. Married persons are taxed jointly, not separately on all types of income. There are different rates for single and married persons. Significant changes to the method of assessing family incomes are planned for the year 2003.

The tax year is the calendar year. Historically, federal and all cantonal income taxes have been assessed for any two-year period on the average taxable income of the previous two-year period (the previous biennium or *praenumerando* method). Following harmonisation, federal income tax and cantonal income tax in all but three cantons are now assessed on the current-year method. The cantons of Ticino, Valais and Vaud still operate the *praenumerando* system but are expected to adopt the current-year method from 2003.

Income tax is levied on the aggregate income of an individual from a number of sources including:

☐ income from employment (salary, bonuses, stock options and so forth) and self-employment;
☐ income from investments (dividends, interests and so forth);
☐ income from real property;
☐ income from pension payments;
☐ capital gains from real property.

A feature of the Swiss tax system is that private capital gains on movable assets (such as shares, derivatives) are in general not taxed.

A federal withholding tax at a rate of 35 per cent is levied at source on income from Swiss movable capital (such as interest, or dividends from a Swiss source), Swiss lottery gains and Swiss insurance benefits. For a Swiss-resident individual taxpayer withholding tax is reimbursed by way of credit against income tax payable. For non-Swiss residents relief may be obtained, depending on the residence of the taxpayer and the provisions of any relevant double tax treaty.

Income from employment

Income from all employment exercised in Switzerland is fully taxable, whether or not the employee is resident, subject to any contrary provisions in a tax treaty. Taxable income from employment includes salaries, wages, bonuses, gains from share options, pensions, director's remuneration and benefits-in-kind.

Generally, income from employment becomes taxable when the right to it arises rather than when it is actually paid.

For federal tax purposes, expenses that the employee incurs directly in the course of his or her duties are deductible, provided that they are of a reasonable nature. For federal tax and in most cantons, there is no ceiling on the deductible amount. The cost of home-to-work commuting generally qualifies for deduction and is normally based on the cost of available public transport.

Regardless of actual expenditure, all cantons and the federation also provide for a standard deduction also, the level of which varies from year to year.

As in France, there is no withholding tax (pay-as-you-earn) system operated on the remuneration of Swiss-resident employees; social security contributions are, however, deducted from earnings. Tax is withheld from the earnings of non-resident employees.

Investment income

Dividends and interest

Both Swiss and foreign dividends received by a resident individual form part of the individual's taxable income. Dividends from Swiss companies are paid after deduction of a 35 per cent federal with-holding tax. The gross dividend is included in taxable income and the withholding tax may be claimed as a credit when filing a tax return.

Interest from Swiss sources is also liable to 35 per cent withholding tax. The same rules apply.

Income from real property

Rental income from Swiss real property is taxable net of related expenses, including interest. In many cantons, a standard deduction is available (the rate varies from canton to canton between 15 per cent to 30 per cent). Rental income from foreign property is exempt from income tax.

Income is imputed to owner-occupiers and is based on the annual rental value of the property. Mortgage interest is deductible from this notional amount. It seems likely that significant changes will be introduced to this system in the near future. Under the proposed new system, imputation of income would cease and mortgage interest would no longer be deductible.

There is no withholding tax on rental income.

Taxes on capital

Capital gains

There is no federal tax or cantonal tax on private gains from movable property. Capital gains from private real property are taxable, however, at cantonal level.

Wealth tax

No wealth tax is imposed at a federal level.

All cantons and communes, however, levy net wealth tax on worldwide assets, with the exception of foreign real property and a foreign permanent establishment. Assets are generally valued at market value. Debts are deductible. In all cantons, tax rates are progressive and a separate scale of rates exists for married persons.

Double tax treaties

Switzerland has double tax treaties with 63 countries, including the UK and the United States. Negotiations are under way with a further eight countries.

For further information on tax and social security, please contact: BDO Visura

French part of Switzerland:

Roland Etienne
tel: +41 22 322 24 24; e-mail: roland.etienne@bdo.ch

Richard Pochon
tel: +41 21 310 23 23; e-mail: richard.pochon@bdo.ch

Other parts of Switzerland:

Hans Peter Mark
tel: +41 1 444 35 35; e-mail: hans-peter.mark@bdo.ch

Daniela Pupo Conesa
tel: +41 1 444 35 35; e-mail: daniela.pupo@bdo.ch

EASTERN EUROPE

Some trends are now beginning to emerge in the expatriate job market in Eastern Europe: Poland, Hungary, the Czech and Slovak Republics, former East Germany, Rumania, Bulgaria, and the former Soviet Union – Russia and the Commonwealth of Independent States (CIS).

A considerable number of American and West European companies have set up offices or bought or invested substantially in enterprises in these countries, but they are moving cautiously in an undercurrent of instability in the economies of several of them. Mostly they are putting expatriates in the top jobs and hiring locally below that level. They are also sending out middle-ranking expatriates as project managers to kick-start or investigate the potential for new enterprises or to fill specific skill gaps and train locals to take over from them. The area most often cited here is in financial management, a discipline unknown under Communism.

This also highlights a cultural problem that Western managers encounter when they go to work in Eastern Europe. People who have had this experience report that their local subordinates and colleagues are largely unfamiliar with concepts like profitability, decision-making, acting on their own initiative or taking responsibility. Though often technically very competent – the standard of education and training in spheres like engineering is very high throughout Eastern Europe – the extent of management in Eastern Europe under Communism was to fulfil the 'plan', or target in Western terms, no matter what. That accounts, for instance, for the appalling environmental pollution to be found throughout much of the area. In fact, environmental clean-up is one of the areas of opportunity for firms and individual specialists from the West.

The impact of cultural factors on economics remained. Hungary, for instance, has a strong entrepreneurial tradition but not a strong corporate one. Small enterprises are doing better than larger joint ventures between Hungarian and Western firms. The unexpected success of the Polish economy has been put down to the readiness of Polish émigrés to return and train their fellow countrymen in Western ways.

Throughout Eastern Europe, crime is now a new factor to be faced by expatriates. It is a product of rising unemployment, coupled with inflation, both of which are generally understated in the official figures. Average inflation throughout Eastern Europe is reckoned to be around 20 per cent. Prices in countries that were comparatively cheap two or three years ago, notably Hungary, Poland and the Czech Republic, are now comparable with those in Western Europe. Rents are high too, but these are mostly paid by the employer, as are local taxes.

On the positive side, increasingly in Russia also, almost everything is obtainable, though quality remains a problem. This is also true of services. Expatriates report long waits and poor workmanship from tradespeople like plumbers, electricians and telecommunications workers. In fact, the poor standard of the communications network is widely cited as a problem in both personal and business terms.

With the exception of Prague, most of the cities are drab and there is little to do, especially for partners, whose employment prospects are very limited unless they can find jobs in another company with Western connections. Even that is difficult unless they have a good command of the local language.

You can get by in the principal cities of most Eastern European countries with English and German, but only up to a point. Ultimately, learning the local language is inescapable and essential for anyone working there. That is why many of the jobs on offer go to former refugees or their children. European emigrants have a good record of keeping up their native language.

At top levels, what companies are looking for are good general managers who are financially aware, have good marketing skills and can provide some evidence of a track record in the field of international management. Functionally, the job opportunity most widely cited is, as stated above, in financial management. There is also a demand for marketing people. Overall, one of the most important generic attributes that recruiters look for is the ability to train local managers in Western practices and attitudes.

The Middle East

The risks faced by expatriates in this region were enhanced dramatically by the terrorist attacks in the United States in September 2001 and the subsequent military action focused on Afghanistan. The long-term effect of these events is uncertain but expatriates will need to be more rather than less sensitive to local cultures. At the same time, the renewed confrontation between Israel and Palestine ensures that the region remains destabilised.

THE ARAB COUNTRIES: SOME NOTES ON ETIQUETTE

One of the things that worries expatriates about living and working in the Arab world is the idea of having to conform to a society whose customs and etiquette are very different from our own. All sorts of stories circulate about niceties of social behaviour, failure to observe which will mortally offend the Arabs, but most Arabs you are likely to meet will have travelled or studied in the West and be quite used to Western ways. Of course, if, while talking to an Arab, you lounge in your chair in an arrogant or disrespectful fashion, it will not go down well. Nor will it be appreciated if you smoke, eat or drink in the presence of Moslems during the holy month of Ramadan, the time when their religion enjoins abstinence from such activities. But what one is really talking about then is simple good manners, and simple good manners will take you a long way in contacts with members of your host country.

This is not to say that there are not some points of etiquette that you should bear in mind on such occasions as you come into social contact with local people. If you are invited to dinner in an Arab country you will be expected to arrive on time (although Arab guests to your home will be much more casual about punctuality). You should be very careful about admiring any object in the house in which you are a guest because your host may press you to take it as a present, but he will, in due course, expect a present of at least similar value from you. When food comes, you will have more heaped on your plate than you can eat. It is not considered bad manners to leave most of it, rather the reverse, because to leave nothing on your plate suggests you think the host has not been sufficiently generous. If food is being eaten with the fingers (or indeed when you are offering anything to an Arab), use your right hand only; the left is considered impure, since it is associated with what one might politely call the exercise of intimate bodily functions.

If there are long periods of silence over dinner, do not consider yourself a social failure. Arabs do not regard constant talk as a social necessity. Nor should you be taken aback if they ask you rather personal questions – this goes for talk between women in particular. They are not restrained as we are about the things concerning other people that we are dying to know but are always too polite to ask – while hoping they will come back to us in the form of gossip. Nor should you feel the evening has gone badly if your Arab guests leave immediately after dinner. This is customary, and they expect you to do likewise. Incidentally, few Arabs, except the more Westernised and sophisticated, will bring their wives in response to an invitation, and neither will they expect the guest to do likewise.

There are other points of social etiquette as well, and if you are being asked into an Arab home or vice versa, you should certainly seek advice from someone who knows the local scene. It is worth acquainting yourself before your departure with the dos and don'ts of everyday behaviour. For instance, all Arab countries, even the more liberal ones, frown on what the Americans politely call 'public displays of affection' between the sexes. Women wearing revealing clothes are apt to attract attention which varies, according to the country, from what would be described in the UK as rude stares to being told by the police to go home and put on something more suitable. It is unwise to argue with the police in an

Arab country since the processes of justice are, to say the least, different from those in the West. This does not mean, even in Saudi Arabia, that they will cut off some valued part of your anatomy if you are found guilty of a crime; but they will unceremoniously put you on the next plane out of the country if they do not like your behaviour. The public flogging incidents which received so much publicity are extremely rare (as far as Westerners are concerned). This sort of punishment would only be put into practice in the face of the most open and provocative breaches of the law. However, in countries where Koranic law is strictly observed, particularly in Saudi Arabia, there is no right to representation in court and lengthy periods of arrest before trial can occur. On the positive side Islamic law lays great emphasis on the fulfilment of contractual obligations – by both parties.

Drinking is severely punished in the various countries where alcohol is forbidden and it is criminal and foolish to try to smuggle it in. This does not mean to say that smuggling of alcohol does not go on. There are a few places where whisky is available, at prices of up to £80 a bottle. But it is best to leave smuggling to others; and if you are offered smuggled booze be very discreet about drinking it – no raucous parties and avoid being seen under the influence in public.

The maxim about good manners getting you a long way also applies to business etiquette. There will be some things about business contacts that you will find frustrating or annoying but you will just have to accept them with good grace. For instance, Arabs are lax about keeping appointments; and when you do get to the person you may have waited hours or even days to see, all sorts of individuals will probably pop into his office while you are there and interrupt your conversation for minutes on end. Arab customs are also different concerning the acceptance of gifts. This is a tricky one for business people, but a lot of what we could castigate as bribery is the normal custom in an Arab country. This is not to say that you should go about trying to bribe people to get favours – this is generally considered to be a bad idea because, as a Westerner, you would not know who to bribe and how to go about it for a start – but if you are offered a present in a business context you should not refuse it, unless it patently *is* a bribe. To a Moslem, the return of a gift implies that it is unworthy of the recipient and can be a tremendous slap in the face for the giver. It is difficult to tread the narrow path between integrity and self-righteousness, but then few things about leaving home to go and work in another country are easy – though they are nearly always interesting.

One final question that tends to be asked now is whether and to what extent the backlash against Western ways and influence which marked the rise of Moslem fundamentalism has spread. Certainly, there is unlikely to be any loosening up of observances regarding alcohol consumption, dress, religious holidays and so on. More doubtful is the long-term outcome of the robust reaction of America and its allies against the terrorist movements associated with the atrocities in New York and Washington, whose roots lie in extremist fundamentalism.

EGYPT

The economy

Economic growth has improved under an IMF reform programme. Theoretically, with its large population, Egypt could become the manufacturing centre of the Middle East. It is here, in construction and in oil and hydro-electric power, that most of the development is going on and where European expatriates are mostly employed.

Working conditions

A work permit is needed, which must be arranged by the local employer. It is advisable to take a plentiful supply of passport photos and duplicates of essential documents as bureaucracy in Egypt is an industry in its own right and there are many occasions on which form filling, supported by documents, is called for.

Useful information

Government offices: 8.00 am to 3.00 pm Monday–Thursday.

Banking hours: 8.30 am to 2.00 pm Monday–Thursday.

Post office: 8.30 am to 3.00 pm Monday–Thursday. Allow 5 days for airmail post to Europe, 8–10 days to the United States.

_____

Shopping hours: 10.00 am to 9.00 pm in winter, 9.00 am to 10.00 pm in summer. Most are closed on Sunday.

Climate: The two main cities are Cairo and Alexandria. Both have long, hot summers, where the temperature averages 32°C and can be higher, and short winters. These run from November to March and though mild by European standards they do require warmer clothing and a certain amount of indoor heating on colder days. In upper Egypt temperatures are much higher, though it is a dry heat. Alexandria, on the other hand, is inclined to be humid because of its position by the sea.

Electricity: 220 V, 50 Hz AC, but power cuts and unevenness in supply can play havoc with equipment. Plugs are usually the two-pin, round variety. A device called a voltage stabiliser is therefore an essential adjunct to any electrical goods you bring with you.

Education: The local situation regarding schools is quite good but they are expensive.

Health care: Medical attention is also good in theory – Egyptian doctors are much sought after throughout the Middle East – but the standards of hygiene in hospitals can leave something to be desired. Private hospitals are much better in this respect. Egypt insists on HIV tests for anyone staying longer than a month.

Alcohol: There are no constraints on the consumption of alcohol and the practice of Islam, though universal, is not exercised with any degree of fanaticism.

Media: Seven television channels, European Radio Cairo 557AM and 95FM, BBC World Service Middle East Broadcast 639 kHz. *The Egyptian Gazette*, English-language newspaper.

Useful contacts:
British Embassy, Ahmet Ragheb Street, Garden City Cairo, tel: 20 2 354 0850.
Embassy of the Arab Republic of Egypt, 2 Lowndes Street, London W1, tel: 020 7235 9777.
Egyptian State Tourist Office, Egyptian House, 170 Piccadilly, London W1V 9DD, tel: 020 7493 5282.

Country information:
www.touregypt.net/
www.idsc.gov/eg/

www.arab.net/egypt
www.class.eng.ohio-state.edu/people/rashad/museum
www.horus.ics.org.eg/ (Web site for children)
Expatriate networks:
www.outpostexpat.nl
www.expatexchange.com
Community Services Association, Cairo, tel: 202 350 5482.
British Community Association, Cairo, tel: 202 348 1358.

PERSONAL TAXATION

Residence

Egypt taxes individuals on a hybrid source and residence basis. Generally speaking, an individual is considered resident in Egypt if he or she is physically present in Egypt for a period exceeding 183 days in the tax year.

Taxation of personal income

Individuals resident in Egypt are liable to unified income tax on their Egyptian-source income and foreign income to the extent that it is remitted to Egypt. Resident individuals are entitled to certain personal allowances depending on their personal circumstances. Non-residents working in Egypt are assessable to tax on their gross income, generally without deductions or allowances (but see below).

Income from employment

Income liable to tax comprises salaries, wages, allowances, gratuities, benefits-in-kind and all other income related to the employment exercised in Egypt. Earnings derived from employment outside Egypt are exempt from tax. Resident expatriates working in Egypt and acknowledged as having expertise in their field are exempt from tax on accommodation allowances. Employees are entitled to a standard deduction for employment expenses. The deduction amounts to 10 per cent of the employee's income after deduction of allowances. Earnings from employment are subject to withholding on account of tax.

Investment income

Dividends received by an Egyptian resident from Egyptian companies are exempt from tax. Dividends received from abroad are subject to a special tax (the tax on movable capital) of 32 per cent. The same rules apply to interest. Interest from Egyptian sources is exempt from tax. Interest earned abroad is subject, as with dividends, to 32 per cent tax but exempt if the interest is not remitted to Egypt.

Rental income from furnished real property situated in Egypt is liable to unified income tax, net of related expenses. Income from foreign property is exempt unless remitted to Egypt, in which case it is taxable. There is no withholding tax on rents and there is no imputed income for owner-occupiers.

Taxes on capital
Capital gains

There is generally no tax on the private capital gains realised by an individual outside the course of a trade or business. However, a 2.5 per cent tax is levied on the gross proceeds from the disposal of urban land and buildings, whether or not in the course of a trade or business.

Wealth tax

There is no wealth tax in Egypt.

Double tax treaties

Egypt has concluded over 25 comprehensive double taxation agreements, including those with the UK and the United States. Both these treaties exempt earnings of a non-resident from Egyptian tax if he or she stays in Egypt for less than 183 days in the case of the UK or 91 days in the case of the USA, and those earnings are not charged to an Egyptian-resident entity.

For further information on tax and social security, please contact:
Tadha M Khaled
BDO Partner
Zarrouk, Kahled and Co
e-mail: tmkhaled@qeqa.net

THE GULF STATES

Economies

Oil is the salient factor in the economies of all the Gulf States, although the level of reserves varies. Most of these countries are making efforts to diversify into other activities and to invest oil revenues in the creation of infrastructure. Bahrain is developing large-scale industrial enterprises, including aluminium smelting and shipbuilding; it has a longer-established trading tradition and is an important offshore banking centre. It is emerging as a regional centre for technology and light industry. Oman, whose oil reserves are modest by Middle Eastern standards, is developing copper mining and smelting, cement production and fisheries; it also has a programme to expand health, education, communications and public services such as electricity and water. Qatar produces fertilisers and cement, and is also making rigorous efforts to develop its agricultural industry.

BAHRAIN

Oil was first commercially exploited in Bahrain in 1932 and now provides 75 per cent of export earnings. Owing to the gradual decline in crude oil production during the past few years and the fact that present reserves are forecast to run out in the near future, the government is actively encouraging foreign investment in diversified industrial development – with some success. Recent estimates put the population at about 550,000, increasing at a rate of 3.5 per cent a year, one-third of whom are expatriates.

Useful information

Tax: No income tax.

Government offices: 7.00 am to 2.15 pm Saturday–Wednesday.

Commercial organisations: Vary but 8.00 am to 12.00 pm and 3.00–5.30 pm normal, Saturday–Thursday.

Banking hours: 7.30 am to 12.00 pm and 3.30–5.30 pm Saturday to Wednesday, 7.30–11.00 am Thursday.

Shopping hours: 8.30 am to 12.30 pm and 3.30–7.30 pm six days a week, plus Friday morning.

Climate: November–April 15–24°C, July–September 36°C (average), high humidity.

Media: Bahrain Tribue and *Gulf Daily News* English-language newspapers, two Arabic newspapers, one television station.

Useful contacts:

British Embassy, 21 Government Avenue, Manama 306, PO Box 114, Bahrain, tel: 973 534404; www.ukembassy.gov.bh

Embassy of the State of Bahrain, 98 Gloucester Road, London SW7, tel: 020 7370 0092.

Country information:

Ministry of tourism, www.bahraintourism.com/

US Library of Congress, www.lcweb2.loc.gov/frd/cs/bhtoc.html

KUWAIT

The rebuilding of Kuwait, liberated from Iraqi occupation in 1991, is generating renewed opportunities. These expenses are a drain on the economy. However, up-to-date information remains difficult to come by. Certainly, it is not likely to attract any but the toughest, single-status, pioneering-minded expatriates – though for them the rewards may well be considerable. Salaries in Kuwait are still high, and there is a high standard of living, including free education and health care.

Useful information

Commercial organisations: Thursday and Friday official days off, but banks and international companies take Friday and Saturday off.

Electricity: 240 V, 50 Hz AC.

Driving: Apply to Traffic Department for Kuwaiti Driving licence.

Health care: Medical insurance advised; Expacare and BUPA can be bought in Kuwait. Local medical schemes available but with exclusions. Medical required for residence, with entrance barred from sufferers of serious infectious diseases.

Useful contacts:
British Embassy, Arabian Gulf Street, PO Box 2 Safat, 13001 Safat, Kuwait, tel: 965 240 3334/5/6.
Embassy of the State of Kuwait, 2 Alberts Gate, London SW1, tel: 020 7590 3400.

Country information:
www.kuwaitview.com
www.arabview.net/
www.info-juwait.org/generalinfo.html

Expatriate contacts: American Women's League of Kuwait, Kuwait PO Box 77, 13001 Safat.

PERSONAL TAXATION

Taxation of personal income

Kuwait does not impose income tax on individuals.

Taxes on capital

Capital gains

There is no tax on private capital gains.

Wealth tax

There is no wealth tax.

Double tax treaties

There are comprehensive double taxation agreements between Kuwait and 32 other countries including the UK but not currently the United States, although negotiations have started.

For further information on tax and social security, please contact:

Hilmi Mukhaimer
Tax Partner
BDO Burgan
tel: + (965) 241 2651 666 9192

OMAN

Anyone going to Oman, even on a non-business visit, must previously obtain a 'No Objection Certificate' issued by the Sultanate immigration authorities and obtainable in the country by the employer or a local sponsor. The NOC is necessary in order to obtain a visa even for family visitors. This proviso does not apply, though, to visitors born in the UK, who can obtain visas in London for visits of less than 14 days' duration.

Useful information

Government offices: 7.30 or 8.00 am to 1.00 pm Saturday to Wednesday, 7.30 or 8.00 am to 1.00 pm, Thursday.

Business hours: 8.00 am to 1.00 pm and 4.00–7.00 or 7.30 pm, except Friday evening. Businesses closed Thursday afternoon.

Banking hours: 8.00 am to 12.00 pm Saturday to Wednesday, 8.00–11.00 am Thursday.

Electricity: 220/240 V 50 Hz, AC

Climate: Summer 31–48°C and humid, winter 20–25°C.

Media: English-language newspapers *The Times of Oman*, *The Oman Daily Observer*.

Useful contacts:
British Embassy, PO Box 300, Muscat, Postal Code 113, Sultanate of Oman, tel: 968 693077.
Embassy of the Sultanate of Oman, 167 Queens Gate, London SW7, tel: 020 7 225 0001.

Expatriate contacts: Muscat Information Network Centre, tel: 986

677197, e-mail: minco@openmail.minco.pdomus.simis.com
Historical Society of Oman, PO Box 3941 Ruwi, Post Code 112.

Country information:
www.oman.org (excellent links from Oman Studies Centre)
www.omanet.com
www.omania.net

QATAR

Situated on the east coast of Qatar is the capital city and chief commercial centre, Doha, a fast-developing, modern metropolis from which 1080 km of excellent roads radiate to the rest of the peninsula. Other important urban centres are Umm Said, also on the east coast, which is the centre for industrial development, and on the west coast, Dukham, which is a major oil-producing centre.

Useful information

Business hours: 8.00 am to 12.00 pm and 5.00–7.00 pm.

Alcohol: Expatriates can obtain a liquor permit from the British Embassy in Doha.

Emergency services: 999.

Airport arrival/departure: 351550.

Directory enquiries: 180.

Useful contacts:
British Embassy, PO Box 3, Doha, tel: 974 421991.
Qatar Embassy, 1 South Audley Street, London W1, tel: 020 7493 2200.

Country information:
www.qatar.info.com
www.arabnet.com

UNITED ARAB EMIRATES

ABU DHABI

Abu Dhabi is the largest and richest of the seven Emirates which make up the UAE.

The main population centre is Abu Dhabi town, which is on an island 10 miles long and which until relatively recently was little more than a fishing port.

A three-lane ring road including an airport link and downtown tunnel is under construction. Most of the rest of the Emirate, which is about the size of Scotland, is desert. The oasis town of Al-Ain, 100 miles inland, is a fast-growing population centre, however, and is the site of the UAE's university. Oil in large quantities has been found both on and offshore, the centre of the offshore oil industry being Das Island, about 80 miles out in the Gulf.

DUBAI AND SHARJAH

The economy

The UAE is one of the richest nations in the world. Investment in productivity and infrastructure are increasing throughout the UAE. Oil is the main commodity. Dubai is an important banking centre, and its harbour is one of the largest in the Middle East. Abu Dhabi has invested in building up its infrastructure – roads, schools, housing, hospitals, hotels – and developing the harbour. Water is in short supply, so the development of desalination plants is another area of investment.

Personal finance and taxation

Expatriates should be earning considerably more than the equivalent UK salary, with generous fringe benefits: certainly free or heavily subsidised accommodation; provision for medical treatment; payment of school fees or help with them; six weeks' home leave a year, with air fares paid in the case of married men and spells of two to three weeks' leave every four months for bachelors; and probably provision of a car and, in the case of a managerial job, at least one servant. There is no personal income tax and there are no restrictions on the amount of currency which may be taken into or out of any of the Gulf States (but check UK tax regulations if employed by a UK-domiciled company).

Working conditions

Work and residence permits, and a medical certificate, are required in every emirate. Dubai will only issue permits if skills are not available locally.

Throughout the Gulf, you would be well advised to take a supply of passport photos with you, to help speed up the process of obtaining official documents. You should also check for last-minute changes to visa requirements, which are apt to be brought in with minimal notice. At present, passports bearing evidence of a visit or a proposed visit to Israel will still cause some problems though this restriction may be lifted; you are advised to consult your nearest Regional Passport Office.

Useful information

Banking hours: 8.00 am to 1.00 pm Saturday–Wednesday, 8.00 am to 12.00 pm Thursday.

Business hours: 8.00 am to 1.00 pm, 3.00 or 4.00 pm–6.00 or 7.00 pm Sunday–Wednesday.

Shopping hours: As business hours but open until 9.00 or 10.00 pm.

Electricity: 220 V, 50 Hz AC in Abu Dhabi, and 240 V, 50 Hz AC elsewhere, but can be unreliable.

Climate: The region is characterised by hot and humid summers, with temperatures over 100°F, the worst months being July, August and September. Air conditioning and lightweight clothing are essential.

Driving: Check with the local police about driving licence regulations; you will be able to obtain a UAE licence on payment of a fee, presentation of a valid British licence and passing an eye test.

Health care: Most expatriates in the UAE belong to private medical schemes, funded by their employers. However, state-run facilities are generally of a high standard. A health card (costing Dh250 per year) is required for non-emergency treatment at government hospitals.

Education: There are a number of British and International schools with three months' summer holiday, although many parents prefer to send their children to boarding school in the UK.

Alcohol: Available in hotel and club restaurants and bars, but non-hotel restaurants are not permitted to serve alcohol. Non-Moslems are usually able to buy alcohol for private consumption, but in the UAE it is necessary to obtain a liquor permit from the police.

Media: Daily English newspapers – *Gulf News, Khaleej Times, Emirates News* and *The Gulf Today.* Four TV channels. English language UAE Radio Dubai on 92 MHz FM.

Useful contacts:

British Embassy, PO Box 248, Abu Dhabi, tel: 971 2 326600; www.britain-uae.org/

Embassy of United Arab Emirates, 30 Princes Gate, London SW7, tel: 020 7 581 1281.

Expatriate contacts: Abu Dhabi Information Network Centre (Shell employees), tel: 971 2 263016, e-mail: nouland@emirates.et.ae, for children: pincokm@emirates.net.ae

Country information:
www.uae.org.ae
www.uaeinteract.com

SAUDI ARABIA

The economy

The backbone of the economy is, of course, oil. The country is rich in other minerals and much is being done to exploit them. Gold, silver and copper are now being produced. The income from oil has been largely devoted to improving the country's infrastructure, developments such as petrol refining, gas liquefaction plant and other petroleum-based activities, and the expansion of a wide range of manufacturing industries. There has also been a good deal of investment in agriculture to increase self-sufficiency. Another major form of investment has been in various measures of water conservation and deployment and there are now 33 desalination plants.

Personal finance and taxation

Salary differentials between Saudi Arabia and the UK are not as high as they were, but you could still expect to increase your UK gross salary by up to 25 per cent, on average. Salaries are highest in the more arduous, inland posts. These high salaries are accompanied by generous fringe benefits, which include furnished accommodation, ample home leave with air fares paid, a car, medical attention, and free or subsidised education for children in the case of more senior jobs. The level of remuneration reflects the rather arduous social and climatic conditions in the country, which women in particular find hard to take.

There is no personal income tax in Saudi Arabia, and no restriction on the amount of currency that may be taken into or out of the country.

Working conditions

Work permits must be applied for by your Saudi agent, employer or contact in the country. When this is forthcoming you must supply its details to the Saudi Embassy which will issue a visa. This is apt to be a lengthy procedure and plenty of time must be allowed for the documentation to come through. It is a good idea to have smallpox and cholera vaccinations, and polio, TB and anti-tetanus are also advisable.

A particular point to bear in mind is that, if you arrive in the Haji (pilgrimage to Mecca) time, special precautions against cholera have to be taken and certified. Check details before leaving as conditions are sometimes changed without notice. The Saudi Arabian Embassy in London requires all expatriate residents in the Kingdom to undergo an AIDS test before they are issued with visas.

_____

The working week runs from Saturday to Thursday. Work often starts early in the morning, at 7.00 or 8.00 am, with a long break in the afternoon, but working hours are variable, depending on region and prayer times.

Foreigners should carry their ID, driver's licence and residence permit at all times. It should also be borne in mind that exit visas are required to leave the country and these sometimes entail bureaucratic delays before you get them. You also need a letter of release if you are changing employers within Saudi Arabia. The conditions under which you can terminate your employment should therefore be clearly set out in your contract.

Many jobs, particularly at more junior levels, are single status. Where accompanying partners are allowed, you are advised to bring several copies of your marriage certificate.

Useful information

Government offices: 7.30 am to 2.30 pm Saturday–Wednesday.

Banking hours: Vary from province to province but generally 8.00–11.30 am and 4.00–6.00 pm Saturday–Wednesday, 8.00–11.30 am Thursday.

Commercial hours: 7.30 or 9.00–11.00 am or 12.00 pm and 2.30 or 4.30–10.00 pm Saturday–Wednesday. During the month of Ramadan official business hours are 10.00 am to 3.00 pm.

Electricity: 110 or 220 V, 60 Hz AC.

Climate: For most of the year the places where expatriates are likely to find themselves in Saudi Arabia are extremely hot and summer temperatures of 42–50°C are usual. Almost all buildings are air-conditioned. Around Jeddah and the eastern province oilfields, humidity is high and even during the winter season (December to March), it is never really cool. The interior is dry and, though equally hot in summer, can get very cold in winter. Thus warm clothing is necessary in winter in places like Riyadh. There is little rainfall anywhere, although irregular heavy showers do occur in the winter months. Prevailing winds come from the north and sometimes produce uncomfortable dust storms.

Driving: Women are not allowed to drive, which means that they must either walk or take a taxi, unless they are lucky enough to have a chauffeur. In fact, although cars are essential and petrol is comparatively cheap, owning one is not without its hazards. Driving standards are poor but improving; there is no legal insurance requirement, but the compensation that has to be paid for an accident involving loss of life is high. Maximum comprehensive cover and third-party liability are most strongly advised, although expensive. However, the consequences of being involved in a traffic accident are always serious and the Saudi police tend to deal more strictly with offenders than is common in the West.

A car usually goes with the job, in any case with executive or supervisory posts. You will need a Saudi licence, which may be obtained, with a three-month delay, on production of a UK one. Eyesight and blood tests are also required.

Health care: Expatriate jobs generally include free medical attention, and hospitals in the main centres are extremely good. Private treatment, of course, is very expensive – even an ambulance journey to hospital costs around SR600. Oculist services are improving but if you need glasses you should bring spare pairs with you. Sunglasses are also a good idea, because of the strong glare.

Education: There are several International and American schools for children up to the age of 15. There are British private primary schools in Jeddah, Riyadh and Al Khobar. Below this level there are playschools run by expatriate wives. On the whole, taking children of school age to Saudi is not a good idea and in any case places are very hard to get.

Alcohol: It must be remembered that the import of alcohol is forbidden and visitors should not try to take alcohol with them, even in small quantities. The penalties are severe.

Banned products/substances: The import of pork, pigmeat products, salacious literature, narcotics, firearms, games of chance and non-Islamic religious symbols/books is also forbidden. No formal religious practices other than Islam are allowed and discretion should be exercised when *informal* religious practices are engaged in.

Clothing etiquette: Men should not wear shorts in public and there are very severe restrictions on what is considered proper for women in public. Thus, no 'revealing' dresses (décolleté or see-through), no hems above the knee, sleeves at least to the elbow, trousers only if worn with a top that goes below the thighs and, on the beach, one-piece bathing costumes only.

Photography: It is forbidden to take photographs of airports, military installations, or other sensitive buildings such as government offices or institutions and foreign embassies. Photography is better tolerated in rural areas than in the city, but care should be taken not to photograph individuals (without their consent) and particularly not veiled women.

Media: Saudi television has an English-language channel. It is generally possible, also, to pick up English TV channels from Bahrain and other countries in the Gulf as well as Sky News.

Useful contacts:

British Embassy, PO Box 94351, Riyadh 11693, tel: 966 1 488 0077.

Royal Embassy of Saudi Arabia, 30 Charles Street, London W1, tel: 020 7917 3000.

Saudi Arabia Information Centre, Cavendish House, 18 Cavendish Square, London W1, tel: 020 7629 8803.

Country information:

www.us-saudi-business.org

www.saudinf.com

Africa

KENYA

The economy

Kenya is best known for its tea and coffee, which form the backbone of the economy. Other crops include wheat, sugar, sisal, cotton, fruits and vegetables. Tourism is the most important source of foreign exchange, having overtaken coffee in 1988 as the main foreign exchange earner.

Eighty per cent of the population derive their livelihood from agriculture, which accounts for 52 per cent of exports.

There are few mineral resources, but the government is encouraging exploration. The manufacturing sector is being expanded – it includes food processing, canning, chemicals, drink, tobacco, car assembly, paper and printing, metal products, textiles, clothing, footwear and cement. An oil pipeline links the Mombasa refinery with Nairobi.

The government welcomes foreign investment, but it is anxious to see that as much commerce as possible is handled by indigenous Kenyans. As part of the ongoing economic reforms, the government has divested itself of many enterprises, some of which have been sold to foreign investors, who consider the Kenyan atmosphere a favourable one.

Economic development is based on national planning, with emphasis on agriculture and manufacturing and on encouraging export and labour-intensive industries.

Britain and Germany are the principal trading partners and the UK a major provider of external aid, particularly in sending experts, teachers and technical advisers.

There are serious balance of payments imbalances and annual inflation is in single digits. Unemployment and under-employment have remained serious problems, particularly among the young. These are exacerbated by Kenya's rapid population growth.

Personal finance and taxation

Most employers provide housing and make allowances for children's education, cars, etc.

Income tax is charged on total income (including benefits in kind) and ranges from 10 per cent to 40 per cent. Personal allowances are given for single and married people, but there are no allowances for children.

Working conditions

A valid passport is needed, but most Commonwealth citizens do not need a visa, except Australian, New Zealand, Sri Lankan, Indian and Nigerian citizens and British passport holders subject to control under the Immigration Act of 1971. Many other nationalities qualify for a visa-free three-month stay. Entry permits vary according to the type of employment. Applicants must show that they have adequate financial resources and that their activities will benefit the country. It is advisable to check immigration regulations with the authorities, as these are liable to change.

A work permit must be obtained by the employer from the Principal Immigration Officer (PO Box 30191, Nairobi) before the employee leaves Britain. The PIO's permission is needed for dependants to work. Work permits for partners, unless they are professionally qualified, are hard to obtain.

Working hours are as throughout tropical Africa, ie 8.00 am to 5.00 or 5.30 pm. There are 11 public holidays, both religious and official.

Useful information

Banking hours: 9.00 am to 3.00 pm Monday–Friday, 9.00 am to 1.00 pm on certain Saturdays.

Shopping hours: Main stores 8.00 am to 5.00 or 6.00 pm, but many have late shopping some nights of the week and some are open on Sunday.

Electricity: 240 V, 50 Hz AC in most centres and the supply is reliable. Lamps are mainly bayonet fitting, plugs are two-pin round and three-pin flat types. Adaptors are useful when travelling.

Climate: Coastal areas tropical, lowlands hot and dry, highlands cooler with four seasons.

Driving: Roads are of fairly high standard. Driving is on the left. There is an AA of Kenya with headquarters in Nairobi. A valid British or international licence, which should be endorsed at a police station on arrival, is accepted for up to 90 days, thereafter exchanged for a Kenyan one – no test is imposed. The AA and RAC have reciprocal arrangements with the Kenyan AA. Distances are given in kilometres, and petrol sold in litres.

Outside the cities, roads are poor. It may be necessary to have a Landrover-type vehicle there. Many expatriates have two cars, though cars are very expensive. If you have to buy your own it is best to go for a cheaper model; otherwise they are difficult to re-sell when you leave the country.

Transport: International and national air services operate from Nairobi and Moi (Mombasa) International Airports. The main railway line runs from Mombasa to Nairobi and beyond and services include sleeping compartments. Local rail and bus travel are usually avoided. State-controlled taxis and international car hire companies are found at both airports. A private car is essential for people staying any length of time and should be tough enough to withstand difficult conditions. Servicing facilities are adequate in Nairobi, but if you are taking your own car it is advisable to contact the manufacturer beforehand about spare parts, etc.

Health: Kenya is, in general, a healthy place in which to live, apart from the risk of AIDS, which is now prevalent in many parts of Africa and is affecting both the male and female population. It is preferable to seek medical treatment only after consultation with the British High Commission. There are the usual tropical hazards, particularly along the coast. Anti-malarial drugs should be taken.

Health care: Medical standards are high, particularly for private facilities in Nairobi. The National Hospital in Nairobi is managed, administered and staffed at senior levels by British staff. Doctors' fees are expensive, however, and medicines, so bring out what you need. Hospital fees can be reduced through the National Insurance fund but, where insurance is not provided in their contract, many expatriates subscribe to a locally available scheme.

There is a network of district hospitals, clinics and dispensaries, and also mission hospitals. Very remote areas are served by a flying doctor service, which requires a small annual subscription.

Education: Most expatriate parents send their children to private primary schools, but many of these have long waiting lists. There is generally no problem about placing children in nursery schools and kindergartens. The Nairobi International School takes in children for both primary and secondary schooling, though fees are high. It follows the US curriculum but most private schools are geared to that of Britain. There are schools in Mombasa and most other centres; some schools take boarders. There are a number of convent schools. Nairobi University, the Strathmore College of Arts and the Kenya Polytechnic admit students of all nationalities.

Media: The main English-language newspapers are the *Standard, Daily Nation* and *Kenya Times*; there are several weeklies and monthlies and most UK papers can be bought in Nairobi and Mombasa. There is one national radio station in Nairobi with provincial sub-stations in Mombasa, Kisumu and Mount Kenya. There are three TV broadcasting stations and one cable station.

Useful contacts:
British High Commission, Upper Hill Road, Nairobi, PO Box 30465, tel: 254 2 714699; e-mail bhcinfor@aficaonline.co.ke
Kenyan High Commission, 45 Portland Place, London W1, tel: 020 7636 2371.
Ministry of Tourism, Utalii House, off Uhuru Highway, PO Box 30027, Nairobi, or the Kenya Tourist Office, 25 Brook's Mews, London W1Y 1LF.

NIGERIA

The economy

Nigeria is a major oil producer, but during the 1980s much of its oil wealth was squandered and a huge external debt built up. To cope with the crisis, austerity measures – endorsed by the IMF – have been implemented since 1986. Further economic reforms were introduced in 1995, but Nigeria's economic prospects remain disquieting. Corruption is endemic, reforms difficult to implement, the infrastructure is deteriorating and unemployment rising.

Successive governments have been aiming to diversify the economy away from oil, to encourage the development of agriculture and industry, and to overhaul the infrastructure – particularly transport, power supplies and water.

Working conditions

All visitors except nationals of certain neighbouring countries require a visa (easily obtainable for nationals of Commonwealth countries). A visitor's permit will last for a maximum of three months. Expatriates working in Nigeria require a resident's permit and this is obtained by the employer within the quota allowed to the company.

Nigeria acknowledges both Christian and Moslem holidays as well as May Day and Independence Day (1 October). Because of the conditions of working in Nigeria, leave tends to be generous, particularly with companies that operate in other overseas markets. Three tours of three months a year with one month's leave after each tour is not uncommon, although a tour of six months is more normal.

Useful information

Money: Credit cards are not generally used in Nigeria and are accepted in only one or two hotels in Lagos. Credit is not usually given. All retail purchases are made in cash. A cheque from one state to another can now be cleared within 10 working days. Only 'certified' cheques, or bank drafts, are accepted as currency. Cheques tend to be used only to draw cash from one's own local branch.

Banking hours: 8.00 am to 3.00 pm Monday, 8.00 am to 1.00 pm Tuesday–Friday. Some banks now offer Saturday banking from 10.00 am to 3.00 pm.

Electricity: The main voltage in Nigeria is 220 V; however, most hotels/flats have outlets for 110 V electric showers. You need a standby generator because of the supply situation.

Climate: Temperature in the south is generally about 84°F with a humidity almost as high. The rainy season begins in April/May and continues until September/October with a short break during August. Temperatures in the north are sometimes above 90°F and rain is restricted to the midsummer months. The *harmattan*, a dust wind from the Sahara, can be a nuisance to air traffic and is prevalent from November to February.

Driving: Trunk roads linking the various state capitals have improved considerably in recent years. A motorway runs from Lagos to Ibadan, and from Lagos to Benin. However, within Lagos itself traffic conditions are horrendous. For instance, you have to allow about four hours to get to the airport. Poor road maintenance can cause some hazards, and road accidents in Nigeria are very frequent. It is not safe to drive after dusk because of the risk of accidents and highway robbery; be cautious about unsolicited assistance with transport or other facilities.

Transport: Travel by rail is slow and not recommended.

Most state capitals now have airports, the most recent addition being Makurdi, Benue State. Regular services are frequent, but delays can occur because of poor weather conditions. Bribery, known as 'dash', may be necessary to clear customs and immigration. In the north, a private airline links the state capitals, in competition with Nigeria Airways, and has a good reputation.

Where airports are some distance from the town only taxis operate. Care should be taken to ensure that the taxi is properly marked and that a reasonable fare has been agreed upon before the journey begins. Ideally, visitors should always be met at the airports.

Health: Anti-malarial pills should be taken regularly. It is also advisable to obtain immunisation against yellow fever, tuberculosis, typhoid, tetanus, polio, cholera, and hepatitis A and B. There were epidemics of spinal meningitis, gastroenteritis, cholera and measles in the north of the country in early 1996. AIDS is also a problem in this area. Water should always be boiled and fruit and salads carefully cleaned. Swimming pools can be a health hazard and advice should be sought from residents. Exposure to the sun can be a danger, particularly in the north. If there is a need to be hospitalised, it is best to return home if possible. AIDS is now prevalent in many parts of Africa, and is affecting both the male and female population.

Health care: It is advisable to seek such treatment only after consultation with the British High Commission. State hospitals have difficulty in maintaining international standards of hygiene, while private hospitals tend to be expensive and commercially orientated.

Education: Most expatriates send their children to UK boarding schools at an early age and certainly for secondary education. There are private International Schools, often staffed by Europeans and which cater well for ages 5 to 9 and provide a congenial atmosphere, in Lagos, Ibadan, Kano and Kaduna. Fees tend to be somewhat higher than in equivalent schools in the United Kingdom.

Communications: The telephone system is notoriously inefficient. While it is now possible, within Nigeria, to call most of the major cities direct in theory, in practice it requires a lot of patience, owing to the overcrowded telephone system. International direct dialling services are being introduced and calls can be made direct to the UK from certain phones, including those at the offices of NITEL (Nigerian Telecommunications).

International post takes a minimum of six days (airmail) and four to six weeks by surface mail. Documents are better despatched by courier, particularly as mail can get mislaid. Internal post takes about 7 to 10 days.

There are some fax machines in Nigeria, but it is not a common means of communication as it relies on an already congested telephone system.

Special note: The newcomer to Nigeria should understand that, while with care he or she will probably have a trouble-free tour, there is a crime problem in Nigeria. While appropriate precautions will vary from time to time, it is generally not considered safe to travel out of town at night.

Useful contacts:

British Deputy High Commission, 11 Louis Farrakhan Crescent, Victorial Island (Private Mail Bag 12136), tel: 234 1 2619531.

British High Commission, Dangote House, Aguyi Uribsu/stret, Maitama District, Abuja, tel: 234 9 413 2010.

Nigerian High Commission, Nigeria House, 9 Northumberland Avenue, London WC2, tel: 020 7839 1244.

PERSONAL TAXATION

Residence

Nigeria taxes individuals on the basis of residence. A person is deemed to be resident in Nigeria if he or she has stayed in the country for a period of 183 days or more within a 12-month period commencing in a calendar year and ending either within the calendar year or the following year. This implies that if the total period of stay exceeds 183 days within 12 months spanning parts of two consecutive calendar years, such individual would be liable to pay income tax in Nigeria for the two relevant years of assessment.

The issue of residence is determined by the state in which an individual is deemed to be resident at the beginning of any particular year of assessment. The tax due on the individual's income is therefore payable to that state and not to the federal government.

Taxation of personal income

Personal income tax is levied under the Personal Income Tax Decree No. 104 of 1993. The Decree regulates personal income tax throughout the federation and establishes the procedure for determining the total income of a taxpayer for tax purposes. There is thus one uniform law throughout the federation, but income tax accrues to each state and not to the federation. The provisions of the decree apply to foreigners working in Nigeria for as long as they are resident.

An individual is liable to income tax on his total income, which consists of earned income (such as income from employment) and unearned income (such as income from investments).

Certain allowances are available to taxpayers depending on their personal circumstances, in addition to reliefs specific to certain sources of income. The tax year is the calendar year. Income tax is charged at progressive rates of between 5 per cent and 25 per cent. An individual is liable to minimum tax at the rate of 0.5 per cent of total income if the reliefs and allowances exceed the total income or the regular tax computed is less than this minimum tax.

Income from employment

Employment income means income derived through working in Nigeria irrespective of whether the employer is in Nigeria or not, and no matter where the income is disbursed.

Taxable income from employment includes all kinds of remuneration, whether in cash or in kind, such as salaries, bonuses, cost-of-living allowances, gains from share options, employer-provided cars and so forth.

Only specific expenses, such as professional subscriptions necessary for the individual's employment, are deductible from employment income. There is no standard deduction.

A pay-as-you-earn system of deduction from earnings operates, and is designed to deduct the correct amount of tax from the employee by the end of the tax year.

Investment income

Dividends and interest

Investment income is income earned outside paid employment such as dividend, rental income, interest income, and so forth, and it is subject to withholding tax in Nigeria at the rate of 10 per cent. For personal income tax purposes, the income is grossed up and forms part of the individual's unearned income. However, the 10 per cent tax withheld from Nigerian dividends is a final tax, and dividends are consequently not aggregated with other income.

However, withholding taxes suffered by deduction at source

from other investment income may be offset against the total tax payable.

Income from real property

Rental income from real property is taxable as unearned income, less relevant expenses. As with other investment income, rents are subject to withholding tax of 10 per cent.

Taxes on capital

Capital gains

Individuals resident in Nigeria are liable to capital gains tax on gains arising from the disposal of their assets worldwide. However, gains from shares and securities and motor vehicles commonly used for carrying passengers are exempt. The rate of capital gains tax is 10 per cent of the chargeable gain and it is payable to the state where the individual resides, and not to the federal government.

Wealth tax

There is no wealth tax either at the federal or at the state level.

Double tax treaties

Nigeria has a limited number of comprehensive tax treaties in effect. There are treaties with the UK, Belgium, Canada, France, the Netherlands and Romania, but not currently with the US.

For further information on tax and social security, please contact:
E O Olabisi
Partner
BDO Oyediren Faleye Oke and Co
tel: +234 1–4922953/4922943/4922964/471069;
e-mail: eo.olabisi@cyberspace.net.ng

SOUTH AFRICA

The economy

Since the lifting of sanctions at the end of 1993, and the election of a government of national unity, inward investment into South Africa has been able to give a boost to industry, and provide funds for housing, jobs and education. However, the impact of the continuing weakness of the rand, while favourable to exports, has been unfavourable to sustained investment and economic growth remains disappointing.

Working conditions

South Africa has lately been declining in the world salary league table. Fringe benefits are not a significant part of remuneration, although managerial jobs generally earn a car and holidays tend to be generous, six weeks a year being frequently quoted. Free or subsidised medical aid schemes are frequently offered to more senior people. If these are not available such costs, and they are considerable, should be borne in mind in assessing the true value of the remuneration package.

There is a wide variety of indirect sales duties, the most significant of which is on cars. The remission of duty on personal effects is marginal and it is not worth bringing a car into South Africa.

If you are an approved immigrant you may, however, import one motor vehicle per family under full rebate of customs duty (but subject to VAT), provided that the motor vehicle has been owned and used by you and registered in your name, in your country of residence, for at least 12 months before your departure and before the date on which it was shipped to South Africa.

There are no restrictions on the amount of foreign currency you can bring in, but strict exchange control regulations are in force on taking money out of South Africa. For this reason, it is advisable to transfer no more of your assets than you need to South Africa unless you are absolutely sure you want to stay there.

At executive and professional level, working conditions (ie hours and leave) are very similar to those in the UK. There has been little industrial unrest in South Africa, though it has increased recently. Wages are fixed by industrial councils and vary according to occupation and region. Welfare benefits are minimal compared with the UK, although healthcare is now free, and numerous private schemes for medical care, pensions, disability, etc do exist on a contributory basis and about 85 per cent of the white population belong to a scheme of some kind.

There is an active immigration scheme and most UK professional qualifications are recognised in South Africa. The scheme is selective, the criteria being primarily the state of the economy at the time and the extent to which the applicant's qualifications and experience fit in with its needs. However, immigrants are not allowed to change occupation without approval for three years after their arrival in South Africa. This is related to the availability of work. Prospective immigrants should write to the Chief Migration Officer, South African High Commission, Trafalgar Square, London WC2N 5DP for further information.

Useful information

Climate: South Africa's climate is excellent, though by no means uniform. There is quite a difference at all times of the year between semi-tropical Natal, the Mediterranean climate of the Western Cape and the dry, cold winters and hot, thunderstormy summers of Johannesburg.

Education: Education in state schools is free, but schools are allowed to charge a small fee to cover miscellaneous expenses. There are, of course, plenty of private fee-paying schools as well. Children who will not have reached the age of six before 1 July of the year of admission will not be allowed to attend school, even if they have done so previously. The school year begins after the Christmas holiday. It should be noted that the syllabus and atmosphere of South African schools is markedly more traditional and restrictive than is the case in most other countries. University education is not free.

Useful contacts:
British High Commission, 91 Parliament Street, Cape Town 8001,
  tel: 27 21 461 7220; www.britain.org.za/
South African High Commission, South Africa House, Trafalgar
  Square, London WC2, tel: 020 7312 5000.
South Africa Tourist Board, 5–6 Alt Grove, Wimbledon, London
  SW19 4DZ, tel: 906 364 0600; www.satour.co.za/; www.satour.org

PERSONAL TAXATION

Residence

The residence basis of taxation of individuals came into effect in
South Africa on 1 January 2001 and applies to tax years
commencing on or after that date, effectively from the tax year
2001–2.

A natural person is resident in South Africa where he or she is
'ordinarily resident' in South Africa or he or she is physically
present in South Africa for more than 91 days in the current year
and in the preceding three years for more than 549 days in
aggregate.

'Ordinary residence' is akin to the UK concept of domicile. An
individual is ordinarily resident in the jurisdiction that he or she
regards as home and to which he or she naturally and eventually
intends to return. Thus an individual who is physically absent
from South Africa for many years may still be considered resident
there for tax purposes.

However, an individual who satisfies the physical-presence test
but is absent for a continuous period of 330 days or more, is
regarded as ceasing to be resident from the day of departure.

Non-residents are taxed on income with its source in South
Africa.

Taxation of personal income

An individual resident in South Africa is liable to income tax on
income from one or more of five distinct sources:

- [ ] income from employment;
- [ ] income from business;
- [ ] income from rents;
- [ ] investment income;
- [ ] miscellaneous income.

The tax year runs from 1 March to 28/29 February.

Individuals are separately assessed for income tax and there is no joint assessment of married couples.

Personal allowances, in the form of tax credits, are available to taxpayers depending on their personal circumstances. There is in addition a tax-free threshold whereby individuals pay no tax if their taxable income falls below that threshold. For 2002–3, the threshold for persons under 65 is ZAR 22,000. Where taxable income exceeds the threshold, income tax is levied at progressive rates ranging from 18 per cent to 40 per cent (on the slice of taxable income exceeding ZAR 240,000).

Income from employment

All types of remuneration, whether in cash or in kind, received by an employee in return for services rendered in the course of the employment are taxable as income from employment.

Taxable benefits in kind include travelling allowances, company vehicles, low-interest loans, subsistence allowances, residential accommodation, entertainment and so forth.

Certain deductions are allowed against employment income, such as medical expenditure, entertainment, donations to public-benefit organisations, and contributions to pensions, retirement annuity and provident funds, subject to certain limits.

A pay-as-you-earn system of deductions operates on earnings, and is designed to deduct the correct amount of tax by the year end.

Investment income

Dividends and interest

Dividends from a South African source (local dividends) are exempt from tax in the hands of a resident individual whereas foreign dividends are taxable in full. Non-residents are also exempt from tax on South African dividends.

Interest earned by a resident is fully taxable except for the first ZAR 6,000 (ZAR 10,000 if the person is over 65 years of age), which is exempt. Interest earned by a non-resident from a South African source is exempt from normal South African income tax.

Income from real property

Rental income from real property is taxable in full, after deduction of related expenses. Residents are liable in respect of worldwide property; non-residents in respect only of property situated in South Africa. There is no withholding tax on rental income and no imputed income from owner-occupation.

Taxes on capital

Capital gains

Taxation of capital gains was introduced in South Africa with effect from 1 October 2001. Residents are subject to tax on worldwide gains; non-residents only on gains made on immovable property situated in South Africa and gains made on assets of a permanent establishment belonging to the non-resident. The rate currently applicable to individuals is 10 per cent.

Wealth tax

There is no wealth tax.

Double tax treaties

South Africa has an expanding network of double tax treaties. Currently, over 50 comprehensive treaties, including those with the UK and the United States, are in effect.

For further information on tax and social security, please contact:
Kemp Munnik
Tax Director
BDO Spencer (Steward) (Johannesburg) Inc
tel: +21 (011) 643 7271; e-mail: kmunnik@bdo.co.za

ZAMBIA

The economy

The economy is based on copper, which accounts for about 95 per cent of foreign exchange earnings, and is highly sensitive to fluctuations in world copper prices. As a result of falling world copper prices and increased oil prices Zambia has faced serious economic difficulties and a huge balance of payments deficit.

About 50 per cent of the people are engaged in agriculture, the main crops being tobacco, sugar and maize. Farming is on a subsistence basis. Like other developing countries, Zambia has adopted national plans to develop and improve its farming, encourage diversification and reduce its dependence on imports. The scale of manufacture is still small, but a wide range of industries has been, or is being, established, such as food and tobacco processing, grain milling, production of steel sheets, cotton, furniture, clothing, plastics, cement, beer, soap and detergents, fertilisers and copper products, and vehicle assembly.

There is still a shortage of technical and qualified manpower. Many white mining technicians have left the country to work in the Middle East or South Africa. Government policy aims to entice back qualified Zambians who have left for other countries offering better wages and conditions.

Outside the Copperbelt and the main towns there is little paid employment and considerable poverty.

Personal finance and taxation

Expatriate employees of overseas companies usually receive benefits such as a car, a house, travel and education allowances, which vary from company to company.

Expatriate inducement allowances are subject to taxation and the government intend to abolish inducement allowances altogether except for those professions such as medicine where there is a shortage of qualified Zambians.

Personal income tax ranges from 15 per cent to 35 per cent.

Working conditions

Visas are not required by holders of valid UK passports. Expatriates need a work permit, obtainable by the prospective employer from the Chief Immigration Officer (PO Box 31984, Lusaka). Dependants are not allowed to work without his permission. There are limited opportunities for women to work as doctors, nurses and teachers, but the authorities can be reluctant to issue work permits to expatriate wives. Voluntary work, however, is possible.

Working hours are as in other parts of tropical Africa, ie 8.00 am to 4.00 or 5.00 pm. There are 12 official public holidays. Leave arrangements for expatriates are negotiated individually.

Expatriates are usually expected to train Zambians working under them to acquire higher skills. This may not be explicitly stated, but it is assumed that sooner or later a job will be 'Zambianised'.

Useful information

Electricity: 230V, 50 Hz AC, available in towns; many people in country areas use bottled gas or paraffin.

Climate: Because of its altitude, the climate is temperate, with extremes of heat and cold in summer and winter. The rainy season is December–March.

Driving: The Zambians are exuberant drivers and have one of the world's highest accident rates. New arrivals in the country would be well advised to hire a car with a driver. Indeed, some companies employ drivers for their staff and these drivers' services may be available, for an additional payment, out of office hours.

If you wish to drive yourself, you could consider bringing your own car. New immigrants are allowed under existing regulations to import one car per family duty free provided that the vehicle has been in their possession, or they have proof that they ordered it before their departure to Zambia, and provided that it arrives within six months of their own arrival in Zambia. Otherwise duty and sales tax will be payable – roughly 84 per cent of the CIF value. There is a further excise duty on saloon cars of 25 per cent on those with 1500 cc or less engine capacity and 20 per cent on those over 1500 cc. (Advice on exporting a car can be obtained from the RAC.)

Foreign exchange payment for imported cars, many of which come from South Africa, must be proved to come from a source outside Zambia. Imported new cars can therefore be purchased partly in foreign exchange (covering the cost of the unit plus freight charges) and partly in kwacha (covering local elements of duty, sales tax, clearing charges, profit, etc). In order to drive in Zambia, you will have to take the Zambian driving test; this takes a long time to arrange and there is a high failure rate. An international permit is valid for one year. Be careful about security – car thefts are frequent.

Transport: There are internal air services serving five major centres. Zambia Airways operates flights to the United Kingdom and leading African countries. There is a single-track railway system from Livingstone to the Copperbelt, and the Tazara railway, covering nearly 1600 miles, serves 147 stations between central Zambia and Dar es Salaam, in Tanzania. Cross-country rail or bus travel is not recommended.

Most main roads are tarred, though secondary roads have potholed gravel or earth surfaces. Express buses link Lusaka with Livingstone and the Copperbelt, but urban transport is not much used by Europeans. Taxis and self-drive cars can be hired in Lusaka and other towns. Most car-hire firms do not permit self-drive.

Health: Health standards have declined in recent years with cholera becoming endemic, particularly during the rainy season, and an increase in strains of choloroquine resistant and cerebral malaria. AIDS is prevalent with an estimated 25 per cent of the adult population being HIV infected. However, Zambia is generally a healthy place, in part because of its elevation.

Health care: Hospital and medical treatment carry only nominal fees, but there is a severe shortage of doctors, nurses, medical equipment and drugs. Dentists are few and far between. Most expatriate employers subscribe to private medical practices. The mining companies have their own hospitals and provide medical services for their personnel and families.

Education: Zambian state schools are geared towards Zambian needs and classes are often overcrowded and facilities poor to non-existent. For expatriates in Lusaka there are four private schools, all of which have long waiting lists. There are also privately run Italian, French and Scandinavian schools and a limited choice of nursery schools for which there are long waiting lists. Elsewhere throughout Zambia there are a few other private schools and in the Copperbelt there are also trust schools and two private schools: Simba and Lechwe in Ndola and Kitwe respectively. Most expatriates send their children to be educated in the UK, Zimbabwe or South Africa from the age of 10, although some use home-teaching methods.

Media: Broadcasting on TV and radio stations is in English. There are two daily newspapers – the *Times of Zambia* and the *Zambia Daily Mail* – and four weeklies – the *Weekly Post*, the *Standard*, the *Financial Mail* and the *National Mirror*.

Useful contacts:

British High Commission, Independence Avenue, PO Box 50050, 15101 Lusaka, tel: 260 1 251133; e-mail: brithc@zamnet.zm

Zambian High Commission, 2 Palace Gate, Kensington, London W8 5NG, tel: 020 7589 6655.

Zambian National Tourist Board, 2 Palace Gate, Kensington, London W8 5NG, tel: 020 7589 6343; www.africa-insites.com/zambia/

ZIMBABWE

The economy and political climate

Under the restrictive regime of Robert Mugabe the economy is disintegrating and democracy is under attack. For the time being Zimbabwe must be considered a hostile environment for European and American expatriates and you should think carefully before accepting any offer of employment there.

Useful information

Shopping hours: 8.00 am to 5.00 pm, though some stores stay open longer.

Duty: You need receipts of purchase on items you bring in that are less than six months old because duty is charged. Personal effects can be imported duty free but be prepared for a long wait to clear customs. The authorities will want serial numbers of luxury and electrical items to check that, when you leave, you take out what you brought in. Come armed with a list of numbers. If any goods are impounded pending customs clearance, ensure that you obtain an official receipt and try to determine where they have been put to facilitate claiming at a later date.

Climate: Because of Zimbabwe's elevation the climate is healthy and pleasant, with a daily maximum temperature of 80–90°F for most of the year. The rainy season is from November to March; it is warm and dry from August to October and cool and dry from May to August. There is no need for air conditioning.

Driving: A private car is essential. Many models can be bought locally and there is a wide choice of French, German and Japanese cars. Automatic cars are also available and taxis are reliable. It is advisable to take a valid international driving permit. Strictly speaking, an international permit is valid for nine months; thereafter you require a Zimbabwe licence for which you will have to take a test. A UK licence is not valid because it has no photograph.

Transport: There is an excellent system of main and feeder roads, with traffic control in cities and suburbs. Rail connections link the country with South Africa, Mozambique, Botswana and Zambia, and there are international flights connecting with the United Kingdom and South Africa, as well as domestic services from Harare to Bulawayo, Kariba, Hwange and Masvingo.

Health care: Medical services were adequate but some Zimbabweans prefer to go to South Africa or Britain for more advanced treatment and there have been some recent shortages of medical drugs. Check whether you are going to a malarial zone. Deltaprim tablets are recommended. There is a medical aid health system.

Education: There are both nursery schools and private schools, fees for which vary considerably with waiting lists for all good schools, both government and private. You would be well advised to see what strings your employer can pull.

Communications: The telephone system is grossly overloaded and is one of the biggest frustrations. Private individuals often put up with party lines. An internal call can take a long time. Sometimes even a call booked with the operator can involve a wait of two hours. International calls are relatively easy provided you dial outside working hours. The postal service is generally good, if a little slow sometimes.

Media: There are two English-language daily papers: the *Chronicle* and the *Herald*.

Useful contacts:
British High Commission, Corner House, Samora Machel Avenue/ Leopold Takarwira Street, PO Box 4490, Harare, tel: 263 4 772990.

Zimbabwe High Commission, 429 Strand, London WC2, tel: 020 7836 7755.

Zimbabwe Tourist Office, Zimbabwe House, 429 The Strand, London WC2R 0QE, tel: 020 7240 6169.

The American Continent

CANADA

The economy

Canada is basically a very rich country, but its economy tends to follow closely that of its neighbour, the United States.

Canada produces 20 per cent of the world's wheat; 42 per cent of the land is forested. Canada is one of the largest producers of valuable minerals and is also a major exporter of automotive, timber and paper products. Most trade is with the USA, particularly following the North American Free Trade Agreement in late 1993. Nevertheless, Canada has suffered recession recently, with some areas being very hard hit.

Working conditions

The general working atmosphere and corporate style in Canada closely resemble those of the United States, but Canadian society is more stable, with lower crime figures. If you go to Canada intending to stay more than three months, you have to register this fact on arrival. You cannot change your status from visitor while in-country. Worker visas or applications for permanent residence must be made beforehand.

An average executive job, requiring graduate or professional-level qualifications and some five years or so of experience, would command an annual salary of between C$75,000 and C$100,000. A senior managerial job would be worth C$125,000 to C$175,000, plus

10 per cent to 30 per cent bonus. By and large, executive salaries are higher than at home, becoming more equal going down the scale.

Professional groups that are in demand include mathematicians, sales and advertising personnel, chemists and physicists. It is also possible to emigrate if you have capital available or intend to run a business in Canada under the business immigration programme. Other schemes include Temporary Employment Authorisation, Student Working Holidays, and Live-in Caregiver Programme.

In the public services preference is given to Canadian citizens and here, as well as in many private sector jobs, a knowledge of French is essential. It should not be assumed that the status of French in Canada is merely a nationalistic gesture. It is the mother language of many Canadian citizens. However, people who do not speak it may still enter public service, as provisions will be made for them to learn the language subsequently.

People who want to exercise professional skills will have to apply to the appropriate professional bodies and institutes to make sure that their qualifications are recognised. In some cases where training to achieve the qualifications in question is substantially different in Canada, further examinations may have to be taken to achieve recognition. In all instances, though, documentary proof of degrees, etc, should be taken with you, as well as such personal documents as birth and marriage certificates. Visit the immigration information Web site at www.canada.org.uk\ visa-info\\

Useful information

Climate: Canadian winters are much colder than anything one is accustomed to in temperate zones, although similar to Scandinavia. This is true even in the population centres in the southern part of the country. If you are to arrive in Canada any time between October and March make sure you have plenty of warm clothes. On the other hand, the summer (June to September) can be very warm, with temperatures averaging around 90°F in midsummer in southern places like Toronto.

Electricity: 120V, 60 Hz; conversion from other voltages is not really possible.

Health care: Canada operates a national health insurance programme, which is administered by the provinces, for both hospital and ordinary medical (though not dental) care. In all provinces except Quebec and British Columbia, which impose a brief residence qualification (though in the case of Quebec only for hospital insurance), these are available to immigrants immediately on arrival and you should be sure to obtain details of registration and premium payments as soon as possible. Many employers pay the employee's contribution as part of the remuneration package and this is a point worth checking in any job offer.

Education: Education is compulsory from 6 or 7 to 16 (15 in some provinces) and is free to the end of secondary schooling. Educational methods are progressive and similar to those in primary and comprehensive schools in the UK. There are also a small number of private schools. For registration you will need birth certificate, visa, vaccination certificate and previous school records. In Quebec and French-speaking Canada the medium of instruction in many schools is French, and the teaching of French is an important part of the curriculum.

Post-secondary education is not free, but repayable loans are available from the province, and there are various other forms of monetary assistance including scholarships for able students. University fees vary but are mainly low.

Useful contacts:

British High Commission, 80 Elgin Street, Ottawa, K1P 5K7, tel: 1 613 237 1530; www.bis-canada.org

Canadian High Commission, Macdonald House, 1 Grosvenor Square, London W1, tel: 020 7258 6600.

Canadian Tourist Board, 62–65 Trafalgar Square, London WC2N 5DT, tel: 0906 8715000.

PERSONAL TAXATION

Residence

Like many countries, Canada taxes on the basis of residence. Tax legislation does not specifically define residence, although it does include several rules under which an individual may be deemed to be resident. Generally, residence is determined by common law principles. Under these rules, an individual is generally considered to be resident if he or she has a 'continuing state of relationship' with Canada as evidenced by a dwelling held for year-round use, the presence of a spouse or other family members in Canada, or the maintenance of personal property or other social ties in Canada, such as bank accounts, furniture, club memberships, and other ties.

Taxation of personal income

Canadian residents are subject to tax on their worldwide income, including remuneration from employment, capital gains, interest, dividends, rents, professional fees, pensions, annuities and alimony. Non-residents are subject to tax only on income earned from Canadian sources.

The tax year for individuals is the calendar year.

There are a limited number of personal allowances, which take the form of tax credits against the individual's federal income tax liability. All individual taxpayers are entitled to a personal allowance ('the basic personal amount') of C$7,634 (2002).

Federal income tax is charged on taxable income at progressive rates of 16 per cent, 22 per cent, 26 per cent and 29 per cent, the top rate being charged on the slice of taxable income in excess of C$103,000 (2002). The taxable income of a Canadian resident is calculated by subtracting from gross income various deductions allowed by the Income Tax Act.

A minimum tax of 16 per cent on adjusted taxable income may apply instead of basic federal tax if the former would be greater than the latter. The tax base for the minimum tax is determined by adding back certain tax-preference items to regular taxable income. After adding back tax preference items, a general exemption of C$40,000 is allowed as a deduction to arrive at adjusted taxable income.

Each province levies its own income tax in addition to federal income tax. Liability to provincial income tax depends on residence as at 31 December of each tax year. Provincial income tax is also charged on taxable income at progressive rates, which vary by province. Each province sets its own personal allowances in the form of tax credits, which are applied against an individual's provincial income tax liability. Certain provinces also levy a provincial surtax on provincial income tax. Provinces also apply a minimum tax similar to the federal minimum tax, and the applicable rate varies by province. Individuals are only required to file one tax return with the federal government, with the exception of individuals resident in Québec, who must also file a Québec tax return.

For the year 2002, combined federal and provincial top tax rates range from 39 per cent in Alberta to 48.64 per cent in Newfoundland and Labrador.

Income from employment

All remuneration, including most benefits, derived from employment is taxable. Taxable benefits include living allowances, housing allowances, vacations, and personal use of employer-owned or employer-leased vehicles. A limited number of benefits are excluded from employment income, such as employer contributions to a registered pension or private health services plan.

Employees may deduct expenses only as prescribed by law. The most significant allowable items are the costs of maintaining a motor car where required for the employment, business travelling expenses (excluding travel between home and work), trade-union and professional fees and home-office expenses where the employee is required to work from home.

Employers are required to deduct federal and provincial income tax from all payments of remuneration made to individuals, as well as Canada Pension Plan/Québec Pension Plan contributions and Employment Insurance premiums as applicable. Tables are provided to employers for calculating these deductions.

Investment income

Dividends and interest

Dividends from Canadian companies are effectively taxed at a lower rate through a dividend gross-up and tax-credit mechanism. Generally, dividends received are grossed up by 25 per cent, and resident taxpayers may then claim a tax credit of 16.67 per cent (one-sixth) of the actual dividends received against the federal tax payable on the grossed-up dividend. Canadian residents are also taxed on dividends from foreign companies. These dividends are not subject to the gross-up and tax-credit mechanism and therefore they are taxed at full rates. Where the dividend has been subject to foreign withholding tax, the dividend amount taxable in Canada is grossed up to include the withholding tax, but the individual will generally be allowed a tax credit not exceeding 15 per cent of the dividend and a deduction for the excess.

Interest income is generally subject to tax on an accrual basis.

Income from real property

Rental income from real property (net of related expenses) is included in taxable income. There is no imputed income from owner occupation.

Taxes on capital

Capital gains

One-half of capital gains realised after 17 October 2000 are included in taxable income (higher capital gains inclusion rates applied for disposals realised prior to 18 October 2000). Resident individuals are entitled to claim an exemption of C$500,000 to reduce gains arising from the sale of qualified farm property or qualified small business corporation shares. In addition, an exemption is available that effectively exempts capital gains arising from one principal residence. There is no adjustment in calculating capital gains to remove the effect of any inflationary increase. Capital losses can generally only be applied to reduce capital gains and any unused portion can be carried back three years and forward indefinitely during the individual's lifetime. Capital losses carried over to the year of death can be claimed against all forms of income subject to certain restrictions.

Wealth tax

There are no federal or provincial wealth taxes.

Double tax treaties

Canada has over 70 comprehensive treaties or conventions in force with other countries for the elimination of double taxation on income, including treaties with both the UK and the United States.

For further information on tax and social security, please contact:
John Wonfor
Tax Partner
BDO Dunwoody LLP
tel: +1 416 865 0111; e-mail: jwonfor@bdo.ca

MEXICO

The economy

Mexico is a major oil producer, but its policy is to maintain oil production at the same level and to diversify its external trade. Other prime industries are agriculture, mining, steel and motor vehicles. The major trading partners are the US and the EU.

Membership of NAFTA, the North American Free Trade Agreement, liberalising trade between Mexico, the USA and Canada, should benefit the economy in the long term. Mexico is also seeking a similar deal with the EU.

Working conditions

Expatriate salaries in Mexico correspond to US levels. A work permit is needed, which has to be applied for by the local employer; it is not easy to get because strong preference is given to Mexicans. The employer has to pay a deposit of US$2000, returnable on the employee's departure. Documentation plays a large part in the settling-in process and it is a good idea to get all major documents (eg birth and marriage certificates) certified by the Mexican Consul at this end before you arrive. It is vital that your salary should be expressed in a strong foreign currency. Tax rates start at 3 per cent and rise to 35 per cent. Tax brackets are adjusted quarterly for inflation. Foreigners employed under a technical assistance agreement are not liable to income tax. Business hours are 9.00 am–2.00 pm and 4.00 pm–7.00 pm. Siestas may be longer outside the cities.

Useful information

Electricity: There are fluctuations in the electricity supply (100–127 V, 60 Hz) so as well as checking that your equipment is adapted to these voltages you should also bring a 1 kW transformer.

Climate: The climate in Mexico is mainly hot and dry, though Mexico City is cooler because of its high altitude, although the level of air pollution is high. Altitude does produce problems of breathlessness, insomnia, etc, and those suffering from anaemia or who are overweight may encounter particular difficulties. The rainy season is from June to October.

Driving: Roads are good and petrol is cheap by European standards. British or international driving licences are valid when driving cars registered abroad, but a Mexican licence is essential to drive cars registered in Mexico. Standards of driving are not good and third-party insurance, though not compulsory, is advisable.

Transport: A major improvement programme for the road network and the railways has recently been launched. Public transport in Mexico City is quick and cheap but is also one of the busiest systems in the world.

Health: Mexico has a reputation for giving foreigners stomach upsets – 'Montezuma's Revenge' and 'Mexican Foxtrot'. But, in the writer's experience, the hazards of diarrhoea are no worse than in any other hot country and, though ultimately unavoidable at some point, can easily be kept in check by common sense about what you eat and drink.

Health care: For more serious ailments, Mexico has a good state medical service, although the degree to which it is free of charge depends on your local employer's contributions to the social security system. Since such contributions are not mandatory it is important to know where you stand in respect of medical treatment.

Education: For people who do take children to Mexico there are a couple of good English schools in Mexico City which go right up to A-level, but fees are high; it is advisable to check the latest position.

Useful contacts:

British Embassy, Rio Lorma 71, Col Cuauhtemoc, 06500 Mexico City, tel: 525 207 2089; www.embajadabritanica.com.mx/

Mexican Embassy, 42 Hertford Street, London W1, tel: 020 7499 8586.

Mexican Government Tourist Office, 60–61 Trafalgar Square, 3rd Floor, London WC2N 5DS, tel: 020 7734 1058; www.mexico-travel.com/

THE UNITED STATES OF AMERICA

The economy

Notwithstanding the weakness and technical recession of the period from the first quarter of 2000, the United States has the richest and most successful economy in the industrialised world. There are certainly longer-term economic problems embedded in the USA's big deficits. However, the sheer size of the American market and the natural wealth of the country make it almost independent of the world economy. At the same time, there are shifts within the US economy that affect expatriates – principally the growing importance of the 'sunbelt' states in the south with their 'sunrise' high technology industries and the relative decline of the old industrial north. Although business in the USA spans every imaginable type, the largest sectors are services, finance and manufacturing. Notable industries include high technology, automotive, oil, mineral extraction, defence, steel, chemicals and agriculture.

Working conditions

American salaries are around 40 per cent higher than in the UK but there is nothing like the range of benefits and degree of employment protection that you get in Europe. The Medicare state health scheme is limited to the elderly and medical treatment is very expensive. Meanwhile, if insurance is not included in the remuneration package this could make quite a hole in an imposing salary. It may not be, because American executive salaries are less perk-laden than those in some other countries: for example, very few American executives get cars unless their job necessitates it.

Job advertisements in the USA, certainly at executive level, tend to demand a lot from the applicant but to be rather coy about what he or she is going to receive. Salaries, for instance, are rarely stated. It is as well to get advice from someone who has worked in the USA before accepting any offer, unless it is from a multinational, where conditions are usually fairly standard.

According to one survey, a typical middle management salary would be around US$75,000, with more senior posts in the US$120,000–$175,000 range plus bonus; bear in mind that the cost of living in the United States is now around 20 per cent lower than in the UK. However, pay rates vary according to position, type of industry and area of the country – New York, for example, is very expensive, as is Chicago. In practice, an expatriate is most likely to find a job in the USA with a multinational unless he or she has special skills in engineering, computing, R&D or electronics, a reputation in an academic discipline or is a qualified doctor (salaries offered to GPs range from £80,000 to £120,000).

There is some evidence that US firms are now seeking British managers with international experience, to establish and run European manufacturing bases. There are also opportunities with US companies that have investments in the UK, although it is also worth noting that the USA is the major destination for UK investment funds.

Visitors to the United States, on business or holiday, no longer need a visa for a stay of less than 90 days.

How you set about applying for a visa that enables you to work in the United States, however, is a matter that requires a good deal of caution. Visas for permanent immigration are extremely hard to get unless you have close family ties there. Furthermore, if you make an application of this kind and are turned down, it then becomes extremely difficult to get a visa of any kind – even as a visitor – because the presumption is that once you get to the USA you will find some illegal way of remaining there.

If you are going to work for the British subsidiary of an American firm, or vice versa, the task is relatively easy. Your firm would apply for an L visa which would grant you residence for up to three years. Similarly, if you are proposing to invest substantial sums, at least $1 million, to start up a business venture in the USA creating employment for at least ten people (unrelated), you could apply for an immigrant investor visa.

People who merely want to go to the USA to take up a job offer must get their employer to file an application for a temporary worker's H visa. If you are going to the USA to look for a job, you have to ask the employer to do this as soon as he or she makes you an offer. These applications are processed within a matter of a few weeks – to months.

Although the 35-hour week prevails, working conditions are a great deal more strenuous and exacting than in some firms here. American employers expect results and are fairly ruthless about removing people who do not deliver them. Senior executives come and go and it is not unusual for a shake-up at the top to work its way right down the ladder. In some firms considerable conformity with the image of the company in relation to dress, lifestyle, etc, is expected, even in the private lives of their employees. Holiday entitlement is low.

There is no VAT in the USA but there are sales taxes which vary from town to town – rates are generally between 2 and 10 per cent. Since they are not shown as part of the price of the goods, as VAT usually is, this can mean a nasty shock when you get your bill for an expensive item.

Useful information

Shopping hours: 10.00 am to 9.00 pm, with later shopping one or two evenings a week. All shops are open on Saturday and most on Sunday.

Electricity: 110–120 V, 60 Hz AC. Flat three-pin plugs are normal.

Driving: Driving is on the right. An international or UK licence is valid for one year, but it is advisable to get an American licence from the state department of motor vehicles – after a test. Most highways and super-highways have several lanes, and lane discipline is very strict, as is the enforcement of speed limits. In 1995 the government repealed the national speed limits. Some states now have no restrictions.

Many expatriates buy a new or used car locally and resell it when they leave. The American Automobile Association (AAA) is an extremely helpful organisation for motorists.

Transport: Americans have taken to the air as naturally as our great-grandfathers took to rail. Flying is the most efficient and speedy (and relatively cheap) way of getting round this vast country. All the main cities are connected by internal flights and there are frequent 'shuttle' services between some cities (eg New York to Washington, New York to Boston, and San Francisco to Los Angeles). Helicopter services are often available, as well as private plane hire.

There has recently been some revival of the railways. Long-distance coaches (usually air conditioned) are the cheapest way of travelling, if you can stand the boredom. Americans are also used to travelling long distances by car.

There are underground trains or 'subways' in New York, Boston, Philadelphia and Washington. The famous cable cars in San Francisco are now back in service. New York city bus services are regular and frequent – you need the exact fare.

Health care: Medical treatment is of a very high standard, but is extremely expensive. If possible, people are advised to get full medical insurance for themselves and their families before departure, even for a short stay. However, many European insurance companies no longer offer cover for expatriates and their families in the USA; instead, they advise that insurance should be arranged with a US company such as the Blue Cross.

Education: Nursery school groups can be found in most centres. All children between 7 and 16 must attend school. The school year lasts from September to June. The system comprises public schools – there are about 90,000 in the whole country with over 50 million pupils – and there are 12 grades, 1–6 elementary, and 7–12 in secondary or high school. After the 12th grade the pupils will probably go to college. Schools are operated by boards of education and are free.

There are fee-paying private schools and a number of boarding schools, modelled on the UK pattern, where tuition and boarding fees are usually fairly high. There are International Schools in New

THE MASTERS SCHOOL

49 Clinton Avenue • Dobbs Ferry, NY 10522, USA
Phone: (914) 479-6400 • Fax (914) 693-7295
Email: admissions@themastersschool.com
www.themastersschool.com

Where the bonds of lifelong friendship are established.

Where intellect and character are developed together.

Where sports are competitive and fitness is friendly.

Where a part can be played on-stage and off-stage.

Where access to teachers, facilities & fun is full time and far-reaching.

We are located just 35 minutes north of New York City on the banks of the Hudson River. Accessible by train and major highways.

York (the United Nations) and Washington. The UN School takes children from kindergarten to high school age and sometimes can take in children whose parents are not UN officials. Instruction is in English and French.

Useful contacts:

British Embassy, 3100 Massachusetts Avenue, NW, Washington DC, 20008, tel: 1 202 588 6500; www.britainusa.com/embassy

United States of America Embassy, 24 Grosvenor Square, London W1, tel: 020 7499 9000.

United States Information Service, 24 Grosvenor Square, London W1, tel: 020 7499 9000.

United States Tourist Board, Tourist Information Line 0891 600530 (premium rate, higher charges apply).

Expatriate contacts:

www.britishinamerica.com

www.britnet.nelgin.nu

PERSONAL TAXATION

Residence

The United States taxes individuals on the basis of citizenship and residence. US citizens are liable to US tax on their worldwide income and assets, no matter where they may be resident. Foreign nationals are considered to be resident in the USA for tax purposes if they meet one of the two separate residence tests. As residents, foreign nationals are taxable on their worldwide income in the same way as US citizens. The residence tests are the 'green card' test and the substantial presence test.

A 'green card', or an alien registration card, is given to a foreign national who is granted lawful permanent-resident status, according to US immigration laws. A foreign national is regarded as a US resident from the first day that he or she is present in the United States, while in possession of a green card, and residence continues as long as the green card is held.

In order to be regarded a resident in the USA for tax purposes under the substantial presence test, a foreign national must meet

the substantial presence test for all or part of the tax year. This test is based on the number of days a foreign national is present in the USA in three consecutive calendar years. To meet the substantial presence test, a foreign national must be physically present in the USA for at least:

☐ 31 days during the current year; and
☐ 183 days during the three-year period that includes the current year and the two previous years, under the following formula:
   − current year = number of days × 1;
   − first preceding year = number of days × $\frac{1}{3}$;
   − second preceding year = number of days × $\frac{1}{6}$.

If this test is satisfied, a person is resident from the first day present in the United States during the current year. However, it is important to note that there is a 10 day diminimus rule which allows a taxpayer to be in he USA for 10 days prior to the start of their assignment without being taxed as a resident for that period. In addition, the first day of residency is determined if the taxpayer spends 31 days consecutively in the USA from that date.

Where a resident alien leaves the USA they will remain a resident of the US during their departure year unless a statement is filed with the taxpayers final tax return breaking residency on the day he/she departs the US.

Taxation of personal income

Individuals resident in the USA are taxable on their worldwide income, irrespective of where it is earned, subject to some expatriate concessions. Non-resident aliens are taxable on all US source income, subject to any available treaty relief.

The tax year is the calendar year. Income tax is levied at progressive rates on the total income of an individual from all sources, after all applicable exemptions and deductions. An alternative minimum tax (AMT) of 26 per cent to 28 per cent (the precise rate depends on the level of taxable income and the filing status of the taxpayer) levied on a special base ('alternative minimum taxable income') may apply if it would produce a greater liability than the regular income tax.

Income tax may be payable at three levels: federal, state and municipal. Most states levy income taxes, as do some cities (such as New York). Residents of an income-taxing state are taxed on their worldwide income. Non-residents (of that state) are generally taxed on remuneration earned in the state and on net rental income derived from real or personal property owned or used in the state. State-tax residence rules may differ from federal rules, so that someone who is a resident for federal tax purposes may still be non-resident for state taxes.

Income tax is generally assessed separately on each individual; however, husband and wife may choose to file jointly, which will generally produce a tax benefit.

Allowances (ie personal exemption) are available to taxpayers according to their personal circumstances, and are given by deduction from taxable income. In the tax year 2001, the top marginal rate of federal income tax was 39.1 per cent.

Income from employment

All forms of remuneration from an employment are in principle taxable. These include salaries, bonuses, benefits-in-kind, gains from share options, termination payments, directors' remuneration and so forth.

Expenses incurred by the employee in the course of the employment are in general deductible to the extent not reimbursed by the employer.

Employers are required to operate a withholding tax on payments of earnings, based on withholding-tax tables supplied by the Internal Revenue Service.

Investment income

US residents' worldwide investment income is taxed as ordinary income, at graduated tax rates.

There is no withholding tax on dividends or interest paid to residents, and US dividends do not carry a tax credit.

Non-resident aliens are only taxable on investment income from US sources. Certain investment income that is not effectively connected to a US trade or business is taxed at 30 per cent (or a lower treaty rate, if applicable). This tax rate is applied to gross income, without taking into account deductions.

Certain interest income and capital gains of a non-resident alien are exempt from US taxation.

Rental income from real property is taxable as ordinary income at graduated rates, net of related expenses. There is no withholding tax on rents and no imputed income for owner-occupiers.

Taxes on capital

Capital gains

Capital gains are distinguished as short term or long term (long-term gains are gains on assets held for more than one year). Long-term gains are generally taxed at 20 per cent, whereas short-term gains are included in ordinary income and taxable at regular graduated tax rates.

There is an exemption of a maximum of US$500,000 (US$250,000 in the case of separate filing) on the gain from sale of the taxpayer's principal residence.

Wealth tax

There are no federal or state wealth taxes.

Double tax treaties

The United States has a wide network of over 50 comprehensive tax treaties, including one with the UK. A new UK treaty was signed on 24 July 2001 and is expected to come into force in April 2002.

For further information on tax and social security, please contact:
Donna Chamberlain
International Tax Manager
BDO Seidman LLP
tel: +1 704 887 4218; e-mail: Dchamberlain@bdo.com

Asia

SOUTH EAST ASIA: SOME NOTES ON ETIQUETTE

It used to be said that Britain and America were two countries divided by the same language: meaning that things which appeared similar were often very different under the surface. This is even more true of South East Asia, where the cities, at any rate, have an increasingly Western appearance that nevertheless masks profound cultural differences between Asians and Europeans. The tendency is for expatriates to feel that these can be overcome by observing the ordinary niceties of social behaviour, Western-style, but these do not always translate themselves readily. In the West, for instance, it has become customary for business dealings to be conducted relatively informally – indeed informality has become almost a style in itself. In the East, a good deal of ceremony is still observed and the more important the negotiations, the more ceremony will be attached to them. This is related to what people in the East would call 'face'.

The notion of 'face' is prevalent throughout Asia and it is a difficult term to translate. It may be, as in the instance above, the dignity of an occasion or it may be, more often, simple human dignity. The reluctance to violate your own sense of 'face' may cause a subordinate who disagrees with you to disobey your instructions, having apparently agreed to follow them. The way to deal with such a situation is not to take issue with him or her in public but to sort it out in circumstances where no loss of face is involved for either party. This has to be done with a great deal of tact – the Western notion of frankness is largely unknown to people in the Far East, who are apt to regard it merely as rudeness.

Another rich area of potential misunderstanding lies in the use of body language. As in the Middle East, it is generally considered impolite to take or offer things with the left hand, though at meals dishes can be passed with the left hand, provided it is supported by the right. Oriental people are also very wary of effusive displays of affection. Even old friends should be greeted with a certain amount of gravity and reserve. Those same qualities should also mark your relations with subordinates – pointing at people with your finger or beckoning them by use of the finger is regarded as the height of bad manners. Indeed, many finger gestures are regarded as obscene, as is making points by pounding the open palm with the fist.

The Asian culture, wherever you go, is in fact one that is very nervous about familiarity and treats as familiarity many modes of behaviour that we would regard as fairly normal.* This also extends to the use of Christian (or proper) names. The Chinese style, incidentally, is for the surname to come first, the middle name second and the equivalent of the Christian name last. Thus a Chinese man by the name Goh Kee Seah would be Mr Goh, not Mr Seah.

Another way in which Asian culture differs from ours is in the importance attached to luck. Again it is important to respect this because to dismiss it as superstition would be a grievous offence against the concept of face. It can, of course, work to your favour; for instance, it is considered bad luck if the first person into a shop each day leaves without making a purchase. In those shops where bargaining is part of normal transactions, this can lead to the often expressed sentiment of 'special price, just for you' indeed having some meaning. Normally you will find that after prolonged bargaining you have ended up paying about the same as in a department store.

A further point about shopping: Asians are, in general, slighter than Europeans, so you would be well advised to stock up on clothes before you leave.

---

*An excellent account of this whole issue is given in a book called *Culture Shock* by Jo Ann Craig, published by Times Books International of Singapore.

BRUNEI DARUSSALAM

The economy

Brunei has one of the highest standards of living in South East Asia. Almost all its wealth comes from oil and gas, but the government has encouraged the use of oil money to foster the development of secondary industries and services such as fishing, agriculture, education and communications. The main trading partner is Japan, followed by the UK and Malaysia.

Personal finance and taxation

The public sector employs about 50 per cent of the workforce. Salaries are good and government jobs usually carry such fringe benefits as subsidised or free housing, an education allowance for children, paid home leave, free medical attention, a car or an interest-free loan to buy one and an end-of-service bonus. There is no personal tax in Brunei. There is also no restriction on remittances.

Working conditions

Entry and exit visas are not necessary for UK nationals. Employment and residence passes have to be obtained on behalf of expatriates by their employer but they are not usually difficult to obtain for UK nationals.

Useful information

Electricity: 230 V, 50 Hz AC, with both round and square three-pin plugs.

Climate: The vegetation, climate and general atmosphere of the country are typical of tropical regions of South East Asia, with high humidity and a temperature that rarely falls below 70°F and rarely rises above 90°F.

Transport: You will need a car and a good choice is available locally. Japanese cars are cheaper than British and much cheaper than European models. A Toyota Corolla costs around B$27,750. Taxis, including water-taxis, and self-drive vehicles are freely available. Petrol is cheap.

Health: Generally, health standards are extremely good. Innoculation requirements are minimal – cholera and yellow fever are advised.

Health care: Charges are made for state medical services but most companies employing expatriate workers provide medical insurance. Standards are reputed to be high, but there are also private medical facilities for those who prefer them. Nursing care is poor.

Education: Most expatriate children of secondary school age go to boarding schools in the United Kingdom, though facilities for secondary education do exist in Brunei. There are several good nursery schools, as well as three good primary schools, of which the International School is the most popular.

Alcohol: Although alcohol is banned, 12 cans of beer or two bottles of wine or spirits may be brought in on first arrival and subsequent visits.

Special note: Women should observe the Islamic dress code.

Media: The *Borneo Bulletin* is the main English-language newspaper. The government-published *Brunei Darussalam* and *The Straits Times* are also available. A range of Australian, British and US programmes are shown on television.

Useful contacts:

British High Commission, 2101 2nd Floor Block D, Komplexs Banunan Yayasan, Sultan Haji Hassanal Boliah, Jalan Pretty, PO Box 2197, Bandar Seri Begawan 1921, tel: 673 2 222231.

Brunei Darussalam High Commission, 35 Norfolk Square, London W2, tel: 020 7402 0953.

THE PEOPLE'S REPUBLIC OF CHINA

The economy

Economic reforms since 1979 have brought the country step by step into line with other economies. Sustained foreign investment has enabled the construction of an industrial and communications infrastructure. In November 2001 China finally gained accession to the World Trade Organisation and committed itself to a firm programme of tariff reductions. There are now two stock markets, in Shanghai and Shenshen, and Shanghai has emerged strongly as China's financial centre.

The economy has been growing steadily at more than 7 per cent, with higher exports every year and soaring foreign investments. The coastal provinces, particularly, are booming and inflation has been contained.

Working conditions

Office accommodation is scarce and very expensive. Many foreign companies still have their offices in hotels. It has been estimated by the *China Business Review* that it costs a company around £400,000 a year to keep a small, one-man office in China. Business hours are from 8.00 am until midday and 2.00 pm until 6.00 pm. All foreign visitors require a visa and, for some destinations, a special permit

Useful information

Transport: Both cars and spares are subject to high rates of duty. Taxis are often the preferred mode of transport.

If you have a car it is becoming increasingly possible to get around. You need a permit to travel but these are generally granted without difficulty.

Health: Cholera and yellow fever innoculations are advisable. An AIDS test may be required.

Health care: Good medical care is available, although the equipment may not be the most modern, and proprietary medication may not be in full supply.

Education: There is an International School in Beijing and American Schools in Guangzhou and Shanghai.

Useful contacts:
British Embassy, 11 Guang Hua Lu, Beijing 100600, tel: 861 06532 1961.
Shanghai British Consul General, www.uninet.com.cn/shangbcg/
Chinese Embassy, 1 Leinster Gardens, London W2, tel: 020 7631 1430.

Chinese National Tourist Office, 4 Glentworth Street, London NW1 5PG, tel: 020 7935 9787.
www.cnto.org (US Web site).
www.china.trav.net (Australian Web site).

PERSONAL TAXATION

Residence

The People's Republic of China (China or the PRC) imposes individual taxes on the basis of residence and domicile. An individual is regarded as being domiciled in China if he or she usually or habitually resides in China due to family relationships or because he or she is a registered householder with a personal residence record. An individual who lives abroad for reasons such as education, employment, work assignments, visiting relatives, or touring, and who thereafter must return to China, is regarded as being domiciled in China. The extent to which individuals who are not domiciled in China are liable to income tax depends on their period of residence in China.

Taxation of personal income

Personal income is liable to individual income tax (IIT). Individuals domiciled in China are liable to IIT in respect of their worldwide income. After five consecutive years of residence in China, a foreign individual will be subject to IIT on his or her worldwide income in the same way as a PRC domiciliary, starting from the sixth year. Subject to the approval of the tax authorities, foreign individuals who have resided in China for between one to five years will be taxed on their PRC-source income and non-PRC-source income borne by a PRC establishment. Foreign individuals who have resided in China for less than one year are liable to IIT on their PRC-source income only. A foreign individual who works in China for less than 90 days (or 183 days if from a tax-treaty country) during a calendar year is exempt from IIT if his or her income is paid by a foreign entity and is not borne by a PRC establishment. There are different categories of income which are subject to PRC IIT including:

☐ wages and salaries – 5 per cent to 45 per cent;
☐ income from personal services – 20 per cent to 40 per cent;
☐ business income from sole proprietorships, contracting and leasing – 5 per cent to 35 per cent;
☐ interest, dividends, royalties and other income – 20 per cent.

Income is computed separately for each category of income and IIT is levied at the appropriate rate on taxable income of each category after deducting allowable expenses. The tax year is the calendar year, but tax returns must be filed and tax paid monthly.

Income from employment

Taxable income from employment includes salaries, wages and bonuses. Housing allowances are also taxable. Although the law provides for the taxation of benefits-in-kind, in practice these are not taxed, if certain conditions are satisfied.

There is no deduction allowed for specific expenses However, a general allowance of CNY 800 per month is deductible by PRC nationals from taxable employment income (in some locations, such as Shanghai and Shenzhen, the amount is greater). Foreign expatriates are entitled to an additional allowance of CNY 3,200 per month, in which case their total allowable deduction per month is CNY 4,000. Bonuses, however, are accounted for separately, with no deduction.

A system of withholding from employee earnings is operated.

Investment income

Interest and dividends are taxable with no allowable deductions. The rate of tax is 20 per cent.

Income from real property is taxable, after deduction of a standard 20 per cent of the gross income, in respect of expenses. There is no income attributed to owner-occupiers.

Taxes on capital

Capital gains

Capital gains derived by an individual are categorised as 'other

income' for PRC IIT purposes. They will be taxed at 20 per cent as indicated above.

Wealth tax

There is no wealth tax in China.

Double tax treaties

China has over 60 comprehensive treaties in force with other countries for the elimination of double taxation on income, including treaties with the UK and the United States.

For further information on tax and social security, please contact:
Katherine Young
Tax Partner
BDO McCabe Lo and Co
tel: + 852 2853 1428; e-mail: katherine_young@bdo.com

HONG KONG

The economy

Apart from its importance as a financial and banking centre (no fewer than 172 banks and 300 insurance companies are incorporated there and it now ranks as the world's third most important financial centre after London and New York), Hong Kong's economy is bound up principally with tourism and other service sectors. The traditional light manufacturing base has largely disappeared to mainland China. The biggest foreign exchange earners are foreign trade and tourism, with more than half coming from other Asian countries. One reason for this is the huge range of consumer goods on sale at prices now expensive to us, but still cheap to the Japanese or Taiwanese visitor. Tourist attractions are much as one might find in, say, Singapore, although perhaps more visually inspiring.

Working conditions

There are no exchange controls in Hong Kong and money is fully remittable into and out of the colony. Broadly speaking, an expatriate employee in the private sector should expect to be earning 40 to 50 per cent more than his gross UK pay. On top of this an expatriate employee should expect to get free or heavily subsidised accommodation and medical and dental attention, an education and holiday visits allowance for his or her children, and possibly further fringe benefits such as a car, servants and a good gratuity at the end of his or her contract. Public sector salaries are paid in Hong Kong dollars.

Hong Kong's largely Chinese population (98 per cent) is impressively intelligent, skilled and hard-working, so opportunities for expatriates are limited. It is the policy of the Hong Kong government to recruit locally whenever possible. Details of teaching, academic and technical jobs are advertised in the appropriate sections of the UK press; there has recently been some demand for expatriates following the initial emigration of residents pre-1997.

Useful information

Special note: The feature of Hong Kong life that strikes a newcomer most forcibly is the population density, impressive even by Asian standards. The population density for Hong Kong Island is 5,380 persons per sq km, including barren areas (three-quarters of the whole). So Hong Kong is no place for people who feel the need for wide open spaces or who are bothered by crowds.

Climate: The climate of Hong Kong – warm and humid for most of the year but with a brief cool winter – makes air conditioning and some heating facilities a necessity.

Electricity: 200–220 V, 50 Hz AC.

Driving: There are very few straight roads in Hong Kong and distances, in any case, are short, so a big car is a status symbol which also attracts a higher rate of registration tax and annual licence fees. UK driving licences are valid for a stay of up to a year,

Companies flock to Hong Kong in record numbers

MORE and more international companies are making Hong Kong their home in Asia.

In the past two years the number of international companies using Hong Kong as a regional base has hit a record since statistics in regional operations were first gathered 11 years ago.

By June 1, 2001, there were 3 237 regional operations – a 7.9% increase over the 3,001 in 2000 and an impressive 30% increase over the 2,490 in 1999.

The number of regional headquarters rose to 944 in 2001 – a 10.4% increase over the 855 in 2000. This bettered the previous record of 903 regional headquarters in 1997. The number of regional offices rose to 2 293 in 2001 – a 6.8% increase over the 2,146 in 2000 and another record.

The Director-General of Investment Promotion at Invest Hong Kong, Mr Mike Rowse, said that over the past two years there had been constant and rising international interest in Hong Kong as a location for regional headquarters.

"More and more multinational corporations are flocking to set up beachheads in Hong Kong, taking advantage of our competitive advantages over other Asian cities, in particular, as a gateway to China," he said.

"The survey shows Hong Kong is again topping the charts as the preferred hub and living up to its role as Asia's world city. With China's accession to the World Trade Organisation, Hong Kong's status as the preferred location for regional headquarters for multinationals will be further strengthened."

Companies considered Hong Kong's low and simple tax system as the most important factor in choosing the location for a regional base. Hong Kong residents pay a maximum of 15% salaries tax, while corporations pay 16% profits tax.

Other important factors included the free flow of information, political stability and security, a corruption free government, and world-class communication, transport and other infrastructure.

And once in Hong Kong, expatriates will find a vibrant and energetic city, rich in culture and heritage, that provides a diverse range of recreational pursuits, some of the finest dining anywhere, large tracts of country park, world-class international schools and easy access to the rest of Asia and beyond.

– *Article supplied by Brand Hong Kong,* www.brandhk.gov.hk.

Asia's world city

"17 years in Hong Kong and I still get a buzz every day."

Nichole Garnaut
Restaurateur. Entrepreneur.
Hong Kong permanent resident.

www.investhk.gov.hk

but can be exchanged for a local licence without a test. Bringing a new car into Hong Kong is hardly cheaper than buying one locally; a first registration tax is charged. However, good second-hand cars are reported to be readily available.

Transport: Public transport and taxis are inexpensive but apt to be overcrowded, and most expatriates have cars, which in many cases are not provided as a perk that goes with the job.

Education: Education in Hong Kong can be a problem and expatriates are advised to make arrangements for schooling as soon as they get there, or before. Prior to arrival it is worth notifying the Education Department (9–16th Floors, Wu Chung House, 197–221 Queen's Road East, Wanchai, Hong Kong), or the English Schools Foundation (43b Stubbs Road, Hong Kong) to ask about places. This is because most of the schools cater for the predominantly Chinese population, so the medium of instruction is either Chinese or, if in English, with the emphasis on English as a foreign language. There are several independent schools offering a UK curriculum, at both primary and secondary level.

Media: Hong Kong has two TV stations and two main radio stations providing services in both Chinese and English. There are two English TV channels and three English radio channels, two of which combine from midnight to 6.00 am, to provide a 24-hour service; there is a BBC World Service relay on another channel at night. Satellite television offers a 24-hour global news service and a cable TV channel carries locally produced programmes.

Useful contacts:

British Consulate General, No. 1 Supreme Court Road, Central, Hong Kong PO Box 528, tel: 852 2901 3000; www.britishconsulate.org.hk/

Hong Kong Government Office, 6 Grafton Street, London W1X 3LB, tel: 020 7499 9821.

Hong Kong Tourist Association, 6 Grafton Street, London W1X 3LB, tel: 020 7533 7100; www.hkta.org; www.hkta.org/usa/ (US Web site).

PERSONAL TAXATION

Residence

The Hong Kong tax system adopts a source concept on taxability of income and residence is therefore not relevant. However, for the purpose of the personal assessment option (see below), the terms 'permanent resident' and 'temporary resident' are defined as follows. 'Permanent resident' means 'an individual who ordinarily resides in Hong Kong'. 'Temporary resident' means 'an individual who stays in Hong Kong for a period or a number of periods amounting to more than 180 days during the year of assessment, or for a period or periods amounting to more than 300 days in two consecutive years of assessment, one of which is the year of assessment in respect of which the election (of personal assessment) is made.'

Taxation of personal income

Hong Kong does not have a general income tax. Rather, those sources of income liable to taxation are each subject to a separate tax. An individual may be subject to salaries tax on employment income; profits tax on business profits if he or she carries on a trade, profession or business in Hong Kong; and property tax on rental income from real property situated in Hong Kong.

The tax year runs from 1 April to 31 March.

Income from employment

Taxable income comprises income from both Hong Kong and offshore employment, 'any office or employment of profit' in Hong Kong, and pension income from a Hong Kong pension fund.

Income from employment includes salaries, allowances, bonuses, leave pay, commission, and benefits-in-kind that can be converted to cash, and so forth. All income from Hong Kong employment is taxable, wherever the duties may be performed. However, if certain conditions in relation to the employment contract are fulfilled and qualified as an offshore employment and the individual provides services outside Hong Kong during the tax year, a portion of income attributable to the offshore services is exempt from Hong Kong tax. This exemption does not apply to income derived from any office, such as directorship, or employment of profit.

Housing reimbursement is not taxable as such, but an employee living in accommodation provided rent free or to whom reimbursement of rent paid is made is taxable on a notional benefit of 10 per cent of total income from the employment.

Expenses incurred wholly, exclusively and necessarily for the employment and charitable donations are deductible. Mortgage interest paid on a property used as the taxpayer's principal residence is deductible, with an upper limit of HK$100,000. As a temporary measure of relief, the cap is increased to HK$150,000 for the years of assessment 2001–2 and 2002–3.

Salaries tax is calculated at the lower of (a) the amount computed at progressive rates starting from 2 per cent to 17 per cent *after* deduction of certain expenses and allowances; or (b) the amount computed at a standard rate of 15 per cent *before* deduction of allowances.

There are a number of personal allowances, depending on the taxpayer's personal circumstances. For example, there is an allowance of HK$108,000 for a single person; HK$216,000 for married couples; and a child allowance in respect of child less than 18 years old of HK$30,000 for each child.

Individuals are separately assessed to salaries tax, but a married couple may elect for joint assessment, where this is advantageous.

Investment income

Dividends and interest

Dividends and interest income from bank deposits are not taxable in Hong Kong, whatever their source.

Income from real property

Rental income from real property situated in Hong Kong is subject, after deduction of a statutory deduction, which is 20 per cent on gross rental income, property rates (local property tax) if borne by the property owner and irrecoverable rent, if any, to property tax at a flat rate of 15 per cent. Mortgage interest on let property is not deductible for property tax purposes but deductible if the individual elects to be taxed under Personal assessment (see below).

There is no income imputed to owner-occupiers.

Taxes on capital

Capital gains

There is no capital gains tax in Hong Kong. However, net gains derived from trading of real property are subject to profits tax at 15 per cent.

Wealth tax

There is no wealth tax in Hong Kong.

Personal assessment

An individual may elect for personal assessment if he or she: (a) is of or above the age of 18; *and* (b) is, or whose spouse is, either a permanent or temporary Hong Kong resident (see definition of residence above).

Under personal assessment, tax on the individual's total income (ie employment income, rental income and profits from business) is calculated at the rates applied to salaries tax, and mortgage interest for financing any real property generating taxable rental income is deductible.

Double tax treaties

Hong Kong has not entered into any treaty in respect of personal tax. There is, however, an arrangement with the remainder of the People's Republic of China (of which Hong Kong is a Special Administrative Region) for the avoidance of double taxation on income. This is applied to individuals working both in China and Hong Kong under the same employment.

For further information on tax and social security, please contact:
Katherine Yeung
Tax Partner
BDO McCabe Lo and Co
tel: +852 2853 1425; e-mail: katherine_yeung@bdo.com.hk

JAPAN

The economy

Despite Japan's almost total dependence on imported energy, the country remains one of the world's economic superpowers. Until recently Japan's readiness to adapt to new technology has been one of the secrets of its success, and the latest sign of this is that it is now the world's largest user of industrial robots. However, after a period of economic growth in the 1980s, Japan is now experiencing the worst economic crisis in its recent history.

Japan is a highly industrialised country, only 14 per cent of which is cultivable. Fish rather than meat is the main source of protein in the diet. Rice is the staple food. Heavy investment in subsidiary manufacturing abroad has led to the peculiarity of Japan importing Japanese goods.

Working conditions

An expatriate executive will need double his or her UK salary to live at a normal standard, entertain as his or her job will require, and provide UK schooling for his children. Tokyo has consistently been one of the world's most expensive cities and a senior expatriate executive should strive for US$180,000–$230,000, plus 15–20 per cent overseas loading. Japanese indigenous salaries, once relatively low, are also now in the upper quartile and well above UK levels. It is advisable to arrange for some salary to be paid elsewhere to ease the tax burden and facilitate the transfer of funds to the UK.

The majority of expatriates working in Japan are employed by foreign companies, particularly as representatives; otherwise, the main source of employment is as an English language teacher. EFL teachers are likely to be recruited by Japanese language schools. Bona fide students in Japan can appeal for permission to work a limited number of hours per week (teaching EFL); pay is from £16 to £25 an hour. Some language schools underpay their full-time staff. Even a primary school teacher should be earning at least £16,000 a year, bearing in mind the cost of living.

A person wishing to enter Japan for the purposes of employment, training or study, must apply for a visa. Requirements are: a valid passport; one visa application form completed and signed; one passport-sized photograph; a certificate of eligibility (original and one photocopy). The certificate of eligibility is issued by the Ministry of Justice in Japan. It is provided by a future employer or sponsor in Japan. In certain cases additional support documents may be required.

Employment patterns in Japanese firms differ from those in the West – recruitment is on traditional paternalistic lines from families with loyalty to the company – and a knowledge of Japanese would be a prerequisite.

Holders of UK passports require no visas for tourist visits under 90 days, which period may be extended to a maximum of 180 days at the discretion of the authorities. A working visa is required by those who have already obtained a post. To obtain a working visa you must first have a definite job appointment in Japan. Your employer should then apply to the Ministry of Justice for a Certificate of Eligibility. Once this is received you must submit, in person, a visa application to the Japanese Consulate, together with the Certificate. Provided the documents are all in order a visa can normally be issued fairly quickly. Information is available from the Visa Section, Consulate General of Japan, 101–104 Piccadilly, London W1V 9FN. Temporary work is not permitted but, if when visiting as a tourist you receive a written offer of a permanent post, a working visa may be obtained by leaving the country and applying from outside (Korea, for example).

Booklets outlining Japanese business practices and attitudes are available for business people from JETRO London, Leconfield House, Curzon Street, London W1Y 8LQ, and may be useful for other visitors.

Useful information

Commercial organisations: Office hours are usually 9.00 am to 5.00 pm; many companies operate a five-day week.

Banking hours: 9.00 am to 3.00 pm Monday–Friday, 9.00 am to 12.00 pm on Saturday.

Shops: Shops and department stores are usually open on Sundays and public holidays, but most other businesses are closed then. There are 14 public holidays a year.

Electricity: 100 V, 50 Hz AC in eastern Japan, including Tokyo, and 60 Hz in western Japan, including Nagoya, Kyoto and Osaka. Hotels generally provide sockets for both 110 and 220 V.

Special note: Expatriate wives may find life difficult because of the position of women in society, where they are expected to be self-effacing. A wife's role might be confined to formal entertaining at home, of which there is a great deal, to promote her husband's interests.

Duty: The expatriate who will be staying longer than a year may bring in household effects, including a car and/or boat, duty free within limits considered reasonable by the customs. The car (or boat) sales receipt must be presented to show that it has been in use for more than one year before its arrival in Japan.

Driving: An international driving licence is valid for one year, after which a Japanese licence must be obtained. This involves both practical and written tests, which may be taken in English. Traffic drives on the left, and tolls are payable for motorway use. The volume of traffic is immense, but Japanese drivers are patient and disciplined, and accidents are consequently few. Signposting is inadequate (supposing one can read them) and a compass might be useful.

Transport: All the usual forms of public and private transport are available.

Health care: Medical insurance for employees and their families is provided either by a government-managed scheme or a health insurance society. There are a number of English-speaking doctors in major cities, and Western brands of drugs are available.

Education: There are many schools for English-speaking children but they are not geared to UK education. Most expatriates leave their children to be educated in Britain.

Media: Four English-language newspapers are published daily: the *Japan Times*, the *Yomiuri Daily*, the *Asahi Evening News* and the *Mainichi Daily News*. For points on etiquette and survival tips, three useful publications for intending expatriates in Japan are *Living in Japan, A Consumer's Guide to Prices in Japan* and *Finding a Home in Tokyo* published by the American Chamber of Commerce in Japan, Bridgestone Toranomon Building, 3–25–2, Toranomon, Minato-ku, Tokyo 105 (tel: 03 3433 5381; fax: 03 3436 1446).

Useful contacts:
British Embassy, No 1 Ichiban-cho, Chiyoda-ku, Tokyo, 102-8381, tel: 813 5211 1100; www.uknow.or.jp/
Japanese Embassy, 101 Piccadilly, London W1V, tel: 020 7465 6500.
Japan National Tourist Organisation, 20 Savile Row, London W1X 1AE, tel: 020 7734 6938; www.jnto.go.jp/

PERSONAL TAXATION

Residence

The extent of an individual's Japanese income-tax liability depends on the individual's residence status. A permanent resident is liable for tax on worldwide income; a temporary resident is liable for income tax on Japanese-source income and foreign-source income to the extent that it is paid in or remitted to Japan; non-residents are liable on Japanese-source income only.

A permanent resident is an individual who is either domiciled in Japan or who has lived in Japan for at least one year and is not a 'temporary resident'.

A temporary resident is an individual who has been living in Japan for less than five years and has no intention of residing permanently in Japan. Most visiting executives are likely to fall into this category.

An individual is domiciled where he or she has his or her permanent home or principal base of life.

An individual is regarded as becoming resident (whether temporarily or permanently) from the day of arrival in Japan if he or she comes to take up an appointment that requires the individual to live continuously in Japan for a period of at least one year. If the assignment lasts into a sixth year, the individual becomes a permanent resident from the end of the fifth year.

Upon departure, residence ceases immediately if it is apparent that the individual will be working abroad for more than one year.

Taxation of personal income

For the purposes of the individual income tax, the tax year is the calendar year.

Income tax is levied at progressive rates on the aggregate income of an individual from one or more of 10 sources:

☐   income from employment;
☐   capital gains;
☐   interest;
☐   dividends;
☐   rental income from real property;
☐   income from a business;
☐   occasional income;
☐   miscellaneous income;
☐   forestry income; and
☐   retirement income.

Husbands and wives are taxed separately, as are their minor children. There is no option for joint filing.

A variety of allowances are available to taxpayers, depending on their personal circumstances. These are given by deduction from taxable income.

Income tax is charged at progressive rates, ranging from 10 per cent to 37 per cent.

Income from employment

Income from employment includes not only basic salary and wages, but also bonuses, commissions, benefits-in-kind, allowances, tax borne by the employer and all kinds of pecuniary benefit derived from the employment relationship.

Remuneration is generally taxable when received.

All resident employees may claim a standard deduction against taxable income from employment. The amount of the deduction varies with gross income. Where specific expenditure directly connected with the employment exceeds the standard deduction, the actual amount may be claimed instead, under certain conditions.

Employers are obliged to withhold salary tax (on account of income tax, inhabitant tax – a hybrid local tax partly based on income and part poll tax – and social security deductions) from all payments of remuneration in Japan.

Investment income

Dividends and interest

Dividends are normally aggregated with a taxpayer's other income and subject to income tax at progressive rates. Dividends from Japanese companies are paid under deduction of 20 per cent withholding tax. The withholding tax may be deducted as a credit against the individual's income tax liability. With certain dividends, resident taxpayers may opt for a 35 per cent final withholding tax.

Deposit and bond interest paid to resident taxpayers is separately taxed at a rate of 20 per cent. Loan interest, on the other hand, is aggregated with other taxable income and subject to progressive rates.

Income from real property

Rental income from real property, net of related expenses, is aggregated with income from other sources. There is no withholding tax on rents paid to residents.

There is no imputed income from owner-occupation.

Taxes on capital

Capital gains

Capital gains from the disposal of real property and of shares are subject to separate rules. With shares, the rate of tax is 26 per cent, although taxpayers may opt for a 1.05 per cent final withholding tax on the gross disposal proceeds. For real property, the rules for computing the gain are complex and the rate of tax varies according to the period of ownership.

All other gains are aggregated with income. Long-term gains (broadly, gains where alienation takes place after more than five years of ownership) are reduced by 50 per cent before aggregation.

Wealth tax

There is no wealth tax in Japan.

Double tax treaties

Japan has concluded over 40 comprehensive tax treaties, including those with the UK and the United States.

For further information on tax and social security, please contact:
Paul Houston
Director
BDO Sanyu & Company
tel: 03 5325 1635; e-mail: paul.houston@bdo.or.jp

MALAYSIA

The economy

Malaysia is a fertile country. Its economy has traditionally been associated with rubber and timber and these are still important products, particularly because of the impact of oil price rises on the synthetic rubber industry. Malaysia is also one of the few remaining sources of tropical hardwoods, grown mainly in East

Malaysia. Oil palm is the most rapidly expanding new crop and Malaysia is now the world's leading exporter of oil palm products. Food crops are also grown extensively and the country is 90 per cent self-sufficient in rice. Recoverable gas reserves, however, have been found on a very large scale indeed and these have spurred industrialisation at a growing pace. Again, this country, like Japan and Russia, is going through major economic turmoil.

The other resource with which Malaysia is traditionally associated is tin, and though facing competition from synthetic substitutes, Malaysia is the West's leading supplier of this metal. The exploitation of bauxite, natural gas and copper ore reserves is growing in importance and the Federation also has oil in modest quantities.

The most rapidly expanding sector of the economy, until the recent collapse, has been manufacturing, which provided 70 per cent of exports, including electronics, office equipment, cars and consumer goods. Development is hampered by acute shortages of skilled labour. Unemployment was officially 4 per cent, but with the collapse of the South East Asian economy this figure is increasing rapidly.

Personal finance and taxation

Broadly speaking, an expatriate should expect to be earning about 50 per cent more than his or her gross UK salary, taking the value of fringe benefits into account. Free or subsidised accommodation and medical care, a car, financial assistance with education and paid home leave every second year are usually provided. Expatriates on contract employment may freely remit money out of the country, though formal permission must be obtained from the Controller of Foreign Exchange for sums over RM 10,000.

Tax is levied on a PAYE basis on any income accruing in or derived from Malaysia; benefits-in-kind, excluding free medical treatment and the payment of passages home, are counted as part of chargeable income. Deducted from chargeable income are a broad range of allowances for a wife, dependent children, contributions to pension schemes and part of the cost of educating dependent children outside the Federation. The rate of tax begins at 2 per cent and reaches a maximum of 32 per cent. The government is encouraging companies to establish their South East Asian headquarters in Malaysia, and expatriates employed in their regional office for a short period (182 days or less) are exempt from Malaysian income tax.

Working conditions

No one may enter Malaysia to take up employment without a work permit and this can only be obtained by the employer. Dependents need a dependent pass and must also obtain permission from the immigration authorities if they wish to take up any kind of paid employment. Separate passes are issued for peninsular Malaysia, Sabah and Sarawak and they are not interchangeable. Sponsorship and a guarantee may be necessary.

The working week is usually Monday to Friday, 8.30 am to 4.30 pm, Saturday until 2.30 pm, but in some states the Moslem week, Saturday to Wednesday, or Thursday morning, is kept.

Useful information

Electricity: UK electrical equipment is suitable for Malaysian supply (230 V, 50 Hz AC), but perhaps not for the climate.

Climate: The climate is tropical, hot and humid, varying little (except in the highlands) from a mean of 80°F. Seasons are more related to rainfall than to temperature. Rain, averaging about 2,300 mm a year, falls in short, drenching thunderstorms: about 60 per cent of it from November to March.

Driving: A private car is considered a virtual necessity and the general opinion is that it is better to buy one of the makes that is locally assembled than to import a car: spares are easier to get hold of, mechanics are more familiar with the cars, and they are better suited to local conditions. Moreover, there is an import duty of 100–350 per cent on cars. In the light of this, employers should be prepared to supply a company car, and as an expatriate employee you can reasonably expect that a car will go with the job. Petrol is cheaper than in the UK. It is advisable to take out a comprehensive insurance policy because local driving standards are poor. You will need to have a Malaysian driving licence eventually but an international driving licence is valid for one year.

Transport: Scheduled coach services and long-distance taxis are cheap and efficient. A small car can be hired for around RM110 a day.

Health: Malaysia's climate is obviously apt to present health problems for those who cannot take long spells of uninterruptedly hot, humid weather. However, the principal disease hazard, malaria, has been largely eliminated, though it still exists in some rural areas. (Yellow fever injections are required before you enter the country, and your doctor will advise you on other precautions.)

Health care: Most expatriates receive free medical treatment in some form or other, either as government employees or as part of the remuneration package. Otherwise, this is a potentially major expense to be budgeted for or insured against. First-class hospital accommodation alone – apart from actual treatment – costs up to RM850 a day.

Special note: Malaysia is very strict about drugs and trafficking in hard drugs carries the death penalty. If you are bringing medicines with you, make sure they are prescribed and labelled.

Education: The schools situation in Malaysia is awkward for expatriates. It is difficult to get into state schools because Malaysian children have priority, and in any case the curriculum is designed for the indigenous population. There are a number of fee-paying schools catering for expatriate children, although only one, the Uplands School in Penang, offers boarding *and* a UK curriculum.

Useful contacts:
British High Commission, 195 Jalan Ampang 50450, Kuala Lumpar, tel: 603 248 2122.
Malaysian High Commission, 45 Belgrave Square, London SW1, tel: 020 7235 8033.
Tourism Malaysia, 57 Trafalgar Square, London WC2N 5DU, tel: 020 7903 7932; www.tourism.gov.my

SINGAPORE

The economy

Traditionally Singapore, with its geographical position at the cross-roads of many international trade routes, its fine natural harbour and its excellent port facilities, has served as the principal entrepôt for South East Asia. It is also an important base for companies operating oil exploration and refining services. To a large extent this continues to be its role, but the government, conscious of the fact that this makes the economy somewhat too dependent on outside forces, has strongly encouraged the development of manufacturing industry. In particular, the government has fastened on to the opportunities created by the 'second industrial revolution' of the new technology. It has deliberately fostered a high wages policy to force manufacturers to move from labour-intensive to capital-intensive activities, particularly in view of the fact that Singapore suffers from labour shortages. However, this policy has had the effect of pricing many Singapore goods out of export markets and their replacement by products from the country's Asian competitors; the rate of growth is now lagging behind that of South Korea and Taiwan.

Manufacturing industry in general has grown rapidly in recent years, sometimes at phenomenal rates. Textiles, printing, electrical goods, electronics, plastics, building materials and foodstuffs are all active sectors. The main slow-down has been in heavy industry. Singapore also continues to be an important financial and banking centre and, as elsewhere in Asia, tourism is a rapidly growing industry. Main trading partners are the United States, Malaysia, the EU, Hong Kong and Japan.

Personal finance and taxation

Managers of medium-sized companies might expect to earn £40,000–£50,000 a year plus fringe benefits such as free or subsidised housing, home leave, free medical treatment, school fees and a car. There are no restrictions on the amount of money that can be taken out of the country.

Individuals resident in Singapore for tax purposes are liable to Singapore personal income tax charged on a sliding scale on income derived in or remitted to Singapore. Accommodation provided by the employer and certain benefits in kind are taxable, but not capital gains. Tax is levied at progressive rates from 2.5 to 30 per cent. There is tax relief for up to three children, but none thereafter – part of Singapore's policy of keeping down family numbers.

Employment for a period or periods that together do not exceed 60 days in a calendar year is exempt from tax.

Working conditions

The British expatriate community is quite large – between 7,000 and 8,000. Jobs are advertised in the appropriate sectors of the overseas press and are usually on a contract basis with a salary plus fringe benefits as indicated in the personal finance section. The major Singapore professional bodies are affiliated to, or otherwise closely connected with, their UK counterparts. People going to work in Singapore must have an employment pass which has to be obtained by the prospective employer. Dependants must also obtain a pass that has to be applied for by the employer. There are various immigration schemes for those with proven technical, professional or entrepreneurial skills.

Useful information

Climate: Singapore is less than 137 km from the equator and is hot and humid for most of the year.

Electricity: 230–250V, 50 Hz AC. Three square pin plugs are common.

Transport: The importing of cars is discouraged, and there is a duty of 45 per cent on imported cars on top of a basic additional registration fee of 150 per cent of the value of any new car, imported or otherwise. Thus it is not advisable to bring a car into Singapore from abroad, even though buying one locally is very expensive. Second-hand cars are advertised for sale in *The Straits Times.* The government is trying to limit car ownership on the island, both by fiscal policies and by placing restrictions on the use of cars in the central business district. On the other hand, both taxis and public transport are correspondingly inexpensive, and indeed are among the world's cheapest.

Health: Singapore has a good health record and the government wages a somewhat draconian cleanliness campaign, which includes hefty fines for dropping even a bus ticket in the street.

Health care: There are no free medical facilities but treatment in government clinics is very cheap, though most expatriates prefer to use private doctors, who charge between S$25 and S$50 (specialists S$45–$80), depending on their qualifications and what sort of treatment is involved. Surgeons' and obstetricians' fees start at around S$2,100 and a private room in a hospital costs about S$180 a day. Medical fees, or insurance premiums to cover them, are often, in the case of expatriates, met by employers.

Education: As with many other jobs overseas, education can be a problem, and arrangements to send children to local schools should be made as soon as possible. Government schools are very cheap, with only nominal fees for the children of Singapore residents. There are three good English private primary schools. The Singapore American School takes all ages up to 18, and there is also the United World College of South East Asia which has facilities for A-level teaching. There is an excellent university in Singapore, at which the standards of entry and the level of the courses are equivalent to UK universities. Fees vary depending on the nature of the course being taken.

Useful contacts:

British High Commission, Tanglin Road, Singapore 247919, tel: 65 473933; www.britain.org.sg/

Singapore High Commission, 9 Wilton Crescent, London SW1, tel: 020 7235 8315.

Singapore Tourism Board, 1st Floor, Carrington House, 126–130 Regent Street, London W1R 5FE, tel: 020 7437 0033; www.newsasia-singapore.com

Expatriate contacts: www.expatsingapore.com

Australasia

AUSTRALIA

The economy

Australia has recovered strongly from the recession of the early 1990s. Indeed, the economy is showing the fastest growth in the Western world, with gross domestic product increasing at an annual rate of 4 per cent. However, balance of trade and foreign debt figures remain poor. The largest export industries are agricultural products and mineral extraction. Primary imports are in transportation and office equipment. Main trading partners are Japan, Korea, the United States and New Zealand. Despite all this, one of the biggest revenue earners is tourism.

Despite a forecast of 4.5 per cent growth, the government maintains a cautious line on immigration policy. Preference is given to people with direct and close family connections, skilled and business migrants, and others accepted under refugee or special humanitarian programmes. A points system is used in some of the categories to determine a person's eligibility based on economic factors such as age, health, education, occupation and the level of skill required to undertake that occupation in Australia. All non-nationals must obtain a visa beforehand.

Additional information can be obtained from the Australian High Commission in London or the Australian Consulate in Manchester.

Working conditions

At executive and professional levels international standards and conditions of work apply. Holidays are normally four weeks a year and some firms pay a holiday bonus. There is also often a form of sabbatical leave after 10 years' service with a company. Flexible working hours are quite common in Australia, particularly in the public sector. The chief difference in working conditions between Australia and other countries is that the concept of status related to specific jobs – and even more, social and workplace behaviour associated with it – has to be discarded. Any tendency to 'give yourself airs' is fatal!

Australian employers will not usually recruit from a distance, but it is possible to get a good picture of the sort of employment opportunities available from Australian newspapers and particularly from the Australian migration authorities. In general the demand is for specific skills and professional or managerial qualifications (in, for example, computer work). Most British professional qualifications are recognised in Australia, but it is necessary to show documentary evidence of having obtained them.

It is fairly easy to get working holiday visas, valid for up to 12 months, if you are under 25. Apply to the Australian Commission or the nearest consulate.

Useful information

Electricity: Electrical goods should be checked with the maker to see if they would work in Australia, because the voltage systems differ (220–250V, 50 Hz AC). Gas appliances are particularly tricky because of differences in pressure and gas composition. British TVs and video recorders do not function in Australia because of different signals and need to be professionally converted to compatibility with the Australian system.

Driving: A car, essential in Australia, is best bought there. If you import a car you will have to make sure that it meets the safety regulations of the state to which you are going. You can drive on a British licence for the first three months. After that you will have to take a local test, but this will only be an oral one if you already hold a British or international licence.

Transport: Interstate transport is usually by aeroplane, although there is also a large railway network.

Education: Education begins at the age of 5 or 6 and is compulsory up to age 15 or 16 (depending on the state). The school session starts early in February, not September as in the UK. It must be remembered that, in the southern hemisphere, the seasons are reversed, hence the Australian Christmas is midsummer. Tuition is free in government schools, but parents generally have to provide uniforms, books and other materials, though such items can be claimed against income tax, up to a maximum of A$250 per child. As many as 25 per cent of pupils, however, attend private schools, particularly in the latter years of secondary education. Fees are reasonable (and subject to tax rebates) because these schools are aided by government grants. Allow A$4000–6000 a year for private secondary school tuition fees.

There are small tuition fees for university-level education, which is very well provided for in all states. Most Australians take a pass degree rather than honours. Standards are similar to those in the UK.

Useful contacts:
British High Commission, Commonwealth Avenue, Yarralumla, Canberra, ACT 2600, tel: 612 6270 666; www.uk.emb.gov.au
Australian High Commission, Australia House, Strand, London WC2, tel: 020 7379 4334.
Australian Tourist Commission, tel: 020 8780 2229; www.aussie.net.au or www.australia.com

PERSONAL TAXATION

Residence

Australia taxes on the basis of residence. An individual will be resident in Australia for taxation purposes if he or she 'ordinarily resides' in Australia or if any of the following tests is satisfied:

☐ the individual's domicile is in Australia and he or she does not have a permanent place of abode elsewhere;

☐ the individual has physically been present in Australia for 183 days or more in the financial year (1 July to 30 June) and does not have a usual place of abode outside Australia; or

☐ the individual is a member of certain Australian Commonwealth Government superannuation schemes.

A place of abode is the place where the taxpayer adopts a habitual mode of living. Whether or not an individual ordinarily resides in Australia is a matter of fact and degree, on which there is a considerable amount of case law. Domicile has the same sense as in the UK – broadly, it is the place that an individual considers to be his or her permanent home.

Where an individual is also resident in another jurisdiction, double tax agreements may apply to demarcate the taxing right of each country in respect of the income derived.

Taxation of personal Income

Individuals resident in Australia are taxed on their worldwide income while non-residents are taxed only on Australian-source income, subject to the operation of double tax agreements, which override domestic tax law.

Taxable income includes income from employment, income from self-employment, investment income (dividends, interest, income from real property, income from trusts and so forth) and capital gains (see below). An individual's total income from these and other taxable sources is aggregated and subject to income tax at progressive rates, after deduction of a personal allowance ('tax-free threshold'). Certain tax credits may also be available to taxpayers, depending on their personal circumstances.

The tax year runs from 1 July to 30 June. For the year 2001–2, the top rate of income tax was 47 per cent, payable on that part of taxable income exceeding A$60,000. Individual residents are generally required to pay a Medicare Levy at 1.5 per cent on his/her taxable income while an additional 1.5 per cent may apply to individuals whose taxable income exceeds a prescribed threshold and who do not have private health insurance.

Only the federal government has the power to levy income tax. The states derive their income from indirect taxes.

Income from employment

Taxable income from employment includes salaries, wages, commissions, allowances (excluding living-away-from-home allowance, which is subject to fringe benefits tax), and bonuses. Non-cash remuneration in the form of benefits-in-kind does not form part of the employee's taxable income but is subject to fringe benefits tax (FBT), which is payable by the employer. FBT is levied at 48.5 per cent on the grossed-up taxable value of benefits provided.

Lump-sum termination and pension payments are also taxable, but at maximum rates lower than the top marginal rate of tax. *Bona fide* redundancy payments are tax-free up to a certain limit. Special taxing rules apply to shares and rights issued under an employee share scheme.

Employees are entitled to claim deductions for expenses incurred in gaining or producing income from employment, but not in respect of private, domestic or capital expenditure.

Employers are required to deduct tax from earnings under the pay-as-you-go system and pay an amount net of tax to employees.

Employers are also required to make a minimum superannuation guarantee contribution to provide for their employees' retirement. The minimum contribution for the 2000/01 year is 8 per cent on the ordinary time earnings for each employee. Limited exceptions may apply that exempt employers from making such contributions.

Investment income

Dividends and interest

Australian-source 'franked' dividends (dividends paid out of profits already subject to corporate tax) are taxable on the grossed-up amount (inclusive of imputation credits). The imputation credit is 30 per cent of the gross dividend ($3/7$ of the net dividend) matching the rate of corporate tax (30 per cent).

Interest income, like dividends, is included in an individual's total taxable income. There is generally no withholding tax on dividends and interest paid to residents if the payee has provided the payer with a Tax File Number.

Income from real property

Residents are taxable on income from real property, wherever situated, less relevant expenses. Non-residents are taxable on their income from real property situated in Australia. There is no income imputed to owner-occupiers nor is there withholding tax on rents paid to non-residents.

Taxation of capital

Capital gains

The net capital gain from the disposal of assets acquired after 19 September 1985 is included in taxable income and taxed at the individual's marginal tax rate. A 50 per cent discount may apply if the asset has been held by the individual for at least 12 months.

A capital loss is carried forward indefinitely and can only offset a capital gain.

Gains from certain assets that have a necessary connection with Australia are subject to capital gains tax, regardless of the owner's residence status. These include Australian real property, shares in Australian private companies, interests in Australian partnerships and trusts, interests of 10 per cent or more in Australian public companies and unit trusts, and Australian business assets.

Wealth tax

There is no wealth tax at either the federal or state level.

Double tax treaties

Australia has double tax agreements with over 35 countries, including the UK and the United States. A new protocol to the treaty with the USA will apply from 1 July 2003.

For further information on tax and social security, please contact:
David Goman
BDO Nelson Parkhill Association Ltd
tel: +61 292 865600; e-mail: dgoman@bdosyd.com.au

_____

NEW ZEALAND

The economy

Economic reforms have changed the economy from being highly regulated and protected to one of market economics. Deregulation, privatisation and the removal of subsidies have brought great changes. The now-independent Reserve Bank has a contract to keep inflation below 2 per cent; the welfare state has been largely dismantled.

Agricultural products continue to form the core of the economy, primarily in dairy products, cattle and sheep. Fish, timber and wood pulp are increasingly important. Natural gas is the most successful resource export. Almost all power is provided by hydro-electricity. Manufacturing is being actively encouraged, but tourism is the fastest-growing sector. Main trading partners are Australia, Japan, the United States and the UK.

Personal finance and taxation

Tax is deducted on a PAYE basis. The basic rates of income tax are 25 per cent and 33 per cent. In addition, there is a goods and services tax (GST) of 12.5 per cent which is similar to VAT.

Working conditions

Applications for work permits must be supported by an offer of employment from a New Zealand employer and must be submitted at least four weeks prior to intended departure from the UK. Accommodation guarantees may be required. Further information may be obtained from the New Zealand Immigration Service, New Zealand House, Haymarket, London SW1Y 4TQ (tel: 020 7973 0366). There are no restrictions about taking money into or out of the country. Visitors from the UK, and many other nationals, do not require a visa but those intending to stay for longer must apply for a residence permit. Consideration is generally only given to applicants with skills on the Priority List.

In general, rates of pay are slightly lower than in the UK, while deductions are at about the same level. The cost of living, however, is less, so that the net result is very similar to working in the UK. Most employees receive at least three weeks' holiday. The 40-hour week is universal.

Useful information

Electricity: 230 V, 50 Hz AC. Most electrical equipment will work in New Zealand, but some items may require a transformer to reduce voltage. British TVs *have* to be adapted as frequencies and line systems differ. However, in some instances it is possible to buy a suitable export model. A VHF modulator is required for video viewing on a normal New Zealand TV set.

Driving: People entering New Zealand to take up permanent residence for the first time may bring in a motor vehicle free of duty and GST if certain conditions are met (a leaflet is available from New Zealand House). UK driving licences are accepted for the first year of your stay, after which you have to take a test (which has written and oral parts) to obtain a New Zealand licence. Although New Zealanders drive on the left and road rules are essentially the same as in the UK, it would be advisable to check out the New Zealand road code – there are differences, especially in the give-way rules.

Transport: Travel by internal airline is very popular, and often the best option to more remote parts.

Health care: Widespread means-testing has been introduced throughout the welfare state, so that only the very poor now receive free or subsidised health care and other benefits. Under a reciprocal arrangement with the UK, health care (including hospitalisation) is available to residents who go to live in New Zealand and have made the necessary National Insurance contributions here. Visits to the doctor, prescriptions and hospital outpatient visits are all charged in relation to the patient's ability to pay.

Education: Primary school education begins at 5, but there is also an excellent network of pre-school education for 3-year-olds upwards. Education is compulsory from 6 to 15 and tuition is subsidised.

Parents are expected to pay some fees and for uniforms, the wearing of which is customary in secondary schools. There are also private schools, mostly conducted by religious bodies. University entrance qualifications correspond to the UK and tuition is subsidised for those who reach top-level entrance qualifications. There are university scholarships for the brightest students. There are seven universities.

Useful contacts:
British High Commission, 44 Hill Street, Wellington 1, tel: 644 472 6049.
New Zealand High Commission, 80 Haymarket, London SW1Y 4TQ, tel: 020 7930 8422.
New Zealand Tourist Board, 80 Haymarket, London SW1Y 4TQ, tel: 020 7930 1662; www.nztb.govt.nz

PAPUA NEW GUINEA

The economy

Until fairly recently, the economy was based almost entirely on agriculture with no cash economy. Most of the population are occupied in this sector. Commercial crops include copra, cocoa, coffee, rubber, tea and sugar. Exports of tropical wood is a mainstay – PNG is one of the few remaining countries in the region exporting unprocessed timber, but restrictions to preserve the forests have recently been imposed. The most important natural resources are copper, gold and silver. The Panguna Copper Mine in Bougainville used to provide nearly half of PNG's national income until closed by rebel action. Large-scale mining has been encouraged elsewhere. Large oil and gas reserves have also been discovered. Other industries are small-scale or absent altogether.

Personal finance and taxation

Wage-earners with only one source of income have tax deducted automatically from their pay, after deductions for dependants. Tax rates go up to 35 per cent.

There should not normally be problems with the remittability of currency from Papua New Guinea.

Working conditions

It is necessary to hold a work permit in order to gain permission to reside in the country. This is obtainable before arrival, either through the Department of Labour and Industry or through the employer. In addition, all foreign nationals must have a valid passport and visa before entering Papua New Guinea.

Many expatriate posts in the country are in government employ, and are well advertised in the UK, typically in *The Guardian*. Salaries are quite high, but the qualifications and experience demanded are equally so.

Useful information

Climate: The climate is typically tropical and cool cotton clothes are normal year-round wear. The Highlands are cooler. Port Moresby has a dry season from May to November, the opposite of Lae's.

Health and security: Malaria is a problem in many areas, although Moresby is now relatively safe. Health problems have now been replaced by domestic and personal security concerns. Violent crime is a particularly serious issue and houses should be well protected. Assaults on women are also a serious problem in the major cities. Curfews are not unknown.

Transport: Travel within the country is usually impossible by road (except from Lae to the principal Highland towns). Consequently, air is the normal medium for transport and Air Niugini flies to all the major centres and to many small towns; other carriers include Talair, Douglas Airways, Bougair and several other charter firms. Hire and radio cars are available in the main towns but bus services are still inefficient. There are some scenic highways, of various quality.

Communications: The telephone service is excellent but all mail must be addressed to PO boxes.

Special note: There is no mains gas supply.

Education: The education system is good, and there is a university with 3,000 students at Port Moresby and a University of Technology at Lae. The language of instruction is English. There are a number of International Schools which follow a broadly New South Wales, Australia, curriculum, but many expatriates send their children abroad for their education.

Useful contacts:

British High Commission, PO Box 212, Waiganis NCD 131, Papua New Guinea, tel: 675 325 1643.

Papua New Guinea High Commission, 14 Waterloo Place, London SW1, tel: 020 7930 0922.

	Annual physical 1	Club membership 2	Company automobile 3	Entertainment allowance 4	Extra vacation 5	Financial counseling 6	Housing assistance 7	Low-interest loans 8	Mobile telephone 9
Argentina	◐	○	●	○	●	◐	○	●	●
Australia	●	◐	●	●	◐	●	○	○	●
Belgium	◐	◐	●	◐	●	◐	○	○	●
Brazil	●	◐	●	○	○	○	○	◐	◐
Canada	●	●	●	○	○	◐	○	○	●
China (Hong Kong SAR)	◐	◐	◐	○	●	○	◐	○	◐
China (Shanghai)	◐	○	●	○	◐	○	◐	○	○
France	○	◐	●	○	◐	◐	◐	◐	●
Germany	◐	◐	●	○	◐	◐	○	○	●
Italy	●	○	●	○	○	○	○	○	●
Japan	●	●	●	●	○	○	◐	◐	◐
Malaysia	●	●	●	◐	○	○	○	◐	●
Mexico	●	◐	●	○	○	○	○	○	●
Netherlands	○	○	●	○	○	◐	○	○	●
New Zealand	○	●	●	○	○	○	○	○	●
Singapore	●	●	●	◐	○	○	○	◐	◐
South Africa	●	●	●	●	◐	◐	○	●	●
South Korea	●	●	●	◐	○	○	◐	○	◐
Spain	●	○	●	○	○	◐	○	◐	●
Sweden	●	◐	●	◐	●	◐	◐	○	●
Switzerland	○	○	◐	○	○	○	○	○	○
Taiwan	○	●	●	○	○	○	○	○	○
Thailand	●	●	●	●	○	○	○	◐	●
United Kingdom	◐	○	●	●	◐	◐	○	○	●
United States	◐	◐	◐	○	◐	●	○	○	◐
Venezuela	●	●	●	○	○	○	○	◐	●

Source: Towers Perrin "Worldwide Total Remuneration 2001–2002"

Chart 5.1 Executive perquisites – 2001/2002

Part Six:

Web Site Directory of Useful Contacts

The Web sites listed are those identified at the time of going to print. Variations in content and changes of address might occur. The publishers cannot take responsibility for the content of the Web sites listed but have tried to ensure, where possible, that the material is of a suitable nature. However, an exemplary illustration of what can be found on the Internet is the *Electronic Telegraph's* expatriate Web site, Global Network, which offers advice, links and country profiles. It can be found at www.telegraph.co.uk or www.globalnetwork.co.uk

INTERNET DIRECTORIES AND SEARCH ENGINES

Alta Vista
www.altavista.digital.com
Britannica Internet Guide
www.ebig.com
DejaNews
www.search.dejanews.com
Search tool for finding news groups.
Excite Search
www.excite.com
HotBot
www.hotbot.com
The Liszt
www.liszt.com
Search tool for news groups and mailing lists.
Regional Directory
www.edirectory.com
Listing of regional Web directories.
UK Directory
www.ukdirectory.co.uk

Who Where
www.whowhere.com
Directory of e-mail addresses to help you keep in contact with friends, family and organisations.
Yahoo!
www.yahoo.com

JOB OPPORTUNITIES

Internet resources

Aboutwork Career Database
www.aboutwork.com/career/index.html
US site with information for jobseekers worldwide. Includes salary details, self-assessment, and access to chat groups on employment-related matters.
America's Job Bank
www.ajb.dni.us
Extensive database of current vacancies in the United States.
Career Mosaic
www.careermosaic.com
Provides regional breakdowns of salary information.
Career Resource Centre
www.careers.org
Index of US and Canadian careers-related Web sites, with more than 2,500 links to related sites.
Cool Works
www.coolworks.com
Provides links to details of 'cool' jobs with emphasis on United States. For example, jobs in national and state parks, ski resorts and ranches. Visa restrictions problematic for Europeans, but worth having a look at this site.
Job Site
www.jobsite.co.uk
Directory of major UK and European recruiters, mainly in IT and human-resource management.

Lifestyle UK
www.lifestyle.co.uk/bh.htm
Vacancies in a range of fields with links to European and US sites.
The Monster Board
www.monster.com
Invaluable resource on international job opportunities and country-specific information. Sites in Canada, Australia, Belgium and The Netherlands.
Prospects Web
www.prospects.csu.ac.uk
Careers information for graduates with overseas sites offering vacancy information.
Purdue University Placement Service
www.purdue.edu/ups/studen/jobsites.htm
US university site with over 1,000 links to job searching sites.
The Riley Guide to Employment Opportunities and Job Resources on the Internet
www.dbm.com/jobguide
Worldwide vacancies with emphasis on the United States.
SYO-Guiden
www.pedc.se/syo/utnavbar.html
Swedish site with links to career guidance sites worldwide.
TV Jobs
www.tvjobs.com/intern.htm
US TV companies offering work experience placements.

Media

The Daily Telegraph
www.telegraph.co.uk
On line version of full paper with recruitment vacancies worldwide.
British Medical Journal
www.bmj.com
Medical vacancies.
The Cell
www.server.cell.com/recruit
International journal of the Biological Sciences with vacancies worldwide.

Construction Site
www.emap.com/construct
Vacancies from *The Architects' Journal, Construction News* and *New Civil Engineer*, updated weekly. Links to other emap sites of specialist journals.

Emap
www.emap.com
Publishers of a wide range of trade and specialist magazines with recruitment sections.

E&P Directory of Online Newspapers
www.mediainfo.com/ephome/npaper/nphtm/online/htm
Reference resource including newspapers on the WWW and proprietary online services. Listed by country with search facilities for specific publications, locations or attributes.

Expat Network
www.expatnetwork.co.uk
Publishes Nexus and offers support service for expats and a register of those looking for work abroad which is sent to recruiters.

Financial Times
www.ft.com
Finance- and business-related vacancies.

The Guardian
www.recruitnet.guardian.co.uk
Vacancies in wide range of occupational areas.

Inkpot
www.inkpot.com/news/weueopre.html
Links to European newspapers.

Irish Times
www.recruit.irish-times.com
Searchable site for jobs in Ireland.

Nature
www.nature.com
International science job listings, updated weekly.

Overseas Job Express
www.overseasjobs.com
Newspaper carrying 1,500 job vacancies and information about working abroad every two weeks.

Physics World Jobs
www.iop.org./cgi-bin/jobs/vacancies

Part of UK's Institute of Physics site with job and research opportunities.

The Scientist
www.the-scientist.library.upenn.edu/index.html
US scientific journal.

Summer Jobs
www.summerjobs.com
Also produced by Overseas Job Express, a database of seasonal and summer jobs.

Washington Post
www.washingtonpost.com/wp-adv/classifieds/careerpost/parachute/front.htm
Reviews of US guidance sites with links to them.

Recruitment consultancies and employment agencies

Au pair JobMatch
www.aupairs.co.uk
Search by country and nationality of families for worldwide au pair vacancies.

CEPEC
www.cepec.co.uk
Lists agencies and search consultants in the United Kingdom.

Crewseekers International
www.crewseekers.co.uk
Work found for amateur crews for leisure sailing, cruising and racing.

Engineering Production Planning Limited
www.epp.co.uk
Agency with offices in Europe, Singapore and the United States. Specialises in vacancies in aerospace, oil and gas, water, power generation, nuclear engineering, production, defence, communications, chemical processing, civil engineering and manufacturing.

European Crew Search
www.eac.co.uk
Matches pilots and flight engineers with airlines looking for crews.

Expats International
www.expatsinternational.co.uk
Provides job information and vacancies for North American, British, Australian and European nationalities.
Hays International
www.hays-ap.com
International vacancies.
Malla Technical Recruitment Consultancy
www.mall.com
Specialising in engineering placements worldwide.
Michael Page International
www.michaelpage.com
Offices in Europe and Eastern Europe.
Reed
www.reed.co.uk
Vacancies, careers information and links to career resources worldwide.
Reed Accountancy
www.reedaccountancy.co.uk
Robert Walters
www.robertwalters.com
European recruitment offices.
TAPS
www.taps.com
Employers using this site include the BBC, British Air Traffic Control, and major scientific, IT and large manufacturing companies.
Veterinary Locums Worldwide
www.vetlocums.com
Site for vets looking for short-term work in practices, wildlife projects or with exotic animals.

Professional Associations

British Medical Association
www.bma.org.uk
Information and advice on working abroad for BMA members.

British National Space Centre – Space Index
www.highview.co.uk
Careers information and links to listings of space-related jobs worldwide.
Institute of Physics
www.iop.org
Physics-related vacancies.
Royal College of Nursing
www.rcn.org.uk
Information and advice on working abroad for RCN members.

Organisations

The British Council
www.britishcouncil.org
Teaching opportunities and voluntary work overseas. Recruits EFL teachers for its own Language Centres.
Committee on the Status of Women in Physics
www.aps.org/educ/cswp/cswp./htm
Arm of the American Physical Society. Information on dual-science-career jobs.
Council in Europe
www.ciee.org/europe/index/htm
Work experience, short-term jobs and worldwide exchange programmes for students and recent graduates.
Doctors without Borders
www.dwb.org
As with IHE, opportunities for medically trained personnel to work in developing countries.
Employment Service Overseas Placing Unit
www.europa.eu.int/comm/dg05/elm/eures/en/indexen.htm
A cooperative network funded by the EC, giving advice on working abroad and job vacancies in other EU member states.
European Commission
www.cec.org.uk
Commission's current vacancies for English-speaking candidates.
The International Health Exchange
www.ihe.org
Health personnel for programmes in developing countries.

Nahat Gateway to the Internet
www.nahat.net/gateway.htm
Medically related careers with links worldwide.
Petroleum Industry
www.discoveryplace.com
Worldwide jobs in the petroleum industry.
United Nations
www.un.org/
Vacancy board for UN departments worldwide.
Women Connect Asia
www.women-connect.asia.com
Network for professional women working in Asia, with current vacancies.

Teaching English as a foreign language

The British Council
www.britishcouncil.org
See above.
The Centre for British Teachers
www.cfbt.com
Teaching vacancies in Brunei, Oman and Turkey and educational specialists in Eastern Europe, Africa, Asia and India.
ELT Job Vacancies
www.go-ed.com/jobs/elt-vac.htm
Teaching English as a foreign language posts worldwide.
International House
www.international-house-london.ac
Recruits teachers for 100 schools in 26 countries.

Voluntary work

British Council
www.britishcouncil.org
See above.
Voluntary Service Overseas
www.oneworld.org/vso/
Opportunities in 58 countries in education, health, technical trades, engineering and other fields.

International companies

Boeing
www.boeing.com
Aviation giant offers internships for college students at US institutions.
British Airways
www.british-airways.com/inside/employme/employme.shtml
Cabin crew, IT and sales vacancies.
Coopers and Lybrand
www.coopers.co.uk
Business advisory organisation with vacancies in accounting, auditing, tax and consulting.
Hewlett-Packard
www.europe.hp.com/jobposting
IT giant with online application forms.
Hoover
www.hoovers.com
Links to Web sites for more than 5,000 of the world's largest companies.
IBM
www.ibm.com
US site has links to global recruitment.
Microsoft
www.microsoft.com/jobs
Information vacancies at the company's different locations.
Shell International
www.shell.com
Superb Web site with access to expatriate information on its 'OUTPOST' and Spouses Support Network Web sites (see expatriate Web sites).
SmithKline Beecham
www.sb.com
Access to both UK and US searches for current vacancies in this pharmaceutical company.

COUNTRY-SPECIFIC DATA

Political information

Foreign and Commonwealth Office
www.fco.gov.uk
Travel Advice Unit provides up-to-the-minute information on political upheaval, natural disasters and epidemics worldwide.
United Nations
www.un.org/
Information on countries in the UN.
US State Department Travel Advisories
Up-to-the-minute information in the same vein as the Foreign and Commonwealth Office.

Economic data

Center for Research on Economic Fluctuations and Employment (CREFE, University of Quebec)
www.er.uqam.ca/nobel/r14160/economics
Index of economic institutions on the WWW. Listing at time of publication included 4,083 institutions in 174 countries.
CIA FactBook
www.oci.ogv.cia/publications/pubs.html
Country breakdown with economic, political, geographic and demographic information available.
Financial Times Country Briefs
www.ft.com
Superb country surveys providing developments and detailed information on regions and countries, including economic indicators and company activity and performance details.
Nanyang Technology University, Statistical Data Locators
www.ntu.edu.sg/library/statdata.htm
An extensive database of information and an invaluable gateway to statistics produced by government departments and international organisations.
Union Bank of Switzerland
www.ubs.com

_____

Produces comparative survey 'Prices and Earnings Around the Globe' detailing costs and earnings in 53 countries.
US Department of State: Country Report on Economic Policy and Trade Practices
www.state.gov/www/issues/economic/trade–reports/98-toc.html
US bias but interesting tables of Key Economic Indicators for 77 countries along with information on custom territories and custom unions.

Business guides

Department of Trade and Industry Export Publications
www.dit.gov.uk/ots/publications
Publications aimed at businesses abroad and for intending expatriates.
Hong Kong and Shanghai Banking Corporation
www.hsbcgroup.com
Publishes 'Business Profiles' aimed at companies and private individuals and contains useful information on living conditions.

General information

The Centre for International Briefing
www.cibfarnham.com
Cultural and business briefings covering all regions of the world. Also customised programmes and language tuition.
Countrynet
www.countrynet.com
Written by Arthur Andersen Consultants with the purpose of providing expatriates with information on relocating to a new country, with 84 countries included.
ECA International
www.eca.co.uk
Relocation company with excellent resources and country briefings worldwide.
Expat Network
www.expatnetwork.co.uk
Among other services provides location reports to members.
Expedia
www.expedia.co.uk
Many links to other travel sites.

Continent-specific information
Africa

Africaonline
www.africaonline.co
Information on African countries.
Commonwealth Institute
www.icol.co.uk
Information on member states of the Commonwealth.
Excite
www.excite.com/travel/regions/africa
Search engine's Web site.
Ourworld
www.ourworld.compuserve.com/homepage/kenya
Yahoo!
www.yahoo.com/travel/regions/africa
Search engine directory of information on the region.

America

US Census Bureau
www.census.gov
US statistics with links.

Asia

Commonwealth Institute
www.icol.co.uk
See above.
East Asia Business Services
www.shef.ac.uk
Tailor-made briefings for expatriates going to Japan, China, Korea or other East Asian countries.
Excite
www.excite.com/travel/regions/asia
Search engine's Web site.
School of Oriental and African Studies
www.soas.ac.uk

Briefing and language service, open briefings on Japan and China, two-day Japan Business Orientation programme.
Yahoo!
www.yahoo.com/travel/regions/asia
Search engine directory of information on the region.

Europe

European Commission
www.europea.eu.int
www.citizens.eu.int
Factsheets and information on working and living in the European Union.

Middle East

ArabNet
www.arab.net

Language tuition

Berlitz (UK) Ltd
www.berlitz.co.uk
Language tuition.
The European Centre
www.eucentre.co.uk
Language consultancy delivery programmes for business and vocational purposes.

EXPAT NETWORKS

British in America
www.britishinamerica.com
Expats in the US link-up.
Britnet
www.britnet.nelgin.nu
Brits Abroad
www.geocitiex.com/TheTropics/2865/pat.htm

Diplomatic Service Families Association
www.fco.gov.uk
Promotes interest and welfare of spouses of serving and retired diplomatic service officers. Provides link between those at home and abroad.
Escapeartist
www.escapeartist.com/
Superb Web site with links to expat forums, country-specific data, advice on relocation and much more.
Expat Access
www.expataccess.com
Expats in Belgium, France, Germany, Italy, The Netherlands and Switzerland.
The Expat Club
www.artinliving.com
Reader exchange available for the swapping of tips and advice.
Expat Exchange
www.expatexchange.com
Comprehensive information source on moving overseas, tax and finance plus much more. Runs an expat network.
Expat Forum
www.expatforum.com
Chat forums in 24 country-specific areas, along with other areas of interest to expats.
Expats International
www.expats.co.uk
Publishes magazine *Home and Away*.
Expat Network
www.expatnetwork.co.uk
Publishes *Nexus* and offers support service for expats.
Expat Online
www.expatriate-online.com
Network for expats living in Belgium.
Expat Resources for Spouses
www.thesun.org
Excellent links to expat forums, products and services, relocation companies and organisations abroad.

Federation of American Women's Clubs Overseas Inc
www.fawco.org
OUTPOST
www.outpostexpat.nl/sec
Shell International's superb Web site providing information to partners who wish to work or develop their skills during expatriation.
TCK
www.tck.world.com
Children's Web site.
Women Connect Asia
www.women-connect.asia.com
Network for professional women working in Asia.

EDUCATION

British Dyslexia Association
www.bda-dyslexia.org.uk
Advice on teaching of dyslexic children.
Cambridge Local Examinations Syndicate
www.ocr.org.uk
Administers the AICE curriculum.
Clarendon International Education
www.clarendon.uk.com
Offers guardianship services.
Department for Education and Employment
www.dfee.gov.uk
Information on maintained boarding schools.
ECIS
www.ecis.org
Details of 400 international schools and Web site access to International Schools Directory.
Gabbitas Educational Consultants
www.gabitas.co.uk
Advice on a selection of suitable schools.
Home School Teaching
www.creshome.demon.co.uk
Provides information and teachers to teach from home.

International Baccalaureate Organisation
www.ibo.org
Joanella Slattery Associates
www.cea.co.uk
Provides free educational advice as well as a comprehensive guardianship service.
National Extension College
www.nec.ac.uk
Offers GCSE and A-level correspondence courses.
Universities and Colleges Admissions Service
www.ucas.ac.uk
Central agency for all UK universities.
The World-wide Education Service (Home School) Ltd
www.weshome.demon.co.uk
Specialises in teaching children with special needs.
World-wide Education Service
www.westworldwide.com
Information on overseas schools.

HEALTH ADVICE

BUPA International
www.bupa.co.uk
Medical insurance worldwide.
Hospital for Tropical Diseases
www.tsonline.co.uk
For access to Health Information for Overseas Travel.
International SOS Assistance
www.intsos.com
Provides emergency help in a time of crisis.
Medical Advisory Service for Travellers Abroad (MASTA)
www.masta.org
Offers health briefs on 230 countries.
Reuters Health
www.reutershealth.com

ENTERTAINMENT

Books

Amazon Books
www.amazon.com
Delivery of over 2 million titles worldwide.
Internet Public Library
www.ipl.sils.umich.edu
Online access to various publications.

Television and radio

BBC News
www.news.bbc.co.uk
BBC Online
www.bbc.co.uk
Radio and World Service programmes online with audio versions.
CNN
www.cnn.com
Soap Digest
www.soapdigest.com
Keep up to date with your favourite soaps.

Newspapers

The Daily Telegraph
www.telegraph.co.uk
Almost entire content of daily newspaper.
The Guardian
www.guardian.co.uk
Selected cuttings.
The Sunday Times
www.sunday-times.co.uk
Full content.
The Times
www.times.co.uk
Full content.

Sport

Skysports
www.sky.co.uk
News on range of sports.
Sportsweb
www.sportsweb.com
As above.
Yahoo!
www.yahoo.com
Comprehensive listings of Web sites covering every type of sport imaginable.

USEFUL MISCELLANEOUS WEB SITES

Allied Pickfords
www.alliedpickfords.co.uk
International removals.
Cybercafe Search Engine
www.cybercaptive.com
Cybercafe locations worldwide to ensure Internet access.
Department for Environment, Food and Rural Affairs
Advice on the transportation of animals overseas.
Expatnetwork
www.expatnetwork.co.uk
Gift service to send gifts or flowers to friends and family.
Expedia
www.expedia.co.uk
Currency converter.
Fedex
www.fedex.com
Web site of Federal Express for your freight needs.
Foreign Languages for Travellers
www.travlang.com/languages
Phrases in many languages.

Kropla
www.kropla.com/
Extremely useful Web site with worldwide electrical and telephone information. Details of electric plugs and voltages used.
Mastercard/Cirrus ATM Locator
www.mastercard.com/atm/
Find automated teller machine in your new location.
VISA ATM Locator
www.visa.atm.locator
Find automated teller machine in your new location.
Visa Service
www.visaservice.co.uk
Specialises in processing applications for business visas and passports.
Visa service.
Worldwide Holiday and Festival Page
www.holidayfestival.com/
Public holidays throughout the world.
Worldwide weather forecasts
www.intellicast.com/localweather/world/
Local weather around the globe.

Index of Advertisers

Index